ZENDURANCE

ZENDURANCE

A Spiritual Fitness Guide for Endurance Athletes

Shane Alton Eversfield

BREAKAWAY BOOKS
HALCOTTSVILLE, NEW YORK
2003

Zendurance
Copyright 2003 by Shane Alton Eversfield

ISBN: 978-1-891369-43-8
Library of Congress Control Number: 2003109382

Published by Breakaway Books
P.O. Box 24
Halcottsville, NY 12438
www.breakawaybooks.com
(800) 548-4348

CONTENTS

FOREWORD

Paula Newby-Fraser

I have been an athlete all my life. The arena of training and competing stretches as far back as I can remember. From early mornings on the pool deck in South Africa to pedaling through the mountains of Colorado—sports have given me the full range of human experiences. This ongoing journey is a very complex one and continues to be my source of intrigue, understanding and evolution.

The tangibles and objectives of training and competing are something that my peers and I have grown to readily embrace and understand. How easy it is to become immersed in heart rates, splits, power outputs, seat angles and every little detail that goes into the preparation to compete in a triathlon to the very best of one's ability. The numbers are all there—to see, to graph, to analyze and dissect. It is difficult to grow up without the ingrained notion that success is *all about results*. Time and splits never lie— they are there for us to see, recording our every effort, and thus setting the standard for us to eclipse on the next go-round.

Having toed the line as many times as I have over the past decades, I realize that all the great performances, results, trophies and accolades are certainly a part of this challenge. However, there is that "something else" that we all know is the *real* essence of our motivation and the synergy that gets us out there to train and race. It is tough to articulate because it is so intangible. Yet this something else is so powerful that we *share the bond* of knowing its existence as a vital part of who we are.

Dare we spend our precious time embracing our *spirit* energy— investigating and understanding it—when there are "real" numbers and facts we can correlate to plot a tangible course to a personal best?

We pay lip service to the mind-body-spirit synergy. There is no doubt for any of us that this elusive balance is what we are all ultimately searching for. In my past five years of teaching in the arena of triathlon, I have clumsily tried to spend time imparting my own intuitive understanding to this synergy. I have been urging fellow athletes to spend time and give commitment to their spiritual and mental harmony—if only a small part. Why spend so much time, money, and energy in total physical preparation—yet roll the dice on our emotional and spiritual readiness? This is the *difficult* challenge. It takes courage and (to borrow an expression introduced in this book) *spiritual fitness* to look within and steer the power of our thoughts and spirit, to understand and accept our strength and value as individuals—even if we do it behind the guise of completing an Ironman. This inner journey is a tough and grueling task in our society today—even in the playground of sports.

We have an over-abundance of technical guidance and reassurance to help us become better physical athletes—but where do we turn for guidance in integrating our spiritual selves on this chosen path? With honor and awe, I have watched Shane Eversfield step up and find a way to offer such a complete work in this area that is so wanting. This is truly an incredible guide for us as endurance athletes and as human beings. *Zendurance* articulates the emotions and intuitions we all feel and lets us put some real understanding to it all.

I invite you to open your heart, your mind and your body—to allow your passion for the practice of endurance to lead you to ultimate intuitive illumination—zendurance.

Paula Newby Fraser

STARTING LINE

The Vision

Thirty-four days before my very first iron-distance triathlon, I awoke on a Sunday morning with a feeling in my chest—a feeling of devastation. In the previous six months, I had been able to tip-toe all the way out to the very end of the plank of over-training. I had cautiously turned around and inched out until only my toes were touching—poised for a graceful back dive or perhaps a daring full gainer into the crystalline pool of racing glory.

Well, sometime during the night, that long and feeble plank of overtraining had snapped. When I awoke on that Sunday morning, I was free-falling deep into the chasm of fatigue. I was no longer invincible. I was terrified. I honestly wasn't sure if I would even be alive in thirty-four days. Amid the tears, I vividly saw that I had trained myself right out of a life.

For the next thirty-three days I balanced almost breathlessly on a very thin line between recovering enough to stay alive so that I could make it to the starting line, and training enough to see the finish line. The day after finishing that iron-distance triathlon, I resolved to address the significant gap between my artistic/athletic endeavors—the dreams and visions that send my spirit soaring—and my health and well-being as an ordinary human being. Zendurance as a vision is born out of the compelling commitment to integrate these two—glorious athlete and healthy human being.

Zendurance is for all endurance athletes—from the novice to the professional elite. The endurance activities we will consider in this book are swimming, biking, and running—combined together as triathlon. Even if you are not a triathlete—or a swimmer, cyclist or runner—take heart. All endurance activities—walking, hiking, skating, cross-country skiing, snowshoeing, paddling, rowing—have the same potential to be practices of zendurance. This book can still be of great value to you for transforming any endurance activity into zendurance.

Defining Endurance

What makes an activity an endurance activity? *Activity*, in our context, is movement. *Endurance activity* is patterned, cyclic movement that is sustained over a period of time. How long must an activity be sustained to be an endurance activity? The duration—based on our unique individual capacities—varies widely with each type of activity. For one individual, completing a one-mile walk or run might be a rich, challenging, and satisfying endurance activity. For another, it might be just part of a warm-up routine before a substantially longer race.

As we transform endurance training into zendurance practice, we are enhancing the quality of our activity more than the quantity. Each of us must appreciate, honor, and respect our own capacities and those of others as well. Any endurance activity twenty minutes or longer affords us the opportunity of moving meditation.

A desirable element to our endurance activity is cross-lateral movements. These are movements like walking strides (left-right) with opposing arm movements (right-left). Cross-lateral movements coordinate and stimulate function of both halves of our brains. These alternating movements balance us out through the left-right opposition. Not all conventional endurance forms incorporate this cross-lateral movement, but it does not diminish their potential for movement meditation.

Generally, the intensity level of endurance activity should not be very high. Low to moderate intensity levels yield the best results—both as physical exercise and as meditative practice.

Function of This Book

This book is not a technical training manual. See Philip Maffetone's books *In Fitness and in Health, Training for Endurance,* and *Eating for Endurance* for excellent guidance on basic, sensible and healthy approaches toward endurance training—regardless of experience or fitness level. For the triathlete with even an introductory level of experience, Joe Friel's *Triathlete's Training Bible* is a masterful, comprehensive training guide towards preparing for and realizing great racing performances.

Zendurance is a guide to transforming endurance athletic activity—both training and racing—into a viable spiritual practice. You need not be afraid or suspicious of the term *spiritual.* This book is not a religious doctrine and does not seek to sway or orient anyone toward any religious doctrines. *Zendurance* is intended to be compatible with your present religious convictions—or their absence.

Spiritual Practice

A spiritual practice is a self-empowering way of gaining insight and wisdom about our true, essential nature. A viable spiritual practice must also empower us with the ability to integrate and apply that insight and wisdom in our everyday lives. This includes our families, relationships, occupation, and so forth—as well as our endurance training. A true spiritual practice should endow us with genuine clarity, happiness, compassion, and calm mindful presence moment to moment.

The Zen Question

What is Zen anyway? The word *Zen* has certainly arisen recently as a fashionable, trendy expression, but what does it refer to? What is it specifically that a Zen practitioner does to progress toward mastery? On the exterior, a Zen practitioner doesn't seem to do anything out of the ordinary—with the exception of meditation, perhaps—and doesn't appear unusual.

As a practice—an activity—Zen is the development and cultivation of a calm, still, silent, open, and empty space of deep inner listening and contemplation. (Get familiar with this phrase. You will read it many times in this book.) The activity of Zen is to cultivate stillness—inactivity. How can stillness be of value in endurance athletics? They seem to be opposites, since endurance requires steady activity for a long duration.

The Paradox of Zen

Zen is illusive and paradoxical by nature. It appears to be one thing and then shifts to appear as just the opposite thing. If Zen is an empowering path toward mastery, it must include the process of activating and dissolving the obstacles and ignorance we possess that—in this present moment—eclipse us from that mastery. Athletic training also works with this same principle when we focus our training on the weakest aspect of our ability in order to improve. In this perspective, Zen and athletic training both approach perfection through imperfection.

Most of us are familiar with this experience: As we become more proficient and knowledgeable in some area, we become increasingly aware of how much we don't know. We have all heard the expression, "The more you know, the more you realize just how much you don't know." As our awareness sharpens, so does our awareness of what we don't know. Zen brings us awareness of our mastery and it also brings us awareness of our naïveté. Zen is not the answer; Zen is the quest, the questioning.

In its most traditional essence, Zen is an investigation—a quest—into the nature of consciousness and awareness. Where does our awareness, our consciousness come from? What principles govern awareness?

The Value of Zen—Effortless Power

What can possibly be the value for us as endurance athletes of gaining awareness about awareness? How can that help us? How can it improve our performance and increase our level of mastery as athletes? If Zen practice is to develop and cultivate a calm, still, silent, open, and empty space of deep inner listening and contemplation, what benefits will we experience as we become more proficient at this practice?

Most of us have—at least occasionally—experienced a time when life seemed effortless, when we were able to just go with the flow. This experience was one of harmony and integration with the people, places and things around us—when our inner universe and our outer universe were in balance. Regardless of whether that experience occurred during an exciting and stimulating time or a quiet and seemingly uneventful time, we felt calm and at ease inside. We were in touch with that calm, still space within. Our relationship with the universe around us seemed effortless. This is an experience of effortless power.

Effortless Power and Our Cosmic Mirror

The experience of harmony and effortless power can only come from a calm, still, silent, open, and empty space of deep inner listening and contemplation. If we are agitated, frustrated, frantic, angry, or frightened inside, it is reflected and mirrored in the universe around us—there is friction, resistance, turmoil and chaos in our outer universe. A principle tenet of Zen—indeed of life itself—is that the outer universe around us accurately reflects and mirrors what is true in our inner universe. This is our cosmic mirror.

Effortless power. Now, that's a very attractive offer, isn't it? Sounds like a great asset for our endurance training and racing, yes? Well, it all starts with that calm, still center. Your universe works from the inside out.

In the reverse flow, we choose to be the victim, to blame the outer universe for the condition of our inner universe. We are simply moving backward—against the flow—disempowering ourselves. The result? We experience friction, resistance, turmoil, and difficulty—conditions that are not at all conducive to great athletic performances or to a full and satisfying life. The practice of Zen begins with the clear recognition of this cosmic mirror and the way in which we each create our universe from the inside out. The most vital and valuable asset in this commitment is our calm, still, silent, open and empty space of deep inner listening and contemplation.

Sounds very simple, yes? Ah, paradox! That which appears most simple can be most difficult. Our commitment must be tenacious. Then again, as endurance athletes, we are already pretty familiar with tenacity.

Effortless Power—Right Here and Right Now

So how is it that we can experience effortless power through a calm, still, silent, open and empty space of deep inner listening and contemplation? When our awareness and our interactions are sourced from this space, we exist very much in the present moment, free of the conditioning of the past and the expectations of the future. When we are present in this moment, we are fully capable and free to respond appropriately rather than reacting through our burden and attachment to past patterns or future desires. Responding appropriately includes yielding, blending, and aligning with the current circumstances as they really are—rather than how we think they should be. We offer no resistance and no struggle. As they say in Jamaica, "No problem, mon."

We often think of power as control. Paradox once again. Power is choice—it is choosing what is so in this moment. It is not necessarily liking what is so. Effortless power is realized through yielding, embracing, blending, aligning, and integrating—giving up our desire to control and accepting what is. Zen as a state of being is open to effortless power and is calm in its presence.

Questions?

Throughout this book, we contemplate many questions. In our modern informational culture, we are conditioned to seek immediate answers, to fortify ourselves with the latest information. We strive to move from question to answer as quickly as possible. Because of our emphasis on answers, we invest little time and energy in actually formulating and constructing questions. There is a tremendous potential for knowledge that lies in the patience and willingness to sit with and contemplate questions without attachment to the immediate gratification of answers. The opportunity for knowledge in this context is an opportunity for wisdom rather than information.

Back to the Beginning

In traditional Zen Buddhism, there is the essential concept of beginner's mind. Suzuki Roshi, who made this notion popular in the West, says, "In the beginner's mind there are many possibilities, but in the expert's mind there are few." As an illustration of this essential quality, consider the name of the most popular Western magazine on Buddhism and spiritual paths: *Tricycle*. A tricycle is a child's vehicle, a beginner's vehicle. Are we willing to swallow our pride, to dismount from our stealthy, road-warrior aero bikes and get back on the tricycle of naïveté—of the beginner's mind?

It takes a tremendous amount of courage, humility, and conviction to embrace our naïveté and to remain open to possibilities. Naïveté and openness are the grounds for creativity and art—our next topic.

As we engage in endurance athletics, we are engaging in a quest. Quest. Question. Coincidence?

What Is Art?

Typically we think of art as a painting, a sculpture, or some other unique, one-of-a-kind object. Art that we appreciate portrays a sense of beauty or grace. We may be familiar with the expressions, "She's got that down to an art" or "He's got that down to a science"—expressions that usually refer to a great level of skill or mastery. But what's the difference between art and science?

Throughout human civilization, we have used both the logical, empirical, left-brain scientific process and the intuitive, creative, imaginative right-brain process to investigate and learn about the universe around and within us. The scientific and the creative processes are not mutually exclusive or separate from one another. Albert Einstein—widely regarded as one of the most brilliant scientists of our modern era—said, "Imagination is more important than knowledge." His scientific discoveries and advancements required a creative approach as well as a scientific one.

Many books have been written about the science of athletic

training and racing—books based on empirical evidence and measurable results derived from well-defined research and experimentation. Studying and interpreting these books and then integrating and applying the knowledge and the principles can be extremely valuable. It can lead endurance athletes, trainers and coaches to remarkable achievements. The same diligent process of study and application can also lead to dismal failure.

If the scientific results are so accurate and predictable, then why is there so much variation? Scientific experiments are conducted in the laboratory—a controlled environment in which certain variables are either manipulated or held constant. Step out of the controlled environment and it's *Welcome to the real world*. Real time, real live circumstances, real athletes with real jobs, real families, and real lives.

The ability to interpret and apply scientific knowledge in the real world requires both accurate observation/perception and creative, intuitive, ingenious response/action. It requires that the athlete creatively implement his or her training program with a healthy dose of flexibility and articulation in the present moment—given the present conditions of both the athlete and the surrounding environment. This is the art of science. Since training and racing are not conducted in the lab, a creative approach is vital.

If the art of science is the perceptive and creative genius to apply and integrate the universal operating principles and laws in this present moment and these circumstances, then what is the science of art, of creativity? Have patience, we will return to this question.

What Is Patience?

What is patience and how do we cultivate it? Where does it come from and how do we source it? What is the value of patience? How does it empower us?

Like most qualities of Zen—of spiritual training—patience is pure and simple and yet it is a subtle and profound power that can be difficult to find. Patience naturally and effortlessly arises when we are—you guessed it—calm, still, silent, open, and empty. As we become progressively more present and engaged in the *now*, with fewer and fewer strings attached to the past and future, we lose or give up impatience. The resulting emptiness? That's patience.

The Value of Patience

Patience allows us to calmly and diligently approach each training session, each task in our lives, and each interaction with others. When we are patient—without attachment to a desired result—we are much more present and aware—more intelligent. Patience is absolutely paramount to quality training sessions and great race performances. One of the occasions when it may be most difficult to practice patience—and the most beneficial—is when we are preparing for and starting a very long training session—say a five-to-six-hour bike-run session.

Our tendency might be to arrive at our staging area, pull out our bikes, and just get on with it. With patience, however, we are more mindful to check over our bikes, to set up our running gear for a smooth transition later on, and to put on that sunscreen and lip "da kine." Our long sessions usually require a bit more preparation—extra water bottles, nutrition and spare tubes, cash and other personals. One suggestion is to start off riding for a mile or two in the opposite direction before turning back and passing our staging area on the way out. This affords us the opportunity to stop for anything we might have forgotten without the psychological glitch of having to turn around and go back. Those first out-and-back miles give us a chance to gently and patiently warm up, to get conscious of our breathing and to begin settling in for the duration.

If you are accustomed to riding with others, arrive well ahead of your departure time (just like the airport) and prepare gently and patiently. Do a little out-and-back ride on your own so you can tune in. When it is time to depart with your friends, you will not be distracted with what you might be forgetting or how your bike setup feels. Every moment of that long session counts. It is important to set that mindfulness in motion right from the start.

Summarizing Patience

Patience requires yielding and surrendering. Patience and presence require that we let go of our attachments, expectations, anticipations, and our desire to be somewhere in the future now. Patience is presence—here and now! How easy it is for us to forget *here and now* during those last few days before a big race. This is a great opportunity to move slowly, deliberately, and gracefully in every moment—practicing patience, patience.

Well, if you are reading this, then you do have patience. Better yet—patience is arising through you. Instead of patiently reading this, you could have been out there clicking off a few more miles on that bike.

In athletics, there are two alternatives to patience—injury and burnout. Impatience demands quantity. Patience embraces quality.

What Is Discipline?

From a child's perspective, discipline is notoriously associated with punishment. Even as adults, discipline is still associated with punishment. We are dishing it out to our own kids and we have our own ways of punishing ourselves—self-discipline, we call it.

Let's refresh our perspective of discipline. How does *discipline* relate to the word *disciple*? A disciple is someone wholly committed—with impeccability and integrity—to a path or process of learning, growing and living. Punishment is not so commonly associated with a disciple as it is with discipline. A disciple may be willing to forgo certain pleasures, privileges, or indulgences as he or she commences along the chosen path. These abstentions are not, however, viewed as punishments—they are not measures to correct bad behavior.

Clear Vision And Intention

A disciple clearly and willingly chooses to forgo certain activities and deliberately and mindfully pursue others. For a disciple, this choice does not require discipline as we usually view it—it requires clear intention and clear vision of where the path or process is leading. It is the exhilarating and clear experience of accomplishment and knowledge that motivates the disciple and inspires integrity.

Here is an illustration of the willful choice—of a disciple in a fairly traditional context: As I am writing this section of *Zendurance*, my wife, Fatima, is engaged in a fairly traditional form of spiritual practice known as a retreat. For one year, she has chosen not to speak and not to leave our farm. In addition to shaving her head once a week (I know triathlon disciples who do that), she chooses to forgo conventional distractions and diversions—TV, radio, magazines, newspapers, most reading material and a majority of our CD collection. She does not eat after 2 or 3 P.M.

For most of us, this may seem like a harsh and austere punishment. However, just like the disciple of endurance athletics, she clearly experiences how this practice is enhancing her human-being-ness and spirituality. Her serenity is remarkable. For exam-

ple, occasionally birds get into our house and then frantically fly at
the closed windows to escape. Fatima can walk right up to them,
place her hands around them, and carry them outside. They have
no fear of her in that calm, serene state. It amazes our friends who
have witnessed this.

Rather than obsessively flailing that punishing whip of discipline
at our training and racing, we can be disciples. As endurance athletes, we can choose to be skillful, committed practitioners. We can
be clear in our vision. We can see clearly the direction of the path
we are choosing. Clarity is a strong motivator—more powerful than
punishment.

Clarity, in this context, is not about having answers—it is not
about knowing with certainty that we will be capable of maintaining a set pace for a specific mileage in order to compete or win
against others or ourselves. Clarity is about seeing the big picture—our quest as endurance athletes and how it enhances and
empowers our human beingness.

Endurance athletics as a viable life style and spiritual practice
does not require the punishment of discipline. It requires that we
become disciples—that we skillfully use our training as a practice
toward our well-being and the well-being of others with clear intention and clear vision. As disciples, let's examine the Law of Creation
as the ancient Hawaiians view it.

The Law of Creation—Hawaiian Style

The ancient Hawaiians refer to the Law of Creation as *Kanawai
Kumulipo* (pronounced: kah-nah-VAI koo-moo-LEE-poh). *Kanawai*
is the Hawaiian word for "law." Within *kanawai* is the word *wai*—
fresh water—a most essential and vital element of life. (Hawaiian is
a sacred and empowering language that is full of this kind of
encoding.) In *kanawai, wai* emphasizes just how vital and essential this Law of Creation is in our lives.

The encoding within the word *kumulipo* is quite profound. The
meanings for *kumu* include "source," "teacher" and "tree." As
Connie Rios explains in her book *Ka Hana Pono*, a tree is "something that has withstood the test of time, has as much below the
surface as above, is firmly rooted in the earth (the material aspect)
and also reaches out to the heavens (symbolizing spirit). 'Lipo'
means deepest darkness. Kanawai Kumulipo: the physical law of
creation from the deepest source of darkness."

So what is the relevance of this law to clarity of intention and

vision as the true source of discipline? When we choose to accept
the challenge of training for and completing an arduous endurance
event, it is our clear intent and vision that effectively motivates us,
rather than the punishment of discipline. We activate and set in
motion the Law of Creation when we generate that clear intent and
vision. We are committed to creating and realizing our goal.

This next important quote from *Ka Hana Pono* reveals just how
powerful our process toward realizing that challenging endurance
goal is: "A deep understanding of the law creates the awareness
that what you've actually energized is the surfacing of every dark
thing ('lipo') within you that stands in the way" of your vision, your
intention or your dream. Pretty powerful stuff, huh? If we look honestly at our own lives, we know this to be true. When we choose to
diligently pursue a well-defined goal, the process of realizing that
goal is a process of clearing and dissolving all the obstacles (internal as well as external) that arise along that path.

The punishment of discipline would stipulate that we beat those
obstacles (those parts of ourselves) into submission—that we wage
war on them, usually to the point of injuring ourselves. The disciple, on the other hand, chooses to embrace those obstacles gracefully and to resolve or dissolve them with patience, humility, and
compassion. This is truly the path of effortless power. Since *kumu*
also means "teacher," *Kumulipo* implies that our deepest darkness
and ignorance is our teacher.

The way in which we treat and honor our own darkness—our
own weaknesses, fears, and obstacles—largely determines how
well we can illuminate our darkness and how we embrace our radi-
ance and light. If we beat ourselves into submission while we are
training toward our goal races—and call it discipline—we will be
lucky to make it to the starting line intact. (I speak from experience
here.) As disciples, it is through our graceful, patient, and compassionate approach—illuminating our darkness and embracing
and dissolving our obstacles—that we shine with brilliance on race
day.

Starting Line

The Law of Creation—as revealed through the wisdom of ancient
and sacred Hawaiian culture—answers our earlier question, *What
is the science of art—of creativity?* As we pursue a vision or a goal,
we are engaging in an act of creativity. As we realize our vision, we
will experience all of our darkness—our fears, ignorance, weak-

nesses, and so on—that have the potential to eclipse our light—our awareness, brilliance, and mastery—from illuminating that vision. This is the science of art, plain and simple. In human terms, as we progress and grow—be it as athletes, husbands, wives, what have you—we will experience our ignorance and obstacles. These obstacles and ignorance may appear from within us or through others and from seemingly external sources—via our cosmic mirror.

We have the choice to ignore the Law of Creation—to go through our lives refusing to acknowledge our own darkness, to wage war upon it, and to view ourselves as victims in our universe. As disciples, we can choose to embrace our darkness as our teacher—our *Kumulipo*—and truly begin to discover effortless power.

This choice is the beginning of our Zen path, our spiritual path. As endurance athletes, it is the beginning of zendurance.

This is the Starting Line. Welcome.

I

TRI-ZEN

ZENDURANCE

WHY TRI?

SWIMMING—YIELDING

BICYCLING—BLENDING

RUNNING—ALIGNING

ZENDURANCE TRAINING SUMMARY

WHAT IS FORM?

WHAT IS FEEL?

INTELLIGENCE OF TRI-ZEN

T-1: TRANSITION ONE

Mind in matter.

ZENDURANCE

Introduction

How are endurance activities such as swimming, biking, running, walking, hiking, skating, cross-country skiing, rowing, and paddling similar to the activities of traditional spiritual and Zen practices? How can they enhance our mental, emotional and spiritual health as well as our physical health? How can we transform these activities into genuine moving meditations—endurance into zendurance? To answer these questions, let's examine the fundamental similarities between aerobic endurance athletics and traditional spiritual practices.

Solitude and the Inner Journey

In the Zen approach to endurance training, solitude is an essential condition. Rather than focusing on interaction and conversation—disassociating ourselves from the movement activity we are engaged in—we turn our awareness inward, experiencing the inner state—the alignment and integrity of body, mind, heart and spirit. This is the first step toward creating and experiencing the movement meditation of zendurance.

As our physical *and* mental strength develop, we are able to sustain the groove of our training session for a longer duration as a moving meditation. Physically we gain strength in our bones, connective tissue, and muscles, we develop metabolic and aerobic capacity, and we improve our efficiency, coordination, and harmony. (These last three are primarily neurological gains.) Mentally we acquire patience, calmness, and concentration, as well as keen perception and awareness. Together, through the integration of body and mind, we cultivate greater sensitivity and intelligence.

Moving meditation is a simple and natural way of tapping into our energetic nature. We discover a profound realization: As we become clear and empty channels or vessels, our capacity to embrace and to flow energy expands and increases. Zendurance is our physical aerobic capacity combined with our mental focus and stamina. It is both the physical and mental skills to sustain this zone—this meditative state of relaxation and emptiness during endurance activity.

For many of us, especially in Western culture, this inward focus can be very unfamiliar and strange. We are conditioned from birth to project our awareness and activity outward. Our inner journey may be regarded only as self-serving and with no outwardly apparent value or productive use. However, as we begin to explore our own inner wilderness through meditation—be it moving/kinetic meditation or traditional sitting meditation—we discover a much deeper awareness and a more tangible presence in ourselves during our meditation and when we return our attention and energy outward again. We develop a greater capacity for patience, tolerance, and attentiveness in our interactions with others through our development of inner focus and awareness.

Finding Balance

This does not mean that we must conduct all our endurance activity and training alone. Especially for the initiate—who has limited experience with this kind of inward journey and meditation—it may be much too monotonous and severe to spend hours at a time in this inner state. For some it may be distressing or discouraging, while others may find it gratifying from the start. As with anything new in life, we gradually familiarize ourselves with our own inner wilderness.

Conversely, we can also cultivate this inner focus and exploration to the virtual exclusion of our interactive, outward attention and activity. We can become disassociated from our surroundings, loved ones, and community. As athletes, this can happen if we become obsessed with increasing our training loads to improve our performances (greed and addiction) or as a way of escaping situations and relationships we do not want to face (avoidance). We may train ourselves right out of a life. This is the scenario that often leads to overtraining and injury.

With both our hearts and our minds, we must remember that we have to be healthy, whole, and balanced human beings before we can be athletes. Then our endurance activities can substantially support and enhance our human-being-ness.

I conduct most of my training in solitude, and I enjoy it immensely. Provided I am not overtraining, I finish my sessions with a clear, open, and receptive mind, an acute and heightened sensitivity to the world around me, and a calm, serene joy in the simplest activities. For me the solitude of training is a privilege and a pleasure. As oriented as I am toward solitude, I also find it very healthy and gratifying to periodically train and race with others for the fellowship and the opportunity to express and share with other athletes the joy of our health and our activity. Our endurance activity must include the healthy and vital elements of play and companionship.

In summary, the solo nature of endurance athletics is a valuable element in our Zen approach. It encourages us to look inward, to explore our inner wilderness and to cultivate inner listening. This inner listening becomes one of the most valuable and essential skills of the accomplished endurance athlete. It is a prerequisite to developing form and feel, two topics we will explore further.

Going in Circles

The second similarity shared by traditional meditative practice and endurance athletics is cyclical repetition. In many traditional forms of meditation, there is the continuous use of a mantra—a word or phrase sounded vocally or repeated silently with the inner voice—usually with slow, calm breathing. In some meditation forms, the cycle of breathing serves as the mantra. In our zendurance approach to aerobic athletics, it is the stride or stroke of our repetitive movement that serves as our mantra. This endless patterning becomes a bridge or a vehicle so that we can disengage from our normal mental activities and distractions. Our mind naturally begins to settle into the cyclical pattern of our movement— as we progress into a subtle, quiet state of consciousness.

The Calm Pond and Clear Thinking

Traditional schools of meditation offer an analogy to describe this process of calming the mind: Let's imagine our consciousness as a pond or lake. In our normal, active thinking state of consciousness, the water in the pond is moving—there is activity in the form of currents within the pond and waves upon its surface. This activity—currents and waves in the water—equates with the complex collage and layering of our conscious thought and activity. In a turbulent pond, sediment is stirred up and suspended, making the water murky. We cannot see through the water and cannot see the bottom. The waves and ripples on the top surface make it difficult even to see our own reflection. With increasing activity, it becomes progressively more difficult to see into the pond—likewise, it becomes more difficult to see clearly into the nature of consciousness.

In our Western culture, we are extremely activity and thought oriented. We hold relentlessly to our busy outward focus and our verbal consciousness. Hence our mental ponds are typically very murky because of the high level of agitation—the high level of mental activity. Culturally this can be a difficult condition to change. We may not see that there is an alternative to this unceasing level of activity. Through meditation, using a repetitive form of mantra—either a word/phrase or a movement—we begin to calm and distill our minds—to bring clarity to our pond or lake of consciousness.

Athletics And Serenity

Herein lies the true beauty of endurance training and events. In the guise of an outward activity leading to a well-defined goal—the finish line of a race, for example—there exists, on a deeper level, a very powerful inner experience of discovering our true calm and serene nature. It is our cultural hunger for such deep inner exploration and serenity that has led to the incredible popularity and rapid growth of endurance events, such as marathons, century rides, and long-distance triathlons.

Many athletes who complete their first long-distance event/race realize that, while the finisher's T-shirt and medal are cherished and well-earned mementos, it is the endurance lifestyle—the day-to-day commitment to training—that brings the real value, satisfaction, love and sense of accomplishment. It is the ordinary and daily practice of developing that inner listening—as we quiet and empty the thinking mind through the repetition of endurance training in solitude—that yields true happiness and satisfaction. This practice of going in circles becomes a powerful and effective tool that enhances all areas of the endurance athlete's life.

Seamless repetition includes the element of circles. The movements of endurance activities are circular—they have no apparent beginning or end. Likewise, in some traditional forms of meditation, the practitioner fixes his or her gaze on an image called a mandala—a symmetrical and circular visual pattern. This image can be a physical image hung in front of the practitioner or an image held purely in the mind. The circular symmetry leads the practitioner inward to the center.

Zendurance: Our Path to Meditation

In zendurance, the seamless, circular motion of our athletic activity brings us to our center as we establish the inner balance and coordination to smooth out and make our activity more effortless. As we train, particularly in our solo sessions, we can begin to locate in our bodies the center point—the origin—of our movements. This solo, inner focus and the repetitive, circular nature of our endurance activity will naturally lead our bodies and minds toward a collective center of movement.

At that center, body, heart, and mind share a kind of unified field—a universal medium—where we experience wholeness and integrity. This experience of wholeness and integrity is also reflected and manifested outwardly, in our relationships with the world around us—with our families and friends, and through our occupations and daily activities. As we go through our daily lives, we begin to abide in that place of stillness—it becomes more tangible for us. Our clarity and integrity of body, mind, heart and spirit promotes a more harmonious dance with the world around us.

Staying on the Path

For those of us ingrained in Western cultural ways, it can be very difficult to gain experience and understanding in the nature of our consciousness and awareness. Through zendurance, we can use our aerobic training sensibly to investigate the nature of consciousness. For many of us, the greatest challenge in this practice is not maintaining the discipline to train and live the endurance Zen life—it is developing discernment and honesty with ourselves. We must be able to distinguish between healthy zendurance practice—that steadily improves our overall health and our athletic performance potential—and the obsessive ego-drive to improve performance no matter what the cost. (Training with a heart rate monitor offers the most accurate physiological criteria.)

I did not have that discernment and honesty thirty-four days before my first iron triathlon . . . Or did I? When I awoke on that Sunday morning, feeling like I had suddenly aged by forty years, the truth is, I was not surprised. My body and my mind had issued clear warnings that I was overtraining—yet I refused to heed them. Why?

Stressing on the Path

Plain and simple: I was addicted to stress. It was the only pattern of existence I had known for years. I was physically addicted to the draining feeling of fatigue, sluggishness, and painful mornings. I was mentally addicted to the agitation, anxiety and obsession. I was chemically addicted to my body's adrenaline and its array of stress-induced hormones, coupled with caffeine for that jump start. I was not even aware of these addictions.

I was a stress junkie. How did that happen? When did it happen? Certainly I did not deliberately and intentionally navigate into this addictive stress pattern. Somehow, gradually over decades of time, I had refined and concentrated this pattern. When continuous and chronic stress is culturally regarded as a normal and natural state of being—a way of living—then it doesn't appear at all inappropriate to tiptoe all the way out to the end of that feeble plank of overtraining in the hope of pulling off a respectable race performance.

Culturally, stress is not only appropriate and encouraged; it is exploited. Billions are spent each year to "relieve" the stress we create for ourselves. This includes medications, vacations, libations and home entertainment stations. It takes tenacious discernment and genuine self-honesty to actually see this latent and insidious disease of stress addiction. Our cultural values and our media encourage and stimulate stress. For many of us, it is literally the only pattern, the only mode of functioning that we know. It is the one that gets us through the demanding challenges and tasks of our lives.

How can we possibly "see the forest through the trees"? How can we transform this unconscious mode of functioning into a healthy and gratifying way of living? Our zendurance approach to athletic activity can be a conscious and deliberate opportunity to transform the stress addiction of our lives into calmness and serenity. Our practice of zendurance can be instrumental in gradually dismantling our addiction to stress and repatterning our lives. The calm, abiding awareness and serenity we develop through the movement meditation of zendurance practice can actually strengthen our tenacious discernment and genuine self-honesty.

The Profound Power of Movement

Just how powerful and effective can a simple physical activity be in developing and directing mindfulness? In my early twenties, I began studying and practicing tai chi on my own. My guidance came from two sources. One was a book with photos and brief descriptions of the movements and a few pages that described some basic principles like breath, relaxation, and attitude. The other essential source of guidance was simply feeling the chi energy and allowing my body and movements to be directed by it.

After practicing for four or five years on my own, I read a book on the philosophy and practice of Taoism—the source of tai chi and the yin-yang symbol. Although I had never before consciously studied Taoism—at least not through the intellectual approach of reading a book—it was incredibly familiar and second nature to me. I felt like I had been a Taoist all along. Tai chi, as physical application of Taoism—as a kinetic activity of body and mind—had deeply instilled and activated these profound and fundamental principles within me. My familiarity with Taoism did not occur as a result of our normal way of learning—by reading and assimilating the principles on a conceptual level, and then filing them in a logical form of memory. It happened through conscious and deliberate movement.

Reading that book on Taoism awoke in me the realization of just how powerful and profound a seemingly physical practice could be for the whole integral self. Our zendurance practice—and the calm abiding awareness we cultivate through this kinetic meditation—offers us a great opportunity to clear our deeply ingrained patterns of stress.

Reclaiming Our Youth

For many of us, swimming, biking, and running were the most basic and familiar youthful recreational activities. As young children, most of us did not engage in these activities as direct and formal competition. Swimming was most often a summertime beat-the-heat activity. Running was a consequence of game playing and team sports. Cycling was a fun and practical form of transportation.

These are all activities we associate with childhood—a time of avid interests, vibrant creativity and imagination, and vivacious physical health and energy. Those powerful memories and associations with youthfulness can be instrumental as adults in breaking our sedentary physical state and our mental resignation to aging, stress, and the burdens and responsibilities of adulthood.

One of the oldest participants in Hawaii Ironman says, "Youth is a gift of nature, age is a work of art." The quality of each of our individual works of art is determined largely by our physical, mental, and spiritual health as well as our playfulness and creativity. Engaging in these simple childhood activities as a practice toward illumination and enlightenment can go a long way toward appreciating the gift of nature and skillfully crafting the work of art. Most endurance activities are so simple and basic that children can joyfully engage in them. They return us to the beginner's mind.

Is the child within you still alive, curious, and playing? Is the artist within you still passionate, searching, and creative?

WHY TRI?

Introduction

Why would a competent single-sport swimmer, cyclist, or runner (or walker, skier, whatever) take on the additional training of one or more activities in which he or she has less experience, competence, and familiarity? Particularly if it appears that this would be at the expense of the single-sport training program—at the risk of diminishing performance? This is completely against our modern trend toward specialization.

For many of us, stepping into unfamiliar territory is difficult and uncomfortable. I am a perfect example of this kind of fixed person. As a consideration of the *Why Tri?* question, I will share with you the circumstances that first "encouraged" me to cross-train, and the results of that first experience.

Personal Experience

I was a very satisfied recreational runner for more than twenty years—I ran every kind of terrain from city blocks to wilderness trails. I had just run my very first race six months earlier (Honolulu Marathon) at the age of forty-one. Now, six months later, I was training for my third marathon, with the intention of actually racing that distance for the first time. In my zeal and obsession, I overtrained, sustained an injury to my right foot, and could not run at all for six weeks. I had run through many injuries before, but the few times I attempted to run with this one, I succeeded only in aggravating the injury. I was psychologically demoralized.

The only choice I had was between torment and depression or the renewal of my other childhood activities—swimming and easy cycling. (Intensive cycling aggravated the injury.) I was also able to water-run—both in the conventional manner of closely imitating my running form in deep water (just my head above) and shoreline running in waist-deep water. None of these activities really provided me with the runner's high that I dearly loved and was addicted to but they seemed to stave off a complete mental breakdown.

My outlook on this training program was skeptical at best and downright disdainful most of the time. In fact, three weeks into this trial, I threw away my two marathon medals as well as a trophy and some awards I had received in shorter races—disgusted with the absence of any indication that my injury was healing. *If I am to gain some kind of beneficial experience from this, it had better be pretty damn good,* I thought as I slogged away in the water, swimming and water-running. The most difficult element to deal with was my attitude and my attachment to running.

With the invaluable support of my wife, I collected the discarded medals and my broken trophy. We took them to a secluded spot near one of my favorite running routes and made a simple shrine offering—including the medals, awards, and some incense. I offered prayers and apologies to the ancestors of that area—an ancient Hawaiian battleground—and resolved to somehow "pull myself up by the bootstraps" and change my attitude. As athletes, our body discipline may be easy, but our mental discipline can be an incredible, intangible challenge. The simple ceremony of offering and resolve, especially in the company and support of my wife, made a big difference in opening my mind and finding vision again.

During my injury layoff, my work as a coffee farm technician necessitated that I continue walking three to five miles a day in the field. This is usually accomplished very slowly as I progress down the rows, working on the trees. While it may have hindered my healing process, it did provide me with very low-intensity aerobic base training. I stayed on my feet and active.

Well, with just two days left before the Kilauea Volcano Wilderness Marathon, I ran pain-free for two or three miles. This was the first time I had attempted to run in more than a month. Two days later, I gracefully finished the treacherous marathon. I walked part of the uphill section that ranges from miles 19 through 24. I finished sore and tired, but injury-free. I was happy, humble, very grateful, and full of joy just to come out and run. It reaffirmed for me that the greatest aspect of an endurance event is not how fast we finish, but the quality of the experience as a spiritual pilgrimage, as a compassionate appreciation for our humility, our strengths, and our weaknesses as human beings. Racing is a celebration of the grace and tenacity we have that allows us to humbly embrace these human qualities and dance through life. Like each and every finisher, I was a winner.

Despite my negative outlook, cross-training had proven very effective, even in this extreme case. Had I not cross-trained I probably would not have completed the marathon. As a result of that experience, I continued to develop a training program where I ran fewer miles than I ran before—at higher quality—supplementing with swimming and biking to maintain my aerobic base. At present, with the exception of run-only races, I rarely run without swimming or biking first. If I have the time before a running race, I will usually do part of my warm-up with my bike. Not a single, impactful step wasted—no "junk" miles.

Flexibility and Adaptability

Perhaps the greatest benefit of multisport training is that I no longer have such an addiction to running. And to my utter amazement, I completed my first Ironman eighteen months after the injury "encouraged" me to cross-train. Once we begin to choose the cross-training approach, we begin to cultivate flexibility and adaptability. These qualities enhance more than just our athletic activities. We begin to enjoy adaptability and flexibility in all areas of our lives. In zendurance, we seek to develop the same mindfulness, attentiveness, and effortless power in all areas of our lives.

Flexibility is tolerance. It connotes an attitude of openness and willingness to accept a wide variety of circumstances without attachment or a need to control the outcome. Flexibility brings us to the beginner's mind and the naïveté to go with the flow. Adaptability is the ingenuity, creativity and attentiveness to call forth our wisdom, insight, and compassion and to engage these skills in this present moment. Patience is a foundation for both flexibility and adaptability.

As we get older and more set in our ways, we come to realize how valuable flexibility and adaptability are for dealing with the most inevitable condition of life—change. Change is inevitable. No matter how insulated and safely we may live, no matter how much money we may have to secure and insure our health, wealth, environment, and surroundings, change is inevitable. Traditional Zen masters have been known to state that there is only one truth: change. Hence, flexibility and adaptability will make us fluid not only as triathletes, but even more so as human beings.

Triathlon challenges our flexibility and adaptability to be proficient at three sports, and to transition fluidly from one to the next. It also empowers our ability to integrate life as an athlete with life as a human being. If cross-training and multisport racing are going to be an integral and enduring part of a healthy life that includes family, friends, and community as well, then flexibility and adaptability are paramount.

SWIMMING—YIELDING

Water

The unique and obvious aspect of swimming is water. Water is not nearly as familiar to us as air because we spend very little time in our lives immersed in this fluid medium. As unfamiliar as this medium seems to us, our bodies are indeed composed mostly of water. Somewhere deep in our cellular memory we have a natural affinity with this fluid medium. We can access that affinity and our natural fluidity through a zendurance approach to swimming.

The most immediate and apparent sensation in our relationship with water is weightlessness. Water is far denser than the more familiar medium of air. The density and fluidity of water afford us some notable opportunities for exercise and for investigation that are unique to this medium.

Water exercise—be it swimming, aqua-aerobics, water-running, or the like—is free of impact. Aside from the potential danger of waves or currents in open water, it offers a safe medium with very little risk of mechanical injury. This may be a significant factor for those of us who are just embarking on an aerobic fitness program. For experienced athletes, this freedom from impact makes any aerobic water exercise a great recovery activity following a race, a hard workout or an injury. It is also the optimal warm-up—most professional triathletes begin their daily training regimes in the water. A session in the water will can gently prepare our bodies for the rigors of cycling or running by activating our muscles and joints and by increasing blood circulation through non-weight-bearing activity.

Open Ocean

Some of us have the fortunate option of conducting some of our swim training in the open ocean. Ocean swimming provides us with minerals and salts absorbed through the skin and membranes of the nose and mouth. This salty medium is a very effective deterrent to the respiratory ailments that can be brought on by a challenging training regime. Clean ocean water is recognized among health care practitioners for its therapeutic value.

If we restrict of our swim training to the open ocean, there is one disadvantage. The high salt content of ocean water provides us with lots of buoyancy. If we ever have the occasion to race in a freshwater lake without the aid of a wetsuit, then the lack of buoyancy—and our lack of experience—will make the swim especially difficult.

There is another very powerful element to open-ocean swimming. Each and every time I step off the Kona coast into the great blue Pacific, I am right in the center of the largest, most vast wilderness left on Planet Earth. Each and every time it is a humbling experience and a vivid reminder that Planet Earth does not revolve around humans. Despite our ability to manipulate and control our environment, we are still, especially as individuals, very small and vulnerable.

In our zendurance training, the experience of vulnerability and insignificance is very valuable. It evokes our compassion and humility and gives us a greater appreciation for the precious and delicate gift of life. Each time we enter the vast ocean wilderness, we confront and embrace our fears. We literally offer our bodies to the ocean and to the creatures within. We offer ourselves to a living entity far greater than our individual selves. The more we dance with our fears, the less our fears will control and limit us.

Fear of Water

Our fear of water can be one of the greatest obstacles to embrace as we embark on a water-based fitness program. With patience and curiosity, we can gradually investigate and move through our fear of water. Beyond the fear of stepping down from the top of the food chain that we associate with open-ocean swimming let's consider for a moment our fears of the medium of water.

When we enter the water and experience weightlessness, we no longer have the stable comfort and security of gravity. Our sense of grounding and stability has been pulled out from under us, as we enter a world that feels more fluid and unstable. This fear may be stronger if we are immersed in an open and moving body of water—a river or an ocean. Our illusion of control and stability vanishes—we are at the mercy of the water's massive strength. As we investigate our fear of this ever-changing and fluid medium, we may discover a deeper underlying fear—the pervasive impermanence and the inevitability of change in our human lives. We would prefer the security of stability and grounding, but in truth this is an illusion in our human existence. Change is inevitable.

Our zendurance approach to swimming offers us the opportunity to embrace and explore our fears of being ungrounded—of impermanence and change. We begin to explore and to bring light to our fears as we become intimately familiar with the medium of water. As we dispel our fears, we can assimilate the fluid and buoyant nature of water into our own being and learn to relax enough to go with the flow—in our swimming and in all the activities of our lives.

Eventually, with patience, compassion and trust, even the most fearful of us can embrace, explore and dispel our fears enough to swim in the clear blue Pacific waters hundreds of feet deep. The company of a few friends or several hundred athletes in a competition makes it far less daunting. With the sun's rays penetrating and undulating deep into the clear blue waters, it is a magical, transforming experience—to see so deeply into our own subconscious and behold the awesome beauty that lies beyond our fears.

The Pool: Our Zen Chamber

Very few of us have the opportunity to train year-round in the open waters of a lake or ocean. For most of us, the pool is our primary water temple. Take heart, for the pool also offers some valuable elements to our zendurance training. In contrast to open-ocean swimming, a pool can make our fears more approachable. Likewise, shallow-water swimming can be far less intimidating.

The most distinguishing element of pool swimming is the well-defined parameters of the pool itself. It is easy to be discouraged by the monotony of endless laps, back and forth in this water chamber. Consider that many traditional meditation practitioners engage in retreats—isolating themselves from any external distractions for a period of time ranging from a few hours to several years. Tibetan Buddhist lamas have been known to retreat to dark caves in the Himalayan Mountains for twelve years or more, rarely if ever engaging in interaction with another human—their simple meals left quietly at the cave entrance by a servant. The starkness of this kind of situation—free from any distractions—compels the practitioner to look deeply inward at the nature of Self, of mind and consciousness. In addition, many practitioners will not even lie down to sleep—resting in a meditative cross-legged posture all night.

When we consider these austere parameters, an hour of laps in the pool is not so extreme. Like a traditional meditation retreat, the pool offers little in the form of variation, diversion, or distraction. It is a very consistent environment. This can greatly facilitate our meditative zendurance approach as we turn our focus inward to subtler levels of awareness and feeling. The calm pool environment supports us in developing our subtle sensitivity—our feel for the water. Sensitivity is perhaps the most valuable attribute for improving our swimming technique. The pool is an excellent environment in which to develop our moving meditation. The practice of counting strokes per lap gives us accurate feedback about the efficiency of our swimming technique and helps us focus on each stroke as a mantra.

Preparing to Enter The Zen Chamber

As conducive as this kind of environment can be for meditative practice, it can easily lull us into autopilot and junk miles. Before beginning our pool swim session (or any training session, for that matter), we can take a few minutes—particularly if we are training alone—to be conscious and to be present in this session. When we pause and clearly identify our objectives, we get the most out of our training. Our objectives may be to address and embrace our fears of water, to build our aerobic base, or to practice and improve specific aspects of our technique. This simple preparation is valuable in cultivating mindfulness rather than monotony.

In addition to the monotony of the pool parameters, there is the sensory deprivation of water, especially in a pool, where the only visual stimulation may be the stripe on the bottom of the lane. As with traditional meditative practice, we are in a truly "solo" environment. This environment and the stringent parameters of the pool may be why so many swimmers and triathletes choose to train, at least partially, with a swim club or under the guidance of a coach—even if they conduct the rest of their athletic training in solitude. This choice provides us with a little more leverage in cultivating mindfulness rather than simply switching on the autopilot.

Balance

Optimally we want to establish a balance between the pool Zen chamber—where we can intimately study and develop our technique, form, and feel—and the animated waters of a natural environment—where we temper our technique with flexibility and adaptability. Swimming in choppy water, swells, and current requires more than just proficient technique. Rough-water swimming also challenges mental composure—the ability to remain calm and relaxed. Together, our swim technique and our mental composure in the swim leg of a triathlon will set the stage for the rest of our race.

Unique Form of Exercise

Physically and mechanically, swimming is quite unique in comparison to biking or running. In swimming we assume a horizontal position. In a conventionally ordered triathlon, we begin in the prone position, then transition to the bike, assuming the aero position—similar to crawling on all fours—and finally to a vertical position for the run. This closely resembles our evolutionary progression—at least so far.

Swimming emphasizes the upper body and works much of the torso in a unique way. Reaching and pulling with the arms and hands is very unique in mechanics and feel, as is the twisting motion of the torso through the water. The subsequent strengthening and lengthening of our torso and arms, as well as their connection to our center of movement in the pelvic region, may also benefit our cycling and running.

One of the most valuable skills we can develop and acquire from swimming is conscious, efficient, and regulated breathing. In the medium of water, where availability of air occurs in a specifically timed and patterned way, our breathing must be coordinated with our movement. Developing the ability to coordinate breathing with movement will greatly enhance our zendurance approach to any form of endurance exercise as well. Likewise, conscious breathing is one of the most essential techniques in any form of meditation—sitting or moving. It is the first step toward mind in matter.

Take a Deep Breath

The reach, pull, and push action of swimming stretches and expands, then contracts and compresses the rib cage and helps improve lung capacity. Let's consider the mechanism for breathing: The lungs are suspended in the airtight chest cavity, a chamber enclosed by the rib cage and separated from the lower abdomen by the muscles of the solar plexus. The lungs themselves have no muscle tissue attached to them and rely solely on the increasing and decreasing volume of the chest chamber to accomplish inhalation and exhalation. The muscular web incorporated in the rib cage and the solar plexus muscles expand and contract to accomplish this volumetric change.

Breathing itself is kinetic in nature—requiring strong, well-conditioned musculature. All the leg strength in the world will not sustain an endurance runner who lacks the strength and capacity to efficiently and harmoniously provide oxygen for the entire duration of the run. Swimming greatly strengthens the breathing musculature. It educates our respiratory process and increases our lung capacity. This will benefit other endurance activities as well.

Resistance and Efficiency

Perhaps the greatest aspect of study and contemplation in the medium of water is the resistance it provides to movement. Herein lies a potent opportunity for zendurance training and study. Consider that the world's greatest runners have been scientifically measured to be 90 to 95 percent efficient—meaning that 90 to 95 percent of the energy they exert propels them forward. By comparison, the world's greatest swimmers are measured to be only 10% efficient—only 10 percent of the energy they exert actually propels them forward. The other 90 percent is lost to the resistance of the medium of water. Where does this leave the rest of us?

Of all the endurance activities, none offers the resistance of swimming and the opportunity to train and to cultivate a feel for yielding and for efficiency—for seeking out the path of least resistance. Water always seeks the path of least resistance. We are learning in an essential way from the water. Remember that pool and fresh water swimming offer less buoyancy—and therefore more resistance—than ocean swimming.

Efficiency is paramount to all endurance activities. Swimming provides us with the "thickest" medium in which to investigate the nature of efficiency and to develop this quality—both its physical and mindful aspects. We begin to discover and develop the humble attitude of yielding. This humble attitude of yielding may seem quite contrary to our belief that speed can come only from exertion and force. Technique is emphasized more in swim training than in any other endurance activity. Even the most elite swimmers constantly focus their training on perfecting technique. The very foundation of swimming technique is efficient and stealthy movement through the water.

Yielding

In zendurance swimming, we approach our training with a humble attitude and a diligent awareness and feeling for yielding, so that we home in on efficiency. (Open-ocean swimming can do a lot to inspire our humbleness.) We let our feel for swimming guide our technique. Good coaching will also provide us with a strong technique foundation as well as valuable guidance and inspiration to initiate and conduct this feeling investigation. We are pursuing a harmony with the water by training our nervous system to feel the disturbance we create in the water and to yield to the water's resistance. We allow the water to guide us on the path of least resistance.

Yielding and Technique

There are many valuable and worthwhile drills and techniques that can significantly improve our swimming performance. Good coaching and swimming lessons that focus on freestyle technique and form are a great place to start. Also, there are several good books and magazine articles that can guide us in the right direction. Our purpose in *Zendurance* is not to provide a technical manual on proper swim technique. Rather, we are examining the qualities of swimming and the medium of water that elicit in us our true essential nature as spiritual beings and how we can develop these qualities.

A consistent study of proper swim technique is one of the best approaches to developing these qualities and to improving our performance as well. In fact, one of the major premises is that any zendurance practice that develops and cultivates our spiritual qualities will also improve our performance. This is a principal tenet of effortless power.

Typically in our training programs, swim technique sessions are appropriately scheduled on recovery or low-intensity days. Although we do not regard them as breakthrough workouts, this does not diminish the significance of these sessions. How we approach these sessions largely determines how much value we gain from them. An open-minded, patient, and diligent approach works best. Our intention during these sessions is not to crank up the ol' heart rate—it is to accomplish the most work with the least amount of effort and therefore lowest heart rate.

Before we begin these valuable technique sessions, it is important to give ourselves permission to move slowly and effortlessly. We are concentrating on feeling, not intensity. If a surgeon were preparing to perform a lifesaving operation on you, how would you like him or her to approach you? Would you prefer sensitivity, patience, and serenity, or would you prefer speed and intensity? Let's breathe slowly and take our time. These techniques sessions offer us the best possible opportunity to transform our swimming into zendurance meditation and to tune in to our effortless power.

Fluid Sensitivity

We are all familiar—tangibly familiar—with the viscosity of water. Water pours, it flows, it yields completely. Water effortlessly takes on any shape. It shape-shifts in an instant. Our zendurance approach to swimming is a process of feeling like water, of taking on the qualities of water—just as fish do. It is a profound and very subtle study in yielding, flowing, and pouring like water. Even our thinking becomes fluid.

As we train, we can investigate the fluidity of water. In this investigation, we are attentive to feeling the movement and flow of water along every part of our skin's surface—every curve, every nuance. We become keenly aware of how water flows over our hand—both the palm and back—as our hand enters, extends, and catches the water.

This hand sensitivity can be very valuable for developing an efficient swim technique and for becoming more fluid. We can devote a few minutes of our swim sessions to just focusing on our hand sensitivity. During this exercise, we diligently concentrate on feeling the relationship of our hand and the water.

The first time we begin this exercise, we can start without the distraction of actually swimming by simply moving our hand through the water to feel how the water flows. In this simple introduction, we can move our hand through the water by leading with our fingertips—as we do when our hand enters and extends through the water during the first phase of our swim stroke. It is important to keep our fingers and hand very relaxed, as this will encourage greater sensitivity and yielding. By moving slowly at first, we can begin to feel even subtle disturbances that our fingers and hands create. We can begin to distinguish between the feeling of smooth flow and turbulent flow around our fingers and hands.

Next, we can practice cupping or catching the water in our hand and moving that cup around. By practicing slowly and gently, we can begin to feel how and where our cupped hand "leaks"—usually out of one side or the other. The purpose of this simple introduction is just to develop a sensitive and intelligent discernment—an ability to distinguish a smooth efficient flow from a turbulent one, a stable and balanced cup from an unstable leaky one.

We continue to develop this sensitive and intelligent discernment in our hands as we apply this exercise to our actual swimming technique—again by diligently concentrating on the sensitivity in our fingers and hands.

By training and developing the sensitivity of first our hands, then our arms, and eventually our whole body, we are also training the fluidity of our attitude and awareness to function quietly and humbly, without generating resistance. We are learning to yield in many ways.

The Power of Sensitivity

Efficiency in our stroke technique combined with a quiet, streamlined, and stealthy form will be far more effective in improving our swimming performance than thrashing and churning the water with a set of weight lifter's arms. That calm, quiet, stealthy zendurance approach is essential not only in our physical form, but in our mental and emotional state as well. A quiet, humble, and stealthy attitude—mentally and emotionally—is basic to our pursuit of effortless power as athletes and as human beings.

Serene and Sensitive—Right from the Start

In a conventionally ordered triathlon, swimming is the first event. This can really support our conscious and deliberate zendurance approach. Right from the start of the race—even with the adrenaline-soaked intensity at the beginning of a big event that includes hundreds of athletes—our focus is on gentle sensitivity and yielding to the resistance of water. In the midst of all these thrashing bodies, we are subtly seeking and intimately feeling out the path of least resistance and most harmony. Does that sound like the way to begin a race?

Wow, what a contrast! What a paradox! Right from the start, our approach is fluid and gentle as we quietly hone the subtleties of efficiency, stealth, and harmony. It takes great tenacity and a calm composure to move through the water with stealth and silence when we are surrounded by mayhem and chaos. In the months and years preceding the race, our zendurance training practice focuses on this fluidity, sensitivity, stealth, and silence—on this subtle yet tangible sense of yielding—so it will be well ingrained in our bodies and minds on race day. The result? Faster swim times, with less effort.

What about every one else? It's a zoo out there! In my experience of large starts, when I am truly swimming from a place of serenity, the water around me is calm—I am rarely struck or grabbed. Even if I do get hit, it's not worth the energy and effort to retaliate. When I start a race in a fit of anaerobic fury, I find myself in the middle of the zoo.

Arriving Late for the Perfect Swim

One of the best race experiences of my life was the 2001 Kealakekua Bay 2-Mile Swim, held two weeks prior to Hawaii Ironman. I arrived a bit late, and by the time I entered the water, everyone had a two- or three-minute head start. I stood waist-deep in the water, relaxed, stretched, and began slowly so that I could warm up. On the way out from shore, I stopped and talked to Mike, who was patrolling on a surfboard. I resumed with a slow easy pace, emphasizing long, slow, and sensuous strokes. My breathing pattern was every three strokes, so that I was breathing bipolar. This, too, kept my rate of exertion low. I made the conscious choice to swim with excellent technique and stealth and not to increase my tempo. If I was going to catch up and pass other swimmers, it would not be through exertion.

Sure enough, I began to pass the slower swimmers after fifteen minutes or so. In the crystal-clear cobalt blue waters, I watched each person's technique. Many were thrashing mercilessly, creating a lot of disturbance. They generated a lot of bubbles and white water in their fury to go faster. As I glided by, I was even more determined to move as effortlessly and quietly as possible—to make it look easy. Several swimmers tried to follow in my draft but could not keep up. Granted, these were the slowest, most inexperienced swimmers in the race. The more they thrashed, the slower and longer my strokes became—still breathing every three strokes.

I progressed through much of the field and observed more than one hundred swimmers. As I advanced through the field, I noticed how the technique of the faster swimmers improved over the slower swimmers, and how much more effortless they appeared. They generated significantly less white water, bubbles, disturbance, and overall mayhem. They seemed much calmer and at ease. This experience is indelible for me. Never again have I raced in the water by thrashing or attempting to speed up my cadence.

Yielding and Efficiency

Seeking out the path of least resistance and most harmony cultivates efficiency. Efficiency is the essence of our zendurance approach to any endurance activity. With swimming, our attention to yielding translates to efficiency when we minimize our turbulence and disturbance, by using our sensitivity and intelligent discernment. The fluidity and resistance of water can really help us hone our skills of yielding—both our physical technique and our mental attitude.

In Western culture, we tend to evaluate our productivity and our performances by how much perceived effort we exert. Often in training or racing, when we conclude a session feeling very tired and sore, we feel satisfied that we are progressing. Conversely, if our timed effort shows a great performance, yet we have finished without feeling utterly wasted, some doubt and suspicion may arise in our minds about the quality of the race or training session.

Culturally, this can be an extremely difficult standard of evaluation to liberate ourselves from. High-performance swimming clearly demonstrates the truth. It bears repeating that even the greatest elite swimmers orient most of their training toward technique and efficiency. If we watch world-class distance swimmers in action, the most noteworthy observation is how soft and effortless their movements appear. There is very little disturbance to the water's surface, even when they are swimming at top speed. If we observe them from under the surface, we see very few bubbles of air around them.

The practice of training our bodies and our minds to clearly feel our way along the subtle path of harmony and least resistance requires sensitivity and intelligent discernment. This can go along way toward repatterning the old "no pain—no gain" axiom. Imagine moving through our lives without experiencing the frustration we usually react with when we encounter resistance on the physical, mental, and emotional levels. Imagine embracing and welcoming our resistance with effortless power—rather than attempting to avoid it. On the path of effortless power we do not seek to avoid resistance completely. Why?

Resistance—Obstacle and Asset

We have considered the resistance that water provides in response to our movements. It is through yielding, sensitivity, and discernment that we can most effortlessly and fluidly pass through that resistance. As our hand enters and extends into the water during the first part of our swim stroke, we are opening a path. This is followed by the catch and pull. What are we actually catching and pulling? Water! That same density of the water that provides resistance is what we are catching in our hand. That ball of water in our hand is what we pull on in order to move ourselves forward.

In our swim training we are learning how to yield and pass through the resistance of the water and then how to grasp hold of that very same resistance to pull ourselves forward. In this way, we transform the obstacle into an asset. If that obstacle—the resistant density of water—is not there, we have no asset, we have nothing to hold on to—no way of moving forward! This is true in life, too. If we have no obstacles, no resistance, no challenges, and no mountains to climb, how can we grow, progress, and move forward—how can we enjoy the beautiful expanded view from the mountain summit? How can we gain knowledge and a sense of accomplishment? If water offered us no buoyancy—no resistance—we would simply fall to the bottom and drown, unable to pull ourselves back to the surface.

As swimmers, the density of water is both an asset and a hindrance for us. As an asset, this density gives our bodies buoyancy, so that we remain at the water's surface. This density also provides us with something to catch and to pull ourselves forward with. As a hindrance, the water's density resists and slows our movements. Efficient swimming results from maximizing the assets while minimizing the hindrance.

Minimum and Maximum

We maximize the assets by keeping all parts of our bodies close to the surface and by gaining as much leverage as we can from each handful of water through the perfection of our stroke technique. Our technique includes the entry, reach, catch, pull, push, exit, and follow-through of each and every stroke—like a perfectly repeated mantra. We minimize the hindrance by presenting the least amount of body surface to the water relative to the direction of travel—by being hydrodynamic—and by minimizing the number of strokes we use to travel a given distance. We seek to minimize the disturbance we cause with each movement. This is a radically different approach than thrashing hard and fast in the water.

If we pause to consider this balance of asset and hindrance, it is amazing that we are able to pull such a large mass (our body) through the water with such a small handful of the same stuff in each stroke. Since we cannot significantly increase the size of each handful of water (without the use of paddles) or the buoyancy of our bodies (unless wetsuits are permitted), then our greatest potential for efficiency and improved performance can be realized by decreasing the frontal surface area of our bodies—by yielding to the water through a more hydrodynamic shape—and by minimizing the disturbance we cause with each movement.

Swimming Our Way Through Life

A zendurance approach to swimming can offer some profound insight and awareness into how we embrace the resistances we encounter in our day-to-day lives—whether we experience those resistances physically, mentally, or emotionally. When we encounter resistance in our daily lives, if we react with physical exertion and force or with negative judgments and emotions, we are increasing our surface area so to speak—offering more fuel for the resistance to feed on. This is similar to thrashing in the water. When we stay relaxed and our attitude remains neutral, open, and sensitive in our daily experiences, it is similar to being soft, stealthy and hydrodynamic in the water. By yielding—physically, mentally and emotionally—we offer the resistance that we encounter a minimum of physical, mental, or emotional surface area to act upon. We minimize our disturbance. In a stealthy and calm way, we slip through the resistance—we glide through.

Our zendurance swim training prepares us to appreciate and respond to the resistance we encounter in our daily lives. We learn to approach the obstacles we encounter with gentle sensitivity and intelligent discernment. We learn how to gracefully, deliberately and stealthily swim through our lives—how to use the resistance and obstacles to lever ourselves through. If we approach our lives with the same humble attitude and keen feeling we develop in our swim technique, we move quickly and efficiently through the resistance. We are less likely to cast negative judgments or to struggle and thrash as we home in on the path of least resistance and most harmony.

With adaptability, flexibility, and fluid mindfulness, we can transfer and integrate the profound skill of yielding into our day-to-day activities and relationships. This is true zendurance

—translating our zendurance training practice into day-to-day fluidity and harmony with our world as we embrace and transform the resistance and obstacles into rungs on our ladder of growth and wisdom.

How gracefully, effortlessly, and instantly can we shape-shift and yield to the present moment? Can we flow as easily, as unconditionally as water?

BICYCLING—BLENDING

Two Circles

Cycling: the word itself connotes circling—seamless, uniform repetition—with no apparent beginning or end. (In the middle of those long century rides, sometimes there doesn't seem to be any apparent end.) In "Zendurance," we considered the circular quality of our endurance activities and the similarity to traditional forms of meditation. Going in circles will naturally draw us toward our center—our calm, still, silent, open, and empty space of deep inner listening and contemplation. Cycling may be the most circular of endurance activities.

Bicycling implies two circles, two cycles. Most obviously this refers to the two wheels of a bicycle. The two circles/cycles of *bicycle* also refers to the circling action of our two legs. Our legs are circling diametrically—as one leg circles forward and down, the other is circling backward and up. In our dualistic perspective, this diametrical arrangement is experienced as opposing and contrasting. In our zendurance approach to athletics, we can train our bodies and our minds to experience this diametrical arrangement as balancing, complementary and harmonious. This translates to efficiency and grace—the path of effortless power.

Yin-Yang

Perhaps the most common image of Eastern philosophy and religion that we see in western culture is the yin-yang symbol. Yin-yang portrays the dynamic balance of opposites. If the yin-yang symbol portrayed a static, frozen, and unchanging balance of opposites, it would appear simply as a circle divided into dark and light halves by a straight line. The dynamic state of flux is represented by the S-shaped division of the light and dark halves, which elicits a swirling, circling movement.

One significant aspect of the yin-yang symbol that we often overlook is the perfect circle that embraces the dynamic relationship of polarities. Our legs—diametrically arranged on the crankset of our bike—can be experienced (in both feeling and concept) as an animated version of the yin-yang. In our conventional Western view of yin-yang, we normally associate or identify ourselves with one of the opposites or polarities: male or female, good or bad, day or night.

Circular Pedaling—The Real Zen of Cycling

This is true in our bicycle pedaling technique—we identify most prevalently with the forward and downward half of the pedal stroke and then shift our awareness to the other leg for its forward and downward motion. The backward and upward motion of the pedal stroke is unconscious motion—the motion that is considered as simply a return. This conventional way of pedaling emphasizes the heavy use of one group of leg muscles to the virtual exclusion of its complimentary opposite group. This type of hammering may successfully propel us through the 112-mile bike leg of an iron-distance triathlon in a respectable time, but it will not leave our bike legs in prime and optimal condition to run a marathon.

Efficiency is best realized on the bike through seamless, circular pedaling. This balanced diametrical application of power throughout the full circle of the pedal stroke is one of the most difficult skills in triathlon. Given that cycling is the longest event—both for time and distance—in conventional triathlons, then an even, circular, and efficient pedal technique is essential for good performance—especially for the ensuing run.

The most obvious way to develop a balanced, circling pedal stroke is to practice and emphasize the backward and upward half of the pedal circle. We can practice this through single-leg drills—providing all the power with just one leg at a time. One variation on this technique is to unclip from one pedal and suspend that leg outside the pedal circle while powering with the other leg. Initially, it may be difficult to balance with only one foot clipped in—so it may be appropriate to practice this on a stationary stand at first. With patience and practice, we can progress to the open road while maintaining a comfortable, relaxed aero position—without a lot of movement in the saddle. Single-leg drills allow us to separately and intimately investigate the complete circle of force for each leg and to equally develop the muscle groups and the neurological coordination necessary to master the backward and upward part of the stroke. This technique for perfecting the left and right pedal strokes is similar to the technique of single-arm drills in swimming.

Power Cranks are now available through many cycle shops. Although costly, these cranks allow us to practice the circular application of force with both legs simultaneously. While conventional crank arms are fixed to the chainring assembly, the individual arms of this set will float or stall if we do not pull back and up on them. This is similar to the way a freewheel floats as we coast downhill. Power Cranks train us to keep our legs diametrically arranged and to develop a smooth application of power around the full circle. With or without this particular crankset, it is a challenge to develop the awareness—both mentally and muscularly—to bicycle gracefully.

As with swimming, our natural tendency with cycling is to exert more effort to improve performance, thus degrading technique and form. In the full-circle pedal technique, we are training the body and mind to embrace and to blend diametrical opposites—a profound practice, even in something as simple as pedaling a bike. We are activating and sustaining an animated yin-yang.

The Feeling of Balance

While experiencing a diametrical balance of two circles simultaneously in our pedaling may be a difficult and illusive pursuit, the most obvious experience of balance with a bicycle is one most of us master at a very young age—balancing on two wheels. Many of us, athletes or not, can recall our first experiences of discovering this balance—the freedom from training wheels. No one can teach us this balance—it can only be discovered through feeling. No matter how much we might study or research the conceptual notion of balance, reading and talking about it will not make it happen. Balance can only happen through feel. Hence we begin to consider how vital feeling is in our daily lives. Through feeling we are able to navigate this vehicle, called the body, through our daily lives.

As we steer our bikes through a turn, our feeling sense of balance guides us. Imagine trying to ride your bike through a curve with only your sense of vision—with no feeling of balance. I doubt we would progress very far without falling over or crashing—yet our feeling of balance makes riding a bike through that curve seem innate, second nature. As a practice when we ride, we can explore this feeling of balance and look for its location of origin, in our bodies. The incredible phenomenon of balance requires that our conscious awareness be well integrated with our body's feeling.

This is mind *in* matter. Balancing and riding a bicycle is one of the most powerful introductory experiences of mind in matter—an experience, a feeling most of us develop early on and never forget. The subject of feel is of major significance in *Zendurance*. We shall explore this vast arena a little farther on in this book.

Blending

The most striking and unique quality of cycling—in comparison to swimming or running—is the bicycle itself. (Paddling and rowing also require a vehicle and are similar to cycling in this regard.) Swimming and running have relatively simple requirements with respect to equipment—not so with cycling. Of the three activities, cycling is the most recently developed. The design and manufacture of bikes continues to evolve through advances in mechanical engineering as well as design and materials technologies. In our zendurance approach to cycling, blending our body, mind, and spirit with the bicycle is an essential part of our cycling skill.

Optimally, the bicycle must become an integral extension, an indistinguishable part of our kinetic/energetic being. There is a methodology to this process—based on our technical intellect—and an intuitive, creative process that relies on our sense of feeling. The methodical approach includes selecting a bike (frame, wheels, components, and saddle) that is appropriate to the rider's anatomy and to the intended activity, as well as the rider's style. In addition, a proper setup that includes saddle and handlebar positioning and cleat-to-pedal position are essential. Of these, saddle position is most crucial. This determines how effectively power is transferred from the torso of the rider to the crankset of the bike.

While there are certain principles and guidelines to our bike set-up along with sophisticated equipment like power meters and wind tunnels to dial it in, our sense of feeling becomes the most essential guidance. By establishing the saddle position, we are determining what we feel is the optimal relationship between our power source—located in the lower torso—and the central receiving unit of the bike itself—the bottom bracket, which holds the crank/pedal/chainring assembly. Beyond the initial setup, we gradually and patiently hone our feeling—our intimate, tangible connection with our bikes. This process of feeling steadily evolves over the course of time—years and perhaps decades. It is the essence of efficiency and effortless power on our bicycles—blending.

In the bigger picture of our lives, this deliberate practice of blending and integrating with our bicycles will carry over into how we blend and integrate with our surrounding environment—both with the instruments and objects of our lives and our relationships with others. In particular, our bicycle blending can be a practice that improves our ability to integrate with technology—with all the tools, equipment, instruments, and vehicles that surround us every day. All these things are literally extensions of our bodies and our senses—whether we choose to be aware of them or not. In our present-day global society, this interaction with technology is inevitable and unavoidable.

Becoming a Bicycle Virtuoso

One of the greatest examples of blending—the ability to extend the human sense of feeling into an object—is a virtuoso musician, such as a violinist. As a virtuoso plays, it is clearly evident how much he or she intimately becomes the violin, extending his or her feeling sensitivity into the instrument, blending and embodying the violin. When we watch a virtuoso violinist, we can no longer distinguish visually or aurally between the player and the instrument. The beautiful voice is a synthesis of both.

As diligent practitioners, we can learn to play our bikes—or any of the instruments or equipment in our lives—with the same mastery and virtuosity as the concert violinist. It simply requires our diligence—our clear presence of mind here and now—as well as our clear intent, our patience, and our infinite, intimate sense of feel. As accomplished cyclists—by blending with our bikes—we can literally *feel* the geometry and structure of the bicycle's frame, the precise location of the bottom bracket, and the axis of rotation for each of the two wheels as well as the contact surface and distance between the two tires. This is not a conceptual process—it is not a process of thinking about our bike and its parts. This is a visceral process, a feeling process.

Blending and Feeling

Blending with our bikes and extending our sense of feeling is strongest through the points of physical contact—most significantly through the saddle, and through the pedals and the handlebars as well. We begin to feel and listen to the vibrations and frequencies that are generated as we ride—just as the concert violinist hears and feels the frequencies and vibrations of the violin. Through feeling we grow to experience our own body not as an object, but as a complex energy matrix or field.

Through the practice of blending, we are able to experience the link-up to other complex energy fields—even those we regard as inanimate objects. This practice of blending occurs by feeling and listening to the frequencies and vibrations. As we develop this sensitivity, we learn to distinguish even the subtlest differences—

changing to a different set of tires on our bike, for example. Observing a proficient cyclist is like observing the concert violinist. It is difficult to distinguish between the rider and the bike—as though the cyclist was just running on his or her own wheels.

Stationary Training

The potential for dangerous, impactful situations is greatest on the bicycle—in view of the relative speed and our attachment to the bicycle via the cleats. Add to this the presence of much faster and larger vehicles as well as road debris and—in the case of mountain biking—radically changing terrain. For the sake of safety out on the open road, our outer awareness must be constantly vigilant and keen. This makes it difficult to focus inward and to find our space of deep inner listening where we can blend and extend our sense of feeling into our bikes.

In "Swimming—Yielding," we considered the strengths and weaknesses of both open-water swimming and pool swimming. A similar comparison can be made between cycling on the open road (or trail) and training with our bike on a stationary stand or rollers. In the case of cycling, the differences are more pronounced. A stationary stand does not provide the feel of cycling on the open road. There is no terrain change, no wind conditions, no lateral movement or dynamic balance (except with rollers). On the plus side, the potential for impact and injury is diminished and flat tires are no longer a concern. A stationary setup also eliminates the need to drive somewhere for training and allows us to train indoors when the weather is not all that inspiring.

Training stationary provides us with the only opportunity to completely go inside—to focus our awareness inward and to explore and develop cycling as a moving meditation. It is certainly the only opportunity to close our eyes and intimately blend with our bike. (This may not be safe on rollers.) We can also look down (or in a mirror) and study how our knees track as we pedal. We can focus on eliminating knee wobble and orienting our feet straight on the pedals. These practices are not possible otherwise. On the stationary, we can intimately explore the subtleties of circular pedaling technique, as well as our breathing, cadence, and aero body positioning—all as aspects of blending and extending our sense of feel.

Going in Deep with Monotony

Like pool swimming, the monotony of stationary cycling makes it easy to slip into autopilot and to simply crank out some junk miles. However, if we approach these sessions with clear intention and present mindful focus—diligence—then stationary training can be a valuable and meditative zendurance practice in blending.

Even traditional spiritual practices can appear monotonous. A devout practitioner of tai chi practices the very same series of movements every day for decades. A casual observer might see little variation or progress in the external appearance from day to day or year to year. The astute practitioner—willing to explore the subtle and intimate levels of her or his movement, even to the molecular level—can discover whole new fields of dynamic energy, balance, and harmony. This deeply internal and subtle progress happens through the same clear intention and diligence we must use in our zendurance training. As athletes, we must be consciously clear and present to this subtle, internal process as an opportunity to practice moving, aerobic meditation so that we blend intimately with our bike.

As with swimming, we strive to develop both the inward meditative awareness and the outward interactive awareness. The balance and simultaneous presence of our inner and outer awareness is essential both in traditional Zen practice and in zendurance. When we are truly present and abiding in our calm, still, silent, open, and empty space of deep inner listening and contemplation, this balance and simultaneity is natural and effortless.

Bike Tai Chi

Let's look at other training techniques that can help us blend with our bikes—techniques that train our ability to be still and calm in the saddle and to apply power more efficiency without excess movement or effort. In *The Triathlete's Training Bible*, Joe Friel outlines many training workouts—including hill climbs—and places a strong emphasis on maintaining a calm, still aero position with minimal movement in the saddle. Even in our recovery workouts, we can include techniques that help us blend with our bikes. We have already considered single-leg circles as an exercise in the even, circular application of force. We have looked at stationary training—monotonous as it may be—as a valuable opportunity to go deeply inside without the need to maintain our outer interactive awareness.

Another valuable exercise for blending is "bike tai chi." In the traditional practice of tai chi, we move very slowly and listen intently to our body's balance and relationship to gravity. We can use a similar approach during our recovery bike sessions. On either flat terrain or, preferably, on a slight incline, we practice riding very slowly in our lowest gear. With a very slow pedal cadence, we focus on perfectly and seamlessly applying circular power with both legs while staying absolutely still in the saddle. As with traditional tai chi, in bike tai chi it becomes more difficult to maintain balance as our velocity decreases.

Through this slow-motion approach, we condition our bodies to deeply relax in the aero position. This combination of deep relaxation and seamless circular pedaling increases our ability to blend with and to feel our bike. It enables us to navigate and to steer our bike more with our hips and lower abdomen through relaxed contact with the saddle—relying far less on our arms to steer.

Tai Chi in the Saddle

As the primary conduit for blending with our bike, our positioning on and contact with the saddle can make or break the blending harmony we are developing. Since most of our navigation and blending occurs through the saddle, we need to be attentive to this marriage. The type of saddle we choose and the shorts we wear are important decisions.

The specific points of contact with our bike saddle form a triangle. The apexes of the triangle consist of the two pubic arches known as sit bones at the bottom of the pelvis—those bone protuberances we feel when we sit down—and the perineum, or cord of muscle between the anus and the genitals. Split saddles are popular with triathletes because they alleviate the pressure placed on the perineum caused by tilting the pelvis forward in aero position.

During our bike tai chi sessions, we practice keeping this saddle contact triangle relatively still. A still and stable contact triangle with the saddle forms our most effective conduit for blending with our bikes and for accurate, effortless navigation. Smooth circular pedaling is essential in developing and maintaining this calm and gentle saddle contact triangle. Likewise, that calm and still contact triangle provides a stable platform for delivering power through the pedals and crankset. Smooth circular pedaling and a calm, still contact triangle with the saddle go hand in hand.

Through bike tai chi we gradually become proficient at relaxing and being still in the saddle. Then we gain the sensitivity to extend our sense of feeling into our bikes and to make our bikes feel like natural extensions of our bodies. Eventually, with patient practice, we can feel this blending even when we are generating a great deal of power. We become very attentive to the feedback that our bike provides through the frequencies and vibrations we feel through the saddle, pedals and handlebars. With bike tai chi, this ability to blend allows us to ride gracefully and calmly at progressively slower velocity. It also allows us to ride gracefully and calmly during racing conditions.

Bike tai chi helps us minimize side-to-side weaving and navigate a straight course from our hips via the calm and still saddle contact triangle. This skill will greatly improve our zendurance approach to high-intensity training and racing. Calm, relaxed sensitivity and blending translates directly to economy and efficiency—a big step on the path toward effortless power. Consider that the 112-mile bike course of an iron-distance triathlon is measured along the straightest path. If we are squirming around on our bikes, weaving side to side, we might add several miles to our trek. Heck, 112 miles is enough already, yes?

A Quiet Setting

It is best to conduct these bike tai chi sessions without the distraction and hindrance of traffic—on a quiet side street or in an empty parking lot. Keep in mind that at very slow speed, balance is difficult. Be cautious and mindful, especially with cleats or toe-clips. Mileage, effort, and speed don't count here. Our focus is precise, relaxed, and graceful navigation by blending with the bike. This is a valuable opportunity to really explore the phenomenon of balance as a feeling of both body and bike.

We can engage in this low-physical-intensity, highly conscious integration with the bike by doing repeated laps on an appropriate stretch of smooth pavement. We don't need a long course at all. A slight incline will provide us with adequate resistance so that our speed can be very slow as we apply seamless circular force on the pedals. Coasting or pedaling against the brakes does not give us the same quality of blending and takes us off the aero bars. It is easiest to practice bike tai chi without wind—at least initially. Even one or two fifteen-minute sessions a week will greatly improve our blending skills. A fifteen-minute session can be mixed into a normal recovery ride, alternating five to ten minutes of tai chi riding with five to ten minutes of conventional easy cycling.

Relax and Slow Down

We focus on retaining a relaxed tai chi-like quality throughout the entire session, at both slow and normal speeds. As we gain blending skills with our bikes through these tai chi slow-motion exercises, we will be able to ride gracefully at increasingly slower speeds. Our circular pedaling skills—smoothing out the application of power through each stroke—will allow us to "tai chi" our way up progressively steeper hills without pedal-mashing.

Spin Free

During these sessions, as we are returning to the bottom of the hill, we can stay in the lowest gear and free-spin without actually engaging the freewheel or applying power. In this downhill free-spin exercise, we practice smoothing out our circular pedal spin without any resistance at all—as though the chain was no longer connecting the crankset to the rear wheel. This free-spin exercise really shows us how uneven our application of force is.

The purpose of this exercise is not to spin as fast as possible; it is to minimize bouncing in the saddle and to smooth out the circular motion of our pedal stroke at all speeds. We can only accomplish this by relaxing our leg muscles as well as our hip, knee and ankle joints and by blending intimately with our bikes—especially through the saddle contact triangle and the crankset.

This challenging exercise does not require tremendous strength, but it does require sensitivity, coordination, and awareness. Free-spinning can teach us how to relax our muscles and joints—even while we are in motion. Neurologically, we can reprogram our old beliefs that motion (especially fast motion) requires tension and exertion. Free-spinning is another one of those seemingly simple exercise techniques that can yield some great results—if we are willing to be patient and gentle in our approach.

Effortless Navigation

As we gain a feeling for bike tai chi in aero position and become graceful at slow speed, we can practice riding a smooth, steady, and straight course on top of or alongside a road or parking lot stripe. We want to notice when tension grabs at our shoulders, arms, and mid- or upper back and immediately relax into the saddle and into the frame of our bike—even if we weave off our line. Once the tension grabs hold, we are not going to stay on that straight course for long, especially at slow speed. As soon as the tension takes hold, we will notice that we lose the blending feel with our bike.

Here is another variation on this kind of precision navigation. As we are riding very slowly, we can visually spot on a mark or stain on the pavement ahead and aim with our hips to pass both tires over these very small, precise targets. In these navigation exercises, we steer with minimal arm movement and tension. Our precise navigation occurs through total relaxation and blending with our bike—especially through the saddle contact triangle. As we condition both our bodies and our minds to navigate by blending rather than controlling, we are progressing along the spiritual path of effortless power.

Keep Breathing

Breath! Let us not forget breath—especially during our bike tai chi sessions. Conscious breathing may just be the oldest and most fundamental of all meditative practices. Relaxed and conscious breathing helps us to release tensions, to truly occupy our bodies and to be fully present in this moment. The continuous moment-by-moment practice of conscious, relaxed, and deep breathing can help us extend our sense of feeling into our bikes, improving our blending skills. Our bike tai chi sessions are a good opportunity to practice conscious breathing.

While cycling, we can coordinate our breath with our movement by inhaling and exhaling for so many revolutions of our pedaling cadence. Unlike swimming—which requires that we coordinate our breath with our swim strokes—it may take some conscious effort to be just as conscious of our breathing as we are of our cycling activity. When we can balance and integrate our awareness of breath with our awareness of cycling—or any other endurance activity, for that matter—we are much more conscious of our effort and intensity level. We are much more apt to settle into a rhythm and a pace appropriate for the distance. Our bike tai chi sessions are a great opportunity to practice conscious breathing and to coordinate breath and movement.

Conscious breathing is the simplest and most effective practice toward the form of blending that is most fundamental in our daily lives—mind in matter. It is the essential practice for being completely conscious and present in this moment through our primary conduit, our strongest link with this reality—our bodies.

Foot Consciousness

Another technique we can borrow from traditional tai chi has to do with our feet. In traditional tai chi, it is essential that our feet remain soft, relaxed, and pliable as they bear our weight. Relaxation and sensitivity in our feet are vital in connecting—blending—with the Earth. As we conduct our bike tai chi, we must begin to relax our feet and feel them spread out in our bike shoes. We want to be continuously aware of and sensitive in our feet. We must be attentive to keeping our feet centered and neutral in our shoes, even when we are applying considerable force to the pedals. When our feet are compressed against the inside or outside edges of our shoes, or our toes are jammed into the front of our shoes, our application of power is no longer efficient.

Foot compression in our shoes and the resulting discomfort indicate unconsciousness and inefficiency in our pedaling technique and are most likely to occur during very long rides. This kind of inefficiency will take its toll not only on our feet but also on our knees. Hopping off the bike after 112 miles to run a marathon may not be such a great running experience if our toes have been crammed and jammed into our shoes for six or seven hours. Practicing feet consciousness during bike tai chi/recovery sessions will help train our mental tenacity so that we retain this awareness and efficiency during both our long and our high-intensity sessions.

As we practice our deep relaxed blending while riding slowly, we extend that relaxation into our feet. This will improve our circular pedaling technique by enhancing our sensitivity and receptivity to the circular path of the pedals. During our bike tai chi, we can experiment with loosening the straps on our shoes so that our feet float freely. We can train our feet—through sensitivity—to remain centered and neutral in our shoes (and on the pedals) and to transfer power efficiently without cramming our feet against the toe or sides of our shoes.

Bike Tai Chi Summary

The techniques of our bike tai chi are based on the principles and techniques of traditional tai chi. Slow, graceful, and seamless movement; deep and complete relaxation of our body's muscle tissues, connective tissues, and organs—along with clear and unclut-

tered consciousness—are all qualities of traditional tai chi. Just as
we are developing the ability to navigate our bikes, traditional tai
chi practitioners also navigate and source their movements from
the hips and lower abdomen. Every movement in tai chi
is breathed. In traditional martial arts forms, breath and movement are inseparable in the pursuit of effortless power and
perfect balance.

The more we practice bike tai chi, the more attentive we become
to the unnecessary and inefficient tensions we generate in our riding form and technique. This includes simple things like gripping
tightly with our hands on the bars. Not only are these tensions
wasteful energy sinks, but they also greatly reduce our capacity to
blend with our bikes. As we become conscious of these habitual
tensions, we will also become conscious of the same kinds of habitual tensions that occur in our everyday activities—that impede our
ability to blend with the world around us.

Inspiration

When it comes to blending with a bike, BMX bikers demonstrate some of the most stunning possibilities for blending—elaborate aerial acrobatics, standstill balancing maneuvers, hopping
and jumping stunts. They are a true inspiration. This kind of bicycle gymnastics takes incredible sensitivity and body-to-bike integration. Working up to these maneuvers takes complete presence
of mind, patience, and creativity in the approach to blending and
developing such intimate sensitivity. Patience, creativity, and
imagination can go along way toward blending with our bikes. Our
bike tai chi sessions constitute a great arena for developing these
assets.

Going Long

In the trinity of swim-bike-run, cycling requires the longest
training sessions and the most total hours of training. In our
Zendurance approach to triathlon, this emphasizes even more the
importance of developing a calm, mindful, and blended cycling
technique. Maintaining a calm, empty, open, and meditative zendurance state for sessions lasting four to eight hours or longer
requires great mental tenacity as well as physical stamina. In traditional meditation practice, long sessions are most effective in
moving through the difficult process of embracing and dissolving
the barriers that obscure clear and present awareness. Going in

circles by endlessly repeating mantras—either sound or movement—with minimal diversions or distractions supports and
encourages the zenduring mind to become empty, clear, and open.
This allows the deep and subtle obstacles and barriers to surface.

We may recall Kanawai Kumulipo—the Hawaiian Law of
Creation: As we progress toward a vision or a goal—as we illuminate our dreams and aspirations—we will dissolve all the fears and
obstacles—the darkness, or *po*—that stands between us and that
vision or goal. In triathlon training, it is our cycling training sessions that are the longest and most arduous mentally. These sessions really test our ability to remain present and mindful as we
bring light to our darkness.

Long On Patience

Developing both the aerobic capacity and the mental tenacity of
zendurance in these long sessions requires endless patience and
diligence. (Remember, *diligence* is our clear presence of mind—here
and now.) You may recall our discussion "What is Patience?" As an
illustration in that discussion, we looked specifically at the process
of preparing for and beginning our long rides. Even just a few minutes of bike tai chi can really "set the stage" for a quality zendurance
session—rather than hours of unconscious junk miles.

Cultivating this zendurance ability begins with very clear intention as we approach our long sessions. As our sessions gradually
increase in duration, we must appreciate the opportunity for such
inner work and deep meditation, rather than regarding these long
sessions as monotonous obligations where we are "strapped on" to
the tortuous bicycle and finish with sore and crammed feet. Each
and every cycle of the pedals must be a conscious and deliberate
"mantra"—a perfect circle. For hours on end, we blend with our
bikes moment-by-moment—going in circles.

The Long Advantage Of Cycling

The gentle, non-impactful nature of cycling affords us the only
opportunity (in triathlon) to engage in such long sessions. Very few
of us have the anatomy and perfect form to run weekly sessions of
four hours or more. Long cycling sessions significantly strengthen
our hip, knee, and ankle joints and—with circular pedaling—balance the muscle groups. Joint strength and balanced muscle
strength comprise a very effective safeguard against injuries more
common to those of us who run without any cycling.

As runners, a great way for us to train for a marathon or ultra is to bike immediately before and/or after a long run. Psychologically and physiologically, this allows us to train for longer hours, simulating a much longer duration than the run itself without the added impact. Weekly four-hour sessions divided into one to two hours of cycling with two to three hours of running will make a 4-hour marathon seem much less formidable both mentally and physically, while sparing our joints from the wear and tear of the impact.

Wind

Unrelenting headwinds and crosswinds can be extremely challenging to our mental composure during those long cycling sessions. Training and racing in windy conditions challenges us to develop tolerance and patience, and to strengthen the mental stamina and grounding to maintain that calm, staid composure. During these windy conditions, we can recall all the skills we have practiced in our bike tai chi sessions—consciously relaxing and blending. This can aid us significantly in progressing through the windy turbulence with grace and efficiency.

Relentless and gusting winds are known to literally scatter our thoughts, like loose pages from a book. In traditional spiritual paths, many practitioners conduct their solitary retreats in mountainous regions such as the Himalayas, where windy conditions prevail—providing a similar opportunity to strengthen mental stamina and grounding.

A majority of Hawaii Ironman athletes are quick to cite windy biking conditions as the most grueling aspect of the entire race—both physically and mentally. Even a marathon in the sweltering afternoon Kona sun is an attractive relief from the treacherous Ho'omumuku winds of the north Kona coast. Locating and residing in a quiet and still center of body and mind, as well as developing a relaxed, efficient aero position, are both effective techniques for embracing this challenge. As we learn to abide in this calm, still, silent, open, and empty space, we develop a relaxed, centered composure—even when we are engulfed in turbulence. This quality is clearly evident in accomplished spiritual practitioners.

Tai Chi Approach to Wind

Through our zendurance approach, we develop the humility to yield to, embrace and dance with the elements rather than to confront and do battle with them. In traditional internal martial arts forms like tai chi, the practitioner learns to embrace and to re-direct the opponent's energy and forces rather than opposing them with equal or greater force of his or her own. The practitioner accomplishes this through a relaxed, open and highly perceptive state of being and presence. This translates to economy and effi-ciency—to effortless power.

The martial artist's focus is similar to our zendurance focus—that of blending and extending our sense of feeling. A truly skillful martial artist can effectively read his or her opponent by blend-ing—by extending his or her sense of feeling into the opponent. This process of blending guides the skillful martial artist in posi-tioning—consciously orchestrating the spatial relationship with his or her opponent. Both blending and yielding are part of the foun-dational groundwork for the skill of navigating the path toward effortless power. As zendurance practitioners, the process of blend-ing guides us in skillfully positioning ourselves on our bikes.

Aerodynamic Position

Developing an aerodynamic position is a combination of yielding to the wind and blending with the bike. We strive to disappear from the wind while delivering power effectively from a calm, relaxed center. If the wind encounters very little cyclist, the cyclist encoun-ters very little wind.

Our aero position must start at the lower torso. The pelvic region is the source of both our power and navigation and is our primary conduit for blending with the bike via the saddle. In an aero posi-tion, the forward tilting of the pelvis slightly changes the alignment and mechanics of delivering power as compared to a conventional upright position—and usually requires a more forward saddle posi-tion. Reasonable spinal alignment is crucial for rides of long dura-tion and is built from the pelvis forward/upward. This spinal align-ment includes shoulder, neck and head position. All of these are vital elements to feel as we develop aerodynamic positioning.

Skillfully changing our relationship with our bike—through body positioning and pedaling cadence, including gear selection—in response to terrain, wind conditions, intensity of power transmis-sion, and muscle group fatigue is truly an intuitive art requiring the same relaxed, open, and highly perceptive state of being as the mar-tial artist. Often the slightest, most subtle response—a small shift of saddle position, for example—can be significant in the quest for greater integration, economy, efficiency, and harmony. Such a skillful response can only be derived from keen, subtle observation and perception as a result of blending. Through blending, we become the dynamic matrix of body, wind, bike, terrain, and wind.

Honoring Turbulence and Wind as Our Teachers

So, the next time we are being slapped around by the wind, we can take a deep breath and return to our calm, still, silent, open, and empty space of deep inner listening and keen observation. This can be a powerful practice anytime we are encountering turbulence in our lives. It is obvious that if we find fault with the wind—if we view the wind as being wrong—it will not improve our conditions.

This is actually true of any turbulence in our lives, especially in our relationships with one another. Turbulence from another is no different from turbulence from the wind. Finding fault or blaming someone else for the turbulence we experience will not improve the relationship. We can choose to take a deep breath, return to our calm center, and practice yielding and blending. This is truly how we navigate the path of effortless power in our day-to-day lives. Our zendurance training is an opportunity to practice blending and yielding so that we are more fluid and capable in our everyday lives.

Praying Mantis

It is an interesting similarity between a cyclist in an aerodynamic position—with arms extended forward on the aero bars—and the posture of a praying mantis insect. Those "aero arms" give the praying mantis its name. In our aero position—this prostrating, praying position, bent at the waist, with hands and forearms together—gives us a sense of humbleness, humility, and yielding as we bow to the wind. In this prayerful position and attitude, we choose to bow down and "make ourselves small" rather than sitting upright to fight or resist the wind—yielding to rather than opposing the wind.

We lead with our head and hands in aero position. That's our intellect (head) and our technical skill (hands) leading us on our path. With head and hands, we have realized a level of masterful manipulation here on Earth beyond any other species. If we navigate our path on this Earth in a prayerful aero position—with gratitude, humility, and yielding—our relationship and integration with Earth become more harmonious and integral. The zendurance approach to any endurance athletic activity is a practice of yielding, blending, and aligning with the elements of our Earth. This is the wisest and most compassionate approach we can practice in our day-to-day lives with this great spherical being that supports and nourishes us all of our lives.

Equipment and Equality

Equipment is such a prominent feature of cycling. Imagine yourself out on the open road during the bike leg of a triathlon. There you are, "zenning along," blending with your bike, when someone in your age group effortlessly whisks by you on an exotic bike worth three times what you paid for yours. According to the rules of the race, "all is fair and just." (Well, at least you were faster on the swim—and it probably wasn't because of your goggles!) In the race rules, no provisions or handicaps have been made to distinguish among the levels of quality of our athletic equipment. And what about flat tires or broken parts? No excuses or time credits here either. Repair the problem and get back in the race.

Should we choose to view ourselves as victims of circumstance? *If only I had a better bike; If only I hadn't flatted.* In the bigger picture of life, an enlightened view allows us to see how disempowering it is to choose the victim role of self-pity. The issue of equipment inequity can even be expanded to include our bodies. We are individually born into the unique bodies we inhabit. With faith and trust, we can view this as our choice and seek out the opportunities that are appropriate for us. While most of us do not have the most genetically superior bodies or the most technically advanced bicycles and equipment, no one places limits on how masterfully and brilliantly we each integrate with and animate the equipment we do have—be it body or bike.

This brilliant and masterful blending is achieved through diligent training. Literally, there is no limit to "experience-ability"—to our human ability to engage, focus, and coordinate our senses, our intellect, our imagination, ingenuity, and creativity. There is no limit to our perceptive ability and skills of observation. Likewise, there is no limit to our expressive ability and skills of activity.

In endurance races, with the exception of gender and age, we are all created equal—equal in this experience-ability and potential for brilliance. The dilemma of equipment inequality points to the relativity of it all. The race is always an individual journey and a collective journey at the same time—an expression of how diligently each of us has trained and how we inspire each other in the moment.

Zen and the Art of Bicycle Maintenance

Perhaps the most notorious criticism of triathletes is the grungy condition of our bikes—poorly maintained and dirty. Many experienced bike mechanics cringe at the thought of having to work on one of these grimy machines. Most of us are so focused on the activity and exertion of training that we ignore the maintenance and cleanliness of our bikes. We are willing to spend hundreds of dollars on the latest high-tech gear—like an aero seatpost—to squeeze a few seconds off our times. Yet we are unwilling to simply keep the chain and driveline clean and lubed—which is far more effective at enhancing our performance, at far less expense.

We want more and better equipment, yet we are unwilling to set aside the time and patience to care for what we already have. We can become so focused and obsessed with the activity and practice of our actual training and racing that we ignore other vital areas of our lives that also have a direct impact on our athletic performance, like bike maintenance. In the bigger picture, this narrow focus and fixation to the exclusion of other areas of our lives—such as our family and relationships and our personal health—can significantly diminish the quality of our lives and, again, our athletic performance.

Our attitude toward maintaining our bicycles—even if this maintenance slightly shortens our training hours—is a great opportunity to look at how we regard our lives outside athletics. Essentially, we are addressing how well we blend our athletic practice with our lives as human beings. If we consciously approach the task of bike maintenance as an opportunity to engage in an activity—other than endurance training—from a calm, still, silent open and empty space of contemplation and awareness, it will support us in applying our zendurance abilities to our lives as a whole. We can clean and maintain our bikes with the same impeccability and diligence we have for our training.

Conclusion

Throughout our lives, we experience the profound condition of duality—the *inner me* and the *outer them*—as illustrated by the yin-yang symbol. This condition of duality provides infinite possibilities for our spiritual growth and progress on the path toward effortless power. Blending, like yielding, is an essential process for experiencing that growth and progress.

Bicycling is a simple and tangible way of developing our blending skills. If we really want to experience these benefits, we must consciously and deliberately approach our bicycle training with clear intent. The rewards for this diligent approach can be profound.

Are we ready to give up the resistance and the opposition?

RUNNING—ALIGNING

Simplicity

Many of us experience a sense of freedom and liberation when we run. Perhaps it is the feeling of mobility that running gives us—to move forward and progress toward some destination without the dependence on a vehicle. We are unencumbered, free from wheels of any kind—no motorized vehicle, not even a bicycle. Of all the endurance activities, running is the simplest and most basic, along with its very close cousin walking. We can simply lace up the shoes and go—rain or shine, hot or cold, urban street or wilderness trail. Unlike a vehicle or bicycle, our running shoes require little if any maintenance. The closest thing to a flat tire in running is the need to stop and retie a shoelace. Unlike swimming, we can commence running almost anywhere and anytime—without pool memberships or ocean access.

As we start out on a run, we make the deliberate choice to temporarily set down our daily concerns and preoccupations for the opportunity to enter a solitary meditative state. It's not that we are running away—we usually finish our run right back where we began. The destination we reach is a transformed state of being—both physically and mentally. Simply put: "Have shoes, will run."

Familiarity

Another aspect that distinguishes running is the similarity to other common daily activities—like standing and walking. When we run, we assume the typical standing posture that is unique to humans as bipeds. This posture is far more familiar to us than the aero position of cycling or the prone position of swimming.

Compared to swimming and cycling, there is less apparent danger with running. We do not have to be concerned with the interface of water and air that is required to breathe while swimming. The potential for collision and the diligence this requires for accurate navigation while cycling are not nearly so critical in running—particularly on even, well-paved surfaces. This relative safety factor—combined with the second-nature familiarity of running—means we can get by with less awareness and attentiveness. Part of the simplicity and liberation of running is the opportunity to switch into autopilot mode.

Familiarity and Autopilot

This second-nature familiarity can also be to our disadvantage, especially in our zendurance approach to running. The practice of zendurance requires our complete presence and diligent attention—regardless of the endurance activity. Slipping into a disassociative state of autopilot diminishes the quality of our presence and awareness in the present moment.

We are much more apt to bring our bad habits and unconsciousness into the activity of running than we are with any other endurance form. This is due to our familiarity with the upright posture of running and the similarity to our day-to-day activities of walking and simply shifting weight from one foot to the other.

Our posture—comprised of our skeletal, muscular, and energetic alignment—is very ingrained and can be difficult for us to clearly perceive. In fact our alignment and our posture actually help shape our perceptions. We can begin to get a sense of how deceptive the familiarity and simplicity of running can be and how this challenges our deliberate and conscious intention to transform running into a practice of zendurance.

The High Stakes of Running

There is another crucial element to the mindfulness equation of running as well. While running may not have the apparent dangers that we experience with swimming and biking, there is actually more potential for injury—due to the impact of landing on the ground with every step. Of all endurance activities, running generates the most impact and requires the most meticulously consistent and deliberate approach to training. Running can be the most costly and the most punishing activity to our bodies—due to our inefficiency.

What is the source of our inefficiency as runners? It begins with the poor alignment and posture that we unconsciously bring from our day-to-day activities into our running. To reiterate, this unconscious inefficiency—this misalignment—is so ingrained in our bodies and our minds that it is nearly impossible for us to perceive. It shapes our perceptions—our misperceptions.

Running is one of the most cardiovascular of all aerobic activities. It may be surpassed only by high-intensity cross-country skiing and by rowing a racing scull. Both of these activities demand high levels of exertion for both the upper and lower body. Due to the high cardiovascular demand as well as the stress of impact, running provides us with the best dopamine and endorphin high. After all, the term *runner's high* is not just coincidental.

Gravity

What makes running so extreme? Why do we find the greatest potential for stress and injury as well as the greatest cardiovascular demand and endocrine-system-derived highs (and lows)? To look at this question, let's imagine the following scenario:

At 6:50 A.M., on a Saturday morning in October—just one day before the full moon—you enter the ocean at Kamakahonu Bay, right next to the Kailua Pier. The sun is coloring the sky from behind 9000-foot-high Hualalai Mountain, but has not yet made an appearance. Then at precisely 7 A.M. just after a quiet moment of prayer, with the boom of the cannon, you and over fifteen hundred other athletes begin Hawaii Ironman. You post a 1:14 for the 2.4-mile swim—a bit slow, since you started out easy to avoid the thrashing zoo.

Three hours and ten minutes later, you pedal your bike into Hawi Town at the northern tip of the island—just to turn around and head back down the coast to Kailua again. The trip up to Hawi included some steady winds coming at you from the one to two o'clock direction as you pushed from Waikoloa to Kawaihae and some nasty head-on blasts for those last six miles into Hawi. Once you turn around in Hawi, it feels as if you have picked up a couple of jet thrust packs—at least for a short time. Then just south of Kawaihae, the winds have made their daily transition from trade winds to thermals—so once again you encounter steady wind resistance coming at you from the two o'clock direction.

You finally reach Kailua and civilization again—after being way out there in the windy wilderness—and pull into the transition area, posting a 5:50 bike split. After lacing up your running shoes, you stand up from the transition bench, trot out of the tent, gulp down some cold water, and begin to run. It's "marathon time," folks, and this is the first time your feet have touched the ground in more than seven hours! Welcome back to the surface of Planet Earth. Welcome back to gravity!

Graceful and efficient running is a function of our alignment with gravity. It is the force of gravity and our relationship with it that makes running extreme—that produces the greatest potential for stress and injury, the greatest cardiovascular demands, and the extreme highs and lows of our endocrine system.

Of all the relationships we engage in during our lives—including our most enduring human relationships—our relationship with Earth's gravitational pull is the most constant and enduring. We are each in a constant and continuous relationship with Earth's gravity from the moment of conception in our mother's womb until the time we vacate our bodies at death. It is an intimate relationship—one that permeates every cell of our bodies, all the way to our innermost core. Despite this intimacy, despite the unrelenting continuity of gravity's presence in our lives, our awareness of gravity is usually relegated to the background of our consciousness at best.

Gravity and Zendurance

Like yielding and blending, our alignment with gravity—our balance—is both a physical process and a state of conscious awareness—an attitude, a choice.

In our discussion of swimming, we considered the empowering qualities of yielding—physically as well as mentally and emotionally—as part of our quest for effortless power. Likewise, in our discussion of bicycling, we considered the empowering qualities of blending—physically as well as mentally and emotionally—in contrast to excluding or isolating. In both of these endurance activities—swimming and cycling—it is clear that the qualities of yielding and blending support us in cultivating gracefulness and efficiency and enable us to become more proficient as athletes. As we diligently investigate and develop the skills of yielding and blending through our endurance training, we are more apt to embrace and to integrate these attributes into other areas of our lives as well.

In this context, we use our endurance training as the proving grounds to clearly demonstrate for ourselves the empowering possibilities of yielding and blending. The same holds true with aligning. Running is one of the ultimate physical proving grounds for investigating, exploring, cultivating, and developing alignment and for experiencing the empowering possibilities of this skill. In our zendurance running, we can intimately listen and respond to gravity.

We usually choose one of two relationships with gravity. One choice is to resign ourselves to it—to go through life regarding our bodies as being anchors or burdens of imprisonment. The other possibility we may choose is to fight or resist gravity. By observing the posture and physical activities of others, we can often see the burdensome resignation or the fighting resistance that individuals choose. Those who resign often seem to trudge and move slowly. They appear tired and usually slump in their postures. Those who fight and resist often overexert themselves and experience the impact of that fight.

Impact

To divert for a moment, let's look a little closer at our notions of impact. War, is essentially impact. In primitive times, the weapons of impact were clubs and rocks. After the development of metallurgy, we graduated to swords. Gunpowder brought bullets and artillery shells into the arena of war—still weapons that produce impact, just more remotely. With firearms, we no longer needed to be within physical striking distance. With the advent of bombs, chemical warfare, and so forth, we are simply able to distance ourselves from the point of impact and to expand the range of impact. Even our latest running shoes—which are beginning to look more and more like high-rise air mattresses—are designed not just to cushion the impact of our strides, but also to distance us from that impact.

Aligning—The Third Choice

Returning to the subject of running and gravity, there is an alternative to resignation and to the fight of resistance. The third choice is to align with gravity. If winning a war seems to be accomplished by delivering the most devastating impact first, how can alignment bring more potential for success—for winning—than striking hard and fast? If we want to run fast, we need to apply more force—impact—as we launch ourselves forward, yes?

Ever Try Running in Space?

To consider these questions, let's investigate the seemingly simple mechanical relationship we have with gravity as we run. To begin, let's imagine running in the absence of gravity: Quite simply, running would not be possible. This scenario is similar to the one we considered in "Swimming—Yielding": Without the resistance of water, we have no substance to catch, pull, and push in order to progress forward—that's what swimming is. Likewise, without gravity, how can we thrust ourselves forward as we run?

The Physics of Running

Running is the articulation of a phenomenon known in physics as *precession.* In precession, a force is translated or transformed by ninety degrees. When we run, we are translating the downward force of gravity into forward motion—a transformation of ninety degrees. Our gravitational attraction to Earth creates the friction between the surface we are running on and the soles of our shoes—endowing us with the perfect conditions for thrust. Without this friction—say, on a glassy-smooth ice rink—running is a slippery proposition.

The friction between our shoe and the road—courtesy of gravity —provides us with a momentary anchor point—much the same way that the resistance of water provides us with a momentary anchor point. With swimming, that momentary anchor point is a temporary handhold; with running it is a temporary foothold. Efficient swimming technique is based on minimizing the resistance our bodies generate as we move through the water—through hydrodynamic positioning—while maximizing the use of that hand full of water—our momentary anchor point. Likewise in running, we want to minimize the negative aspects of gravity while maximizing the use of our momentary foothold.

So, what are the negative aspects of gravity? Impact—with its great potential for injury and damage—can be a negative aspect. Friction is another negative aspect—the very same friction that provides us with the momentary anchor point of our stationary platform. Quite simply, if our feet are in constant contact with Earth's surface, we are not moving forward. Once we have launched ourselves forward from our stationary platform, if we can stay aloft, we will continue to move forward, encountering only the friction of the air. However, just as the resistance of water slows our forward progress after each swim stroke, gravity pulls us down after each run stride.

Essentially, as we run, we use the stationary platform of foot contact to propel or launch our body forward. Our body's center of movement is located in the lower abdomen—so when we run, we are essentially moving our hips forward over the stationary platform that our foot briefly provides. We run efficiently and effortlessly by minimizing the two basic negative aspects of gravity—impact and friction. We can minimize impact by avoiding extremely long strides, by landing softly and by smoothing out the vertical up and down amplitude of each stride, as we leap forward. We can minimize friction by decreasing the time we actually spend on the ground. When we run efficiently and effortlessly, our foot contact is as brief as possible. During that brief contact, we move our body forward over the foot platform with minimal up-and-down bounce.

Applying the Physics

Expressing these techniques verbally and actually implementing them in our running form are two very different things. As a way of approaching this implementation, we can deeply contemplate this question as we run: *What does my relationship with gravity feel like when I am running efficiently and effortlessly?* After all, running is first and foremost a dynamic and continuous relationship with gravity. At any given moment, our relationship with gravity may be one of resignation, resistance, or alignment. If we intend to minimize impact and friction, then alignment is our best choice—a choice we make continuously, moment by moment.

Pinpointing Gravity

So if effortless and efficient running is founded upon a precise alignment with gravity, what does that feel like? It feels like *pinpointing gravity*.

In swimming, we strive to become hydrodynamic by exposing a minimum of our body's leading surface to the water's flow around us. In bicycling, we strive to become aerodynamic by minimizing our body's surface area to the airflow. In running, we strive to become "gravi-dynamic" by stacking up or aligning our body so that gravity "sees" very little of our body's surface. If someone were to observe us from Earth's center as we ran overhead, we would want that observer to see very little of our body— just the soles of our feet. We want to appear to that observer as a *pinpoint*.

Small and Humble

There is a common element to our hydrodynamic swimming technique, our aerodynamic cycling technique, and our gravi-dynamic running technique. In all three, our intent is to make ourselves appear small to the potential forces of resistance and/or impact inherent in the water, wind, and gravity. The notion of becoming small—of minimizing our disturbance or impact—is quite foreign to our conventional attitude as athletic warriors. Yet it is an undeniable aspect of both efficiency and grace, and these are two essential elements in endurance athletics.

Our practices of yielding, blending, and aligning—reducing our impact and disturbance—are very humbling practices. The choice to cultivate and strengthen our calm, still, silent, open, and empty center of deep inner listening and contemplation requires humility. Yielding, blending, and aligning require that we relinquish our ego—the real source of our resistance and our desire to create impact. It requires brevity, tenacity, and courage to disengage our ego so that we may yield, blend, and align. Our ego views these practices and attitudes as a threat to our bigness—our significance. Ego regards these practices as a complete surrender and resignation—ultimately as death.

As we diligently practice yielding, blending, and aligning through endurance training, we very gradually build our familiarity and our trust in that calm, still, silent, open, and empty space of deep inner listening and contemplation. We begin to realize through experience that this process of making ourselves small is not so much a death as it is a liberation because we are discovering our true nature beyond ego identity.

Yielding, blending, and aligning are essential practices in all areas of our lives. The zendurance approach to athletic activity is simply our formal training grounds for consciously and deliberately developing our skill and fluency in each of these processes. Then they will become second nature—so that we are able to easily call upon them when we are encountering resistance and impact in our daily lives. As mentioned earlier, our athletic training serves as the proving grounds where we demonstrate for ourselves the empowering qualities of yielding, blending, and aligning. These are the ways of the inner warrior—the gentle warrior on the path toward effortless power.

Aligning as a Study and Practice

Our conscious choice to study and practice alignment with gravity is a profound one since we are in a continuous and dynamic relationship with gravity throughout our lives. Running is one of the greatest opportunities of our lives to study alignment. As we develop this ability—both as a physical skill and as a mental attitude—we will experience great rewards. We will become more graceful and efficient as runners, and we will experience less pain and injury in our running. Our awareness of and sensitivity to gravitational alignment will also carry over into our daily activities and attitudes. We will begin to minimize the impact and friction in our relationships and ordinary tasks as we begin to align with the forces at work in our daily lives and the events we are experiencing. We will recognize the opportunity in each moment to choose alignment rather than resignation or impact.

Let's examine some techniques that can help us to pinpoint gravity—to align with and to make ourselves appear small to gravity.

Pelvic Alignment and Core Strength

In our bodies, aligning with gravity begins with pelvic alignment.
Our pelvic girdle—that big bowl of bone in our lower torso—is the
interface of our upper body with our lower body. The skeleton of
our upper body—the spine—fuses into the pelvis at the lower back.
Our legs—comprising our lower skeleton—connect at the hip sockets, located at the sides of the pelvis and farther forward, toward
the abdomen. Take a moment right now to feel the shape and size
of your pelvis. Feel where your spine fuses to the pelvis and where
your legs connect at the hip sockets. Feel the spatial relationship
among these three connecting points in your lower abdomen.

The tilt of our pelvis—its front-to-back orientation—determines to
a great extent our alignment with gravity and the integrity of the
upper and lower halves of our body. Correct pelvic position—or
tilt—requires both physical core strength and core intelligence. We
can develop both core strength and intelligence through conscientious exercise. Basic Pilates matwork is an excellent exercise program for developing both core strength and intelligence. Cultivating
core strength and intelligence is the first essential technique in
developing an articulate ability to align with gravity as we run.

As we develop the articulation of our core strength and core
intelligence, we will notice gradual changes in our running form.
We will begin to clearly feel the location of our body's center of
movement in the lower abdomen and pelvic region. As we run, we
will be able to place our awareness in this region and feel this center of movement passing over the stationary platform temporarily
provided by each foot. Feeling this dynamic relationship between
the grounded foot and our abdominal movement center is essential to pinpointing gravity.

Getting Our Feet on the Ground

Runners who land on the back edge of the heel—called heel
strikers—tend to spend more time on the ground during each
stride. Heel striking is caused by landing while the pelvis is *behind*
the grounded foot. In this scenario, the foot must remain on the
ground until the lower abdomen has passed over and in front of the
foot. Because the moment of impact occurs while the body's pelvic
center of movement is behind the foot's point of contact, there is

deceleration until the pelvis has passed over the foot. This deceleration results in a greater force of impact. In summary, heel striking typically magnifies those two negative aspects of gravity—impact and friction. Our gravitational profile is much larger than a pinpoint.

With sufficient core strength and core intelligence, our alignment with gravity improves and we are able to keep our abdominal center of movement over our feet instead of lagging behind. With this improved alignment, we are more apt to land on the midfoot or forefoot—since our pelvic center of movement remains over our foot. We spend less time on the ground with less impact. We begin to feel that we are pinpointing gravity; that we are becoming gravidynamic. Precise pinpointing requires accurate alignment of our entire spine over the alternating stationary platforms that are temporarily provided by our feet.

The sensation of pinpointing gravity can be felt throughout our well-aligned spine. At the instant that our foot contacts the ground, our spine is directly over the point of contact. The duration of ground contact for each foot is minimized. We feel less impact at touchdown and we bounce up and down less. Pinpointing gravity enables us to become more proficient at translating Earth's gravitational pull (vertical force) into forward motion (horizontal force)—precession. Precession is the essence of efficient running and walking.

Core strength and intelligence are essential in our zendurance approach to running. Pinpointing gravity is the gateway to efficient, graceful, and effortless running. Now let's explore two techniques that can help us to develop our running intelligence.

Water-Running

It seems odd that we might choose to engage in water-running if we intend to study our relationship with gravity. After all, the buoyancy of water diminishes the effects of gravity. However, water-running does allow us to study the mechanics of our running form without the distraction of impact. It also allows us to run at any tempo—from slow motion to sprint speed.

Let's begin with a general description. Water running is conducted in a body of deep water, so that our feet do not contact the bottom surface. In order to practice water-running, we must first regulate our buoyancy so that our head stays above the water—at least when we are in motion. High salt content promotes buoyancy; therefore, ocean water-running may not require any buoy-ancy aids. Pool water-running may require some aid. There are commercially available buoyancy aids specifically for water-run-ning. You might also experiment with holding an empty water bottle in each hand.

As with any training session that focuses specifically on tech-nique, water-running can be a highly effective tool or it can be a complete waste of time. Clear intention, diligence, and focus are essential for getting the most out of any technique session—water-running included.

Initially, brief water-running sessions are a great recovery activ-ity the day after a long duration or high-intensity bike and/or run session. Even ten minutes of easy water-running can help process out lactic acid and loosen tight, sore muscles and joints. The cold water will also reduce inflammation. These short recovery sessions are easily added to the end of a swim session.

Start with the Core

The emphasis of water-running—be it a short and easy recovery session or a longer interval session—is on gaining awareness, strengthening and improving our running form. This emphasis begins with core alignment of the spine and pelvis. We focus on keeping our hips forward as we generate our strides from the pelvic region. It takes core strength and intelligence to maintain our ver-tical alignment while we run suspended in the water.

Next, we concentrate on correct leg movement—really bending at the knee as our leg moves forward, then lengthening and extend-ing out as we plant our foot. As we refine this leg movement, we want to feel our pelvic center stay directly over our legs, without lagging behind. We apply power from the pelvic region to pull or thrust the leg back—while maintaining our pelvic and spinal align-ment. Finally, we expand our awareness to include our arm move-ment—also sourced from our abdominal core. Arm movement can help us to maintain our turnover rate.

In developing our water-running technique, it is best if we con-centrate on one element at a time—just as we do with our swim-ming or cycling technique. The primary emphasis is good pelvic and spinal alignment—feeling as much length in our spine as pos-sible from the top of the head, through a long straight neck, and continuing all the way to the base of the spine. We want to feel strong abdominal stability without immobility and stiffness. We can also investigate leg mechanics—paying attention to the timing of the hinging knee as the leg moves forward and the extension of the leg as the foot contacts. Feel how this forward movement is generated in the abdomen, in balance with the opposite leg thrusting back.

Water-running is also a safe opportunity to close our eyes in order to conduct some internal feeling investigation. It is much easier to focus inward with our eyes closed. Most importantly, we want to locate—by feeling—our abdominal core center of movement. We want to observe how the mechanics and the coordination of our running form—for both the upper and lower body—are sourced from this intelligent center.

By emphasizing vertical length and alignment all the way from head to foot, we can enhance the strength and intelligence that will improve our ability to accurately pinpoint gravity when we run conventionally. This verticality throughout our body should include a distinct feeling of length through the front of the hip sockets. We want to feel a connection from that long open hip socket all the way to the ball of the foot as we plant and pull back. Again, we can close our eyes and deeply investigate this lengthening.

Tempo Variation

Water-running allows us to exaggerate some of the parameters of our running form that are impossible when we get back to Earth. We can slow our tempo considerably so that we can explore intimately the mechanical complexity of running. Our intention here is similar to bike tai chi. With a very slow tempo, we can focus on smoothing out our running form and making it more seamless. We begin this process in our abdominal core and expand outward.

In contrast, we can also emphasize a very rapid turnover rate through interval training in the water. With this technique, we use the high degree of resistance in the water to challenge and improve our ability to maintain a quick turnover. These moderately high intensity intervals allow us to develop faster leg turnover without impact or extremely high cardiovascular demand. It is important to feel the resistance of the water and to use it as a guide for developing good leg tracking—eliminating wobble or side-to-side movement of the legs. Another opportunity for exaggeration is in stride length—usually at a slow-to-normal tempo. In this exercise, we stretch out the leg extension, as if leaping forward, and then pull back the extended leg using our abdominal core.

After building a base and gaining some familiarity with water-running through short, easy sessions, we may choose to lengthen the duration of these sessions and to include the rapid-turnover intervals mentioned above. Keep in mind that going into autopilot will make these sessions a waste of time and may even strengthen bad habits. Approach these sessions earnestly with an open, inquisitive mind.

Amphibious Running

With adequate base building, we can begin to develop some key running workouts in the water. One example is to substitute a long water-run for a conventional long run every other week. We can build up the duration of this water-run to equal half or more of the total duration of a conventional long run. During this session, we diligently concentrate on various technique aspects and include frequent intervals of rapid leg turnover. Rather than measuring clock time, it will be easier to time these intervals by counting strides.

Upon finishing this session we can transition quickly into a conventional run. In this transition, we want to carry over the technique and core strength we have been focusing on during the water run. By maintaining the vertical length and alignment from head to toe from our water-run, we can refine and enhance our feeling of pinpointing gravity in this follow-up run. We might include a tempo run while diligently focusing on alignment and form.

Another great complement to the water-run is to include plyometric drills in this follow-up run—one-leg hops, two-leg jumps, long leaping strides, skips, high knee drills, and so on. Refer to a good training manual such as Joe Friel's *Triathlete's Training Bible* for a more specific and detailed explanation of plyometric workouts. Water-running maximizes resistance while minimizing impact. Plyometric drills increase impact during short intervals. With care, these plyometric drills can strengthen our joints for impact.

Innovative and Creative

It takes patience, diligence, and creativity to develop unconventional and unfamiliar training sessions, such as bike tai chi and water-running. We must be just as consistent with these sessions as we are with our conventional workouts if they are going to be an effective and integral part of our overall training program. As we approach these training sessions—all of our training sessions, for that matter—our intention and objectives should be clear so that we are not simply going into autopilot to log some junk miles. We want to make the most out of the time we spend training.

Tai Chi Principles and Running

In the "Bicycling—Blending" entry, we examined a slow-motion low-intensity approach to cycling—bike tai chi. The emphasis in bike tai chi is to practice blending with our bikes by integrating and practicing some of the principles of this traditional soft martial art form. Water-running allows us the only practical opportunity to explore slow-motion running since we cannot slow down gravity—without using the resistance of water. More importantly, it offers us an opportunity to develop the core strength and intelligence that will improve our alignment and therefore our relationship with gravity. It does not, however, offer us the opportunity to really develop our sensitivity for gravity and to practice gravitational alignment. Since gravitational alignment is the essence of efficient and effortless running, it is advantageous to develop and practice some running techniques that can improve our sensitivity to alignment.

During every activity of our lives—even breathing—every cell of our bodies is engaged in a relationship with gravity, be it harmonious or burdensome. This is a very profound truth that we must explore thoroughly and diligently in our zendurance training and in our quest for effortless power. Gravitational alignment is an important and fundamental form of intelligence in tai chi and other traditional internal martial arts forms. Since ancient times, practitioners have earnestly studied and trained in this form of intelligence.

Grounding and Sinking

One of the most valuable and profound books I have read in my study of zendurance is Peter Ralston's *Cheng Hsin: Principles of Effortless Power*. Peter considers deeply the nature of gravity and our notions and assumptions about it. According to Peter, grounding and gravitational alignment are absolutely essential in our pursuit and realization of effortless power. Grounding is the feeling of blending with the Earth through the energetic field of gravity. This feeling of blending begins with our deliberate intention to sink our physical weight and our awareness—including our sense of feeling—not just onto the Earth's surface, but into the Earth.

Sinking, just like yielding and blending, seems completely contrary to our natural ego-driven tendencies. How can we possibly realize effortless power by sinking? That is the same as lowering and humbling ourselves, as giving up our superiority—our position of being above everyone and everything. We like to associate our superior source of intelligence with our brain—located at the top of our bodies. Sinking and grounding—as the energetic processes of blending with the Earth—require that we literally lower our awareness instead. By lowering our awareness, we create an alliance with gravity—our principal resource and primary potential for all kinetic activity.

The apparently simple act of shifting our weight from one leg through the other (rather than onto the other) is the most common technique we use to move our bodies. We learn to shift our weight from one leg through the other as we master the arts of gravitational alignment and grounding.

Activating the Gravity Laser

How does gravitational alignment make our movements more effortless, graceful, and efficient? As we align—by pinpointing gravity—we are focusing and concentrating the force of gravity. This process of pinpointing is similar to focusing and concentrating photons of light into a coherent laser beam. Our ability to pinpoint gravity can be felt in much the same way—as though we are creating a narrow laser beam of gravity through our bodies. The only real difference between a conventional light laser and our "gravity laser" is the directional flow. With a light laser, the beam of energy is flowing outward, away from the light source. With our gravity laser, the beam of energy is flowing inward, toward the gravitational source, the center of Planet Earth.

How does grounding make our movements more effortless, graceful, and efficient? Let's investigate this question by continuing on with our laser beam analogy. Let's say we have gained the ability to pinpoint gravity—to create that gravity laser beam through our bodies. What happens when we obstruct or block a laser beam? The path of light—or gravity in our case—is cut off. If the conventional laser light beam is strong enough, it will burn a hole through the obstruction. If not, it will remain cut off.

How do we obstruct our gravity laser, even if we are well aligned? We obstruct it with tension—by holding tension in our muscles.

The process of grounding—of blending energetically with the Earth—is a process of yielding and relaxing, of draining tension. This process of relaxing and draining is just as much mental and emotional as it is physical. If we are experiencing mental or emotional tension and anxiety, we are almost certainly mirroring that in our bodies, as some form of cellular tension—either in our muscles and joints or in our organs.

Even if we are able to focus our gravity laser through perfect anatomical alignment with gravity, if we are not yielding—by relaxing and draining our tensions—and energetically blending with the Earth, then our potential for effortlessness, grace, and efficiency is obstructed. While our gravity laser will not burn a hole through our obstructive resistance, we are likely to experience impact injuries at the sites of obstruction or misalignment.

Running—as a practice of zendurance—includes yielding (relaxing), blending (grounding), and aligning. This zendurance practice can minimize the physical, emotional, and mental impact we experience in our daily lives as we transform our overall awareness and intelligence.

Tai Chi Walking Practice—Transferring Weight

Here is a very simple technique we can use to begin the vast and profound exploration of relaxing, grounding, and aligning with gravity—one I call the "tai chi walk." We want to practice this slow-motion walk in a quiet place, with a smooth flat surface—a floor or a lawn works well. Optimally, it is nice to have a length of twenty feet or more, but a shorter span will work.

Begin standing at one end of the walkway, feet parallel to one another, with your feet spaced just slightly wider than your hips and your knees slightly and softly bent. We begin the process of grounding by relaxing and softening the soles of our feet. Imagine the soles of your feet as two pats of butter, softening and melting in the bottom of a warm skillet. Allow your feet to relax and spread out on the floor. Begin to simply shift your weight alternately from one side to the other—keeping both feet on the ground at hip width.

There are two distinct ways to shift your weight. One way is to push off one leg and onto the other. The second technique is to relax and to "let go" of one leg, allowing the weight to drop into and through the other leg. Close your eyes and try both of these techniques. Notice if you can feel a distinction between them. The second technique—relaxing and sinking through the other leg—

is fundamental to our grounding process. In this simple practice of side-to-side weight transfer, what distinguishes dropping through our leg from pushing onto the other leg is relaxation. With effective alignment, we can thoroughly relax and stand through our leg and foot, into the Earth—allowing the muscle cells of our legs to compress without tension. This is grounding. To repeat, this relaxation must be mental and emotional as well as physical. Be patient and consistent with this apparently simple exercise. The process of grounding—like yielding and blending—is subtle, yet profound. Remember to keep your knees slightly and softly bent, your hips level, and your feet soft and relaxed.

Weight Transfer and the Gravity Laser

In transferring your weight from one leg and foot through the other, imagine a laser beam originating at the hip socket, projecting unobstructed down through your leg, the sole of your foot, and deep into the Earth. Use this image to extend your sense of feeling into the Earth. Then slowly sink and drop into the other leg and foot. Feel the unobstructed laser beam from that hip socket project deeply into the Earth.

When you gain some proficiency at feeling these alternating gravity lasers projecting from the hips and extending deep into the Earth, you can move the source of the lasers to each shoulder socket. This relocation will enable you to extend the deep relaxation and alignment up through your torso. Remember, on the cellular level, this process of deep relaxation allows your weight to compress and to pass through the muscle cells without holding tension. You begin to distinguish the subtle yet profound difference between tension and compression. In a state of tension, the muscle cells are blocking the energetic flow of grounding. In a state of compression, the cells simply pass the energy through without any energy given to resistance. Compression—deep cellular relaxation—is possible only through correct alignment.

These very simple exercises may appear too elementary for us as competent endurance athletes. I have been working with simple techniques like these for well over twenty years. The intelligent processes of alignment do not develop overnight, any more than our swimming technique will develop overnight. These are lifelong studies—be patient. It may be helpful to close your eyes in order to feel this process of yielding (relaxing), blending (grounding), and aligning.

Do the Twist

Now let's throw a little twist into this basic transfer of weight. As you alternately drop from one leg through the other, you can begin to rotate in your hip sockets so that your torso rotates slightly from side to side. There are two distinct ways to accomplish this twist. One is to twist at the chest and upper torso, on top of the hips, as we transfer our weight. The second way is to generate the twist by rotating in the hip sockets as we are transferring our weight, so that our upper torso follows the abdominal movement. We want to generate the rotation from our hips and pelvic region, rather than twisting the chest and shoulders over the hips. This requires that we sink our awareness and relax our upper torso down into our hips. Our process of grounding always moves from the ground upward into and through our body side to side.

Adding in the hip socket rotation to the weight shifting greatly increases the complexity. Not only are we bearing weight—actually passing weight through each hip socket—but we are also rotating the socket at the same time. In this practice, we must relax the connective tissues of the hip socket in order to allow for rotation—just as we are bearing weight. This seemingly simple exercise may actually take years to master, since our conditioning is usually to tense our muscles and connective tissues as they bear weight.

Joint mobility—especially in the hip and shoulder sockets—is a precious physical asset in any zendurance quest. We can recover some of the joint mobility of our youth through a long-term commitment to deep and permeating relaxation. By cultivating an attentive, intimate, and harmonious relationship with gravity, we can receive valuable guidance in our quest for mobility and relaxation. We can allow gravity to actually pull and drain the tensions out of our bodies. Gravity is a profound guide and teacher.

Let's continue with our tai chi walking technique—after all, we have been exploring intimately the transfer of weight through one leg and then the other, but we have yet to move our feet or take a step.

Tai Chi Walking Practice—Moving Forward

To start the tai chi wave walk, center your weight through both hips, both legs and feet—this time with your feet precisely below your hip sockets (hip width). To express this more accurately, each hip socket is stacked up and rests precisely above and through the corresponding foot. Remember, grounding happens from the ground up. Again, your knees are gently, softly, and slightly bent.

Your feet point straight ahead, parallel to each other.

Now shift all your weight through your right foot and then pivot your left heel so that your left hip, leg, and foot rotate outward about thirty-five to forty-five degrees. It is very important that this rotation or turnout originates in the hip socket and not the knee and ankle joints. Do not turn out too far. By pivoting on the heel, you will maintain hip width between your heels. Slowly drop all your weight into your turned-out, soft, melting, buttery left foot and slowly peel your right foot off that warm skillet, lifting the heel first and toes last. Take a small step forward, keeping that right foot parallel (pointing forward) and maintaining hip width between your heels, as you place your foot—heel first—back on the ground. In other words, even though you are stepping forward, do not start walking on a single-line tight wire, with one heel aligned directly in front of the other. This will compromise your balance and will prevent your weight from draining and dropping through your hip sockets, through your feet, and into the Earth.

As you take this first step forward, gently place your right foot completely on the ground before you slowly shift and drop your weight through that right leg. You want to contact the ground completely with that soft buttery right foot while all the weight is still completely on the turned-out and relaxed back left foot. You must keep your back left knee softly and slightly bent and keep your step small in order to do this. Slowly and gradually shift 60 to 70 percent of your weight through your right front hip, leg, and foot.

How do you know when you have shifted 60 to 70 percent of your weight? Your kneecap will be just behind or over your toes. If you feel the weight coming forward and pressing through the ball of your foot, you have shifted too far.

Now shift slowly back again to your back left foot, allowing 100 percent of your weight again to pass through that back hip, leg, and foot. Once more, peel your soft right front foot up and turn it out—rotating from the hip socket. Place it softly back on the floor where it was—turned out now—maintaining hip width between the heels. Slowly shift all your weight through that turned-out right front foot, bending your knee slightly and softly while keeping it aligned over your turned-out foot. Peel your back left foot up and slowly move that leg forward. Gently place that left foot down, toes pointing forward, in parallel position and maintaining hip width—just as you first did with your right foot. Slowly and gently shift 60 to 70 percent of your weight through that front left foot.

Wave Walking

To summarize, each forward progression begins by first shifting just 60 to 70 percent of the weight through the parallel front foot. Retreat the weight completely to the back foot, lift the front foot, place it back down again in the same place—but turned out now—and shift completely forward. Each forward progression consists of two waves—a 60 to 70 percent wave into a parallel foot, then a complete retreat (without actually retracting the lead foot back in), followed by a 100 percent wave into a turned-out hip-leg-foot.

Repeat this two-wave tai chi walk slowly, gracefully, and smoothly across the floor. Try to keep the wave cycles seamless and continuous without pauses or lurches. Coordinate the bending of your knees so that your hips, torso, shoulders, and head remain level, without rising and sinking through each step and without tilting from side to side. Your approach and your breath should be relaxed, slow, and smooth. This is a moving meditation—a practice of total body awareness as we move. As we gain proficiency and skill in this practice of aligning and grounding while walking, we will be able to walk progressively slower with very little effort expended for support or balance. Our goal here is to develop an intimate sense of balance, alignment, and grounding through very slow movement. The intelligence we can gain through this study will greatly enhance the efficiency of our running.

Professor Gravity

If you are really earnest in this exercise, you will begin to diligently listen to gravity as a guide. Gravity is our most thorough, intimate, and permeating teacher for alignment and for the relaxation of grounding. This very simple yet profound exercise is a great opportunity to home in on transforming movement into meditation.

We can practice this tai chi walk just about anywhere and anytime. Remember that the real practice here is not the actual walking, it is the inner listening, the meditation. In this practice, we honor gravity as our brilliant and masterful teacher—a teacher that we listen to with every cell of our body. Gravity helps us to develop the intelligence to move from our calm, still, silent, open, and empty space of deep inner listening and contemplation. This is the essence of any zendurance practice—moving meditation. Spending just five to ten minutes in this slow, smooth, and graceful exercise just prior to a running session can enhance our sensitivity to gravitational alignment and grounding during our run.

Applying Tai Chi Principles to Running

Transitioning from a ten-minute tai chi walk session into a run is a very effective way of integrating the traditional principles of grounding and alignment into our running. We need not consciously go through a mental checklist as we begin our run, since the principles of grounding and alignment are already "circulating" through our bodies, through our neurological and muscular systems.

There are also a few specific techniques we can implement during our running. As we have considered, grounding is a bottom-to-top process. It begins with our feet. In our practice of bike tai chi, we include the technique of foot consciousness—keeping our feet relaxed and centered in our bike shoes, without jamming our toes or squashing the sides of our feet. During our running, we can also be attentive to our feet. We begin by feeling and releasing any tensions we hold in our feet and toes as we run. As with our tai chi walk, we can use the image of soft, melting butter in a warm skillet. We strive to maintain that soft, buttery feeling in our feet during our running strides—particularly as we land and take off from each foot.

During recovery sessions, we can practice draining our bodies of tensions and completely relaxing from head to toe. Even our faces and hands can be relaxed. Many of the world's most accomplished runners look as though they might be holding a delicate silver spoon in each hand as they run—even during the most intense races.

The quality of our breathing is also a part of this running relaxation. When we are truly relaxed, right through the core of our aligned torso, our breath can be deep and smooth, without gasping. It is best to initially practice and implement these relaxation techniques during low-intensity recovery sessions when we are not distracted with achieving performance standards or responding physiologically to high levels of exertion and stress. As we gain a feeling of familiarity, we will gradually integrate these relaxation techniques into our more demanding training sessions and our race performances. This process of introducing and implementing the tai chi relaxation techniques will begin to transform all our training and racing activities into zendurance practice.

Another foot-consciousness technique we can implement that will minimize our impact and improve our ability to blend with the Earth is to discern precisely—through feeling—when our lead foot will touch down upon the ground. Pinpoint precisely where the first point of contact will occur on the sole of the shoe and foot. Since our gravitational alignment requires a long, straight spine—including a long and relaxed neck—we do not stare down at the ground right in front of our feet. We develop this foot consciousness through feeling rather than watching.

As we run, our visual gaze may be fixed on the ground farther out ahead—as long as our neck is aligned—or may be on the horizon. Either way—as long as the terrain permits—we can keep our focus soft and relaxed. This will help us tune into the feeling of inner listening. As we gaze at the horizon, we can observe any up-and-down bounce in our gait. With this visual indication, we can refine and smooth our strides to minimize this vertical amplitude. This usually requires strides of moderate length rather than extended, reaching ones.

As we develop gravitational alignment and soft grounding, our footsteps will become very quiet—without much impact *thud* or scuffing movement along the ground. This is a clear sign that we are minimizing both impact and friction. Our zendurance running form becomes as silent and stealthy as our swimming and biking forms.

As we gain core intelligence and strength and begin to integrate them within our running form, our tactile feeling of pinpointing gravity will become more distinct and sensitive. We may be able to develop the feeling of our gravity laser switching on for an instant and passing through from head to foot to ground—as each foot softly contacts and lifts off. This is as indication that we are pinpointing—concentrating and focusing the force of gravity—and that we are grounding effectively by thoroughly relaxing and draining out any tensions and obstructions.

On a wide, smooth, and traffic-free running surface, it may be possible to close our eyes for at least a few strides so that we can clearly feel the sensations of pinpointing gravity and activating the gravity laser. We can simply run back and forth over this safe stretch—practicing brief intervals of blind running to really develop the feel of running. We may also practice this blind technique on a treadmill.

Professor Gravity—One Last Time

Our relationship with gravity has been the principal focus in this discussion on running. As the most permeating, constant, and relentless relationship of our embodied lives, gravity is our most intimate reality check, our most familiar sounding board. We can tell when we are exhausted because we feel gravity's strong pull. Likewise, we can tell when we are fresh and energized because we feel the rebounding potential of gravity. No wonder we use expressions like "Come on back down to Earth" to express the process of grounding—of being realistic and returning to this moment—here and now. Running is one of the ultimate dynamic practices for studying the nature of gravity and for transforming our relationship with gravity and our bodies. Through the careful and subtle study and practice of alignment and grounding, gravity becomes an infinitely powerful energetic resource.

This kind of zendurance practice will gradually and subtly permeate into the rest of our lives. As we gain proficiency at gravitational alignment and grounding, as well as yielding and blending, we begin to minimize the elements of resistance, friction, and impact in our lives—not just physically, but emotionally and mentally as well.

ZENDURANCE TRAINING SUMMARY

Inner Intelligence

A key focus in our zendurance approach to aerobic training is to strengthen our inner focus and awareness. This inner intelligence is essential for us to develop our calm, still, silent, open, and empty space of deep inner listening and contemplation. From that calm and still place within, we are able to enter the zone—where our endurance activity settles into a natural rhythm and an effortless groove. In this state of moving meditation, we experience harmony, grace, and balance in our aerobic activity and with our surrounding environment.

Training in solitude can help us develop the mindfulness—the diligent, focused awareness and keen perception—that is essential to this inner intelligence. When we train alone, we are more likely to turn our awareness inward and to seek out that calm, still, silent, open, and empty space of deep inner listening and contemplation. If we always train with others—diverting our attention to conversation and interaction—we tend to disassociate ourselves from our actual aerobic training. We switch into autopilot.

Zendurance does not mean that we must always train alone or that we must develop only our inner intelligence. Companionship is a good and healthy practice that is also part of our zendurance approach to athletics. Each of us must find our own unique balance of solitude and communion.

Review of Zendurance Training Techniques

We have briefly considered other techniques that can also help us develop our inner focus and intelligence. Let's review them now: First, we have identified our recovery sessions as the best opportunities to really focus inward—without the distraction of performance levels or training agendas. We can use these low-intensity recovery sessions as mindfulness training sessions.

During these low-intensity workouts, we must give ourselves permission to relax completely, so that our awareness—our conscious feeling awareness—can permeate and fill each and every cell of our bodies. We consciously release each muscular and joint tension so that our inner focus and awareness can circulate freely and easily throughout our body as we train. As we relax each and every part of our body—our neck and facial muscles, our hands and feet, and so forth—we also relax our minds. Mental and physical relaxation are very closely linked.

Our conscious breath is another valuable asset in this process of relaxation and mindfulness. Conscious breathing serves as a vehicle that helps us turn our awareness inward so that we can mobilize and articulate our *feeling awareness* within our bodies. Zendurance is a practice of mind *in* matter—and conscious breath is the vehicle that transports our awareness into our bodies.

We have also identified certain environmental factors that can aid us in developing our inner focus and awareness. For our mindfulness training sessions, it is best to use training routes that are very familiar to us—ones that are relatively free of distractions and technical challenges. Swimming in a pool during off-peak hours is a good example. The stable conditions provided by bicycle stationary trainers and running treadmills can also provide us with unique opportunities for developing deep inner awareness, since we not required to direct much of our attention outward. We may even close our eyes with relative safety.

Such stable and consistent conditions can be monotonous. Every time we notice ourselves slipping into autopilot during our mindfulness training sessions, we gently return to our inner focus and feeling as well as our conscious breath. Our primary objective during these sessions is to strengthen and develop our calm, still, silent, open, and empty space of deep inner listening and contemplation.

In the beginning, we conduct our mindfulness training sessions at very low levels of physical intensity. Through relaxation we can easily find and sustain the zone. We want to emphasize the quality of our inner focus and our feeling awareness, rather than our physical performance.

Our mindfulness training sessions are not for junk miles. While they may not challenge our body's physical capacity, they do provide us with tremendous potential for developing our intelligence. This intelligence includes our inner focus and awareness and the skills of yielding, blending, and aligning. We can approach these sessions with the same level of conscious preparation, enthusiasm, focus, and diligence that we have for our more physically demanding breakthrough sessions.

Three Intelligent Skills of Zendurance

Each and every form of endurance athletics provides us with a unique opportunity to investigate the nature of yielding, blending, and aligning. This investigation is just as much a mental and emotional investigation as it is a physical one. Through a zendurance approach to our aerobic training, we can effectively develop these functional and intelligent skills of yielding, blending and aligning. Then we can begin to integrate each one into all areas of our lives.

The aerobic activities of swimming, biking, and running all feel uniquely different from one another. This unique feeling for each includes our mental and emotional attitude as well as our physical sensations. The zendurance skills of yielding, blending, and aligning also feel uniquely different from one another. Each of these three skills requires a unique attitude as well.

To our ego, these intelligent skills may seem threatening and diminishing. They seem to contrast with our sense of strength and power—as though we are making ourselves small. Disengaging from the ego is essential in transforming our athletic training into a practice of zendurance and in our pursuit of effortless power. As we gain practical experience and familiarity with the skills of yielding, blending, and aligning, we begin to trust in these skills. We begin to glimpse a sense of freedom and liberation as we disengage from those fears and desires. Gradually we discover the courage and compassion to venture progressively farther along the path of zendurance and effortless power.

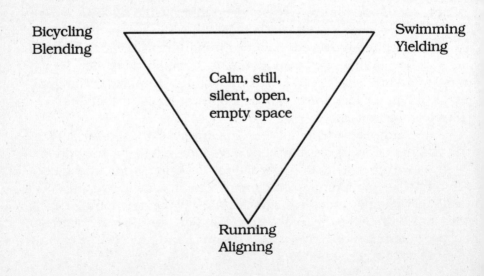

Bicycling
Blending

Swimming
Yielding

Calm, still,
silent, open,
empty space

Running
Aligning

Intelligent Skills of Zendurance

Our athletic training serves as a proving ground for the skills of yielding, blending, and aligning. Using these intelligent skills, we transform our athletic training into the practice of zendurance. Our performances will most likely improve while our perceived exertion levels decrease. We will begin to follow a path of less resistance and more harmony. Our intelligent skills of yielding, blending, and aligning will enable us to more accurately navigate that harmonious path. We will train and race with less wear and tear. Proficiency and a sense of trust and confidence will help us integrate the skills of yielding, blending, and aligning into our daily lives outside our zendurance training.

Just The Beginning

Zendurance begins by transforming our athletic training into zendurance practice. We realize this transformation by practicing yielding, blending, and aligning from our calm, still, silent, open, and empty space of deep inner listening and contemplation. However, this is only the beginning of true zendurance. Zendurance continues as we carry this practice into our ordinary human lives. We will explore the integration of our zendurance skills into our ordinary human lives in the next section, "HeartCore Zendurance." Before we jump into that vast ocean, we have a few more key elements of Tri-Zen to explore.

WHAT IS FORM?

Magnetic Compass Metaphor

How can we define swimming, biking, or running *form*? To explore the element of form, we are going to use the metaphor of a compass. Suppose we are in the middle of nowhere, orienting our way through unknown territory—without the convenience of a grid layout of numbered city blocks, road signs, or mile markers. The only tool we have is a magnetic compass that indicates north and demarcates by degrees all directions relative to north.

Here we are, in the great unknown, orienting our way to a finish line. That finish line could be our comfortable, well-lit, environmentally controlled home—complete with our high-tech home entertainment center and our well-stocked refrigerator. In this scenario, we are fortunate enough to know which direction we must go relative to north.

If our finish line is only a short distance away—say, a few hundred meters—then a casual bearing and sighting from our compass will set us in the right general direction. If we travel in a reasonably straight line in the general direction of our bearing for those few hundred meters, chances are we will pass close enough to our intended destination that we will arrive in familiar territory and easily zero in on that refrigerator.

A Long Way Home

Now let's change the scenario a bit. Let's say the distance just increased from a few hundred meters to 100 kilometers. In order to arrive at our intended destination, we are now required to take frequent and accurate bearings and sightings. If we end up diverting from our required direction by even a few degrees and inaccurately judge the distance we have traveled, we may end up in Timbuktu or upper Saskatchewan—far from our precious refrigerator.

In this metaphor we can correlate the compass with our swimming, biking or running form. At progressively longer distances, it becomes more imperative that our form remains accurate—just like the compass bearing. If our form does not remain dialed in and accurate, we will begin to fatigue, become inefficient and increase our risk of injury as the distance and duration lengthen. To prevent this decline, we must use our compass—our memory of form—accurately and frequently to check and maintain the alignment of our movement form.

Feeling the Internal Compass

Optimally, with a compass it would be nice to hold it in front of us continually and never divert from our required bearing. This might be impractical in the forest where trees or impassable terrain can obstruct our optimal path—not to mention that after a hundred kilometers our eyes and arms would be greatly fatigued from constant sighting and aiming. However, with our endurance athletic form—walking, swimming, and so on—we *can* develop the ability to listen and monitor our form continuously step by step or stroke by stroke, as though our magnetic compass is built-in. Our form compass is integral to our *feel* and our inner listening.

Form and Flexibility

Just as in orienting through the woods with a compass, the terrain that we are moving through varies and changes. In swimming, for example, fresh and salt water, with or without a wetsuit, chop, surge, current, and wind as well as congestion from surrounding athletes in the water will necessitate flexibility and adaptability in our form. On our bike, such factors as wind, topography, surface terrain, and curves will require the same adaptability and flexibility. In running, the variables are similar to biking. Just as with orienting through the woods with the compass, there is the optimally efficient straight line in our endurance form and composure—from which required variations and diversions must be graceful, effortless, and minimal. Flexibility and adaptability are just as important mentally as physically. We can distinguish the physical aspect as *form* and the mental aspect as *composure*.

Distance and Speed

To continue on with our metaphor, one of the circumstances of compass orientation in the forest is the absence of distance indicators. In this situation, it might be difficult to judge when we have traversed the distance. Fortunately, in most endurance races we are provided with accurate distance indicators. However, we do need to choose a form that is appropriate for the distance. We must be able to judge pacing and to keep the optimal form dialed in for the required distance.

Is our compass metaphor as relevant to speed as it is to distance? As we first considered, the accuracy of our bearing and our ability to stay on the optimal path may not be so important in a few hundred meters. But let's say you and a friend are a few hundred meters from your home. Situated in front of that high-tech home entertainment center you have one deluxe recliner and one bare wooden bench. In the refrigerator are one bottle of the finest micro-brewery beer and one bottle of outdated mass-produced swill. *Now* the accuracy of your compass bearing and your ability to stay aligned may be very important as to who gets there first—by even a few seconds. Both endurance and speed are contingent upon a smooth and graceful form that is appropriate for the distance and intensity.

Transition

In multisport events like triathlon—ranging from sprint to iron or ultra distance—we add in yet another element to this quest for effortless power through form: *transition.* We can illustrate this in our compass analogy as the ability to change course and direction. In orienteering through the wilderness, we use the compass to progress along one course for a given distance and then dial-in on our compass and sight along a new course. Our ability to transition smoothly and efficiently in triathlon is analogous to the ability to quickly set our compass up for the change in course and direction.

As experienced triathletes can attest—regardless of distance—the skills to seamlessly transition from swimming to biking and particularly from biking to running are essential to successful triathlon racing. With compass orienteering, all that is required is our memory of how to reset our compass bearing and sight a new course from that new bearing. In multisport transitioning, our memory is a bit more complex. With each endurance activity, we must be able to recall and dial in a form appropriate for the intensity and duration of that activity and then, when transitioning, we must instantly recall and dial in the next one. This is like a language translator who is not only fluent in two languages but can effortlessly transition from one to the other.

What is the nature of this ability to instantly transition from one activity to another—even if we have been engaged in the first one for several hours? The basis for that memory is our *feel* for each activity—our *tangible, intimate familiarity* with each. *Feel* is perhaps the most essential aspect of zendurance. It is our ability to physically *and mindfully* hone the efficiency and effortlessness of our endurance activities. This is the subject of our next inquiry, "What Is *Feel*?" and truly begins our journey along the path of zendurance.

WHAT IS *FEEL?*

Feel

Many coaches and experienced athletes talk about developing a *feel* for swimming and for the water, a *feel* for cycling, for the bike and the terrain, a *feel* for running and for the running surface. What exactly is *feel* and how do we go about developing and cultivating it? Typically we identify a feeling as our perception and our reaction or response to a specific stimulus or sensation—a stubbed toe or the taste of salt. Feeling is also associated with emotional disposition—*I feel happy.*

How about the feeling of *balance?* Remember the first time you actually balanced on a bicycle? This is an easily recollected and particularly powerful experience—perhaps the first conscious recognition of *feel* as we are referring to it here—as a dynamic state of being that is far more than a single focused stimulus. To balance on a bike requires that we be conscious and attentive to more than one sense and more than one single stimulus. It requires a complex coordination of the senses—primarily the senses of touch/kinesis and sight—responding to a number of ongoing, changing stimuli.

The mechanism within the body most often identified with our sense of balance is the fluid chambers, located within the inner ears. These fluid chambers function much in the same way as a builder's level. A builder's level has a transparent chamber filled with fluid and a bubble of air. The builder works to assure that when the straight edge of the level is placed against a surface, the bubble is centered within the fluid chamber. Likewise—as we walk, run, ride a bike, stoop over to pick something up, and so on—we are subconsciously working and adjusting to maintain our sense of balance. If we were to stop and analyze all of the individually perceived stimuli along with each and every minute response and adjustment required to maintain our balance, we would be amazed at the complexity of that process.

The Medium and Language of Feel

Our primary means of communication between one another is through verbal and written language. We transmit and receive verbal and written communications by assembling and interpreting a string of sequentially arranged sounds (verbal) or visual symbols (written). Therefore, our communications are *linear*—a series of single events lined up one after another. Perhaps 99 percent of our interactions with one another are conducted in this linear fashion. Hence much of our shared existence relies on our proficiency in this linear mode.

The language of *feel* however is spatial rather than linear. It is a challenge to discuss *feeling* because this spatial nature makes it illusive in our linear communication—unless we "talk in circles." Talking in circles is a popular technique among wise, enlightened teachers.

Knowing Left from Right

Another consideration in this distinction between linear and spatial experience is the left and right hemispheres of our brain: The left half is most functional during linear thought, perception and expression. The right half is most functional during spatial thought, perception, and expression. The left linear brain is associated with our analytical, deductive process while the right spatial brain is associated with our creative, intuitive process. Even our eyesight has these two distinct modes. Focused eyesight tends to be associated with the left-brain linear process, while peripheral eyesight is associated with the right-brain spatial process.

Much of our conventional educational, occupational, and cultural concerns engage the focused, linear left brain. This may explain the predominance of right-handed people. (I practice left-handed writing and have studied various art forms that exercise and strengthen my right-brain processes and improve the integration and coordination of the two halves of my brain and the two polarities of experience.)

An Introduction to Feel

My initial discovery and study of *feel* began during my undergraduate studies at college. For the first three semesters, I majored in *confusion*. I was in that state of beginner's mind—open and inquisitive rather than closed and full of answers. One question I pondered was my purpose for being in college. I was already working part time for UPS, making a great hourly wage with benefits—more than most college grads could make at the outset of a career. So for me, college was not about collecting a suitcase full of facts that would qualify me for a well-paying job.

As I contemplated my purpose, I discovered that college provid-ed me with an opportunity to *learn how to learn*. I began exploring the processes of learning—of becoming intelligent and functional—specifically the processes that worked best for me. What I wanted most from my university educational experience was a compre-hensive sense of *how* I learned, so that life itself would become a continual educational process.

In my fourth semester, I signed up for an introductory modern dance technique class. That's where I experienced the greatest dis-covery of my educational career—*Aha, I can actually think in some-thing other than words!* Within one week I declared my major: visu-al and performing arts, with an emphasis in dance. My study of dance (and, soon after, tai chi) gave me more *functional* intelligence than any other formal study. I realized that my process of learning was most effective when I was *moving*. That initial discovery opened up a whole new universe to me. It is one that, to this day, I continue to explore and study passionately—the spatial medium and the kinetic language of *feel*.

As my study in dance expanded, I also took a few ballet classes. I began to see two clear distinctions between modern dance and ballet that reached far beyond style or form. Ballet works with a well-defined set of very specific movements—*each with a verbal name*. A ballet teacher or choreographer has only to verbally trans-mit a sequence of words to define a series of movements. The dancer must then translate that linear sequence of words into a spatial sequence of movements—a transformation from linear dimensionality to spatial dimensionality. This lays the groundwork in dance for a *spatial language*.

Modern dance goes one step farther in developing kinetic, spa-tial language. In modern dance, the movements are free form—with no well-defined vocabulary, no rigid set of specific movements. There are no verbal tags to identify the movements. A teacher or choreographer *must demonstrate* the movements, and the dancers must each devise internally a spatial means of recording and recalling those movements. The craft of the modern dancer includes not only the physical fitness and versatility to accurately execute a diversity of movements, but also the *integrated* physical and mental capacity to record and recall the dances *without* the use of words.

Muscle Memory

This ability to record and to recall movement is the phenomenon known as muscle memory. It is immeasurably valuable in endurance athletics. Muscle memory is, quite literally, the collective memory of all the individual cells of the muscles and nerve endings—a spatially arranged matrix of impulses—*electrical* impulses.

As an analogy, you may recall watching on TV a grandiose halftime show for a Super Bowl. Hundreds of dancers and musicians move around on the football field metamorphosing through a sequence of beautiful visual patterns. These are quite striking when viewed from a distance above—as the big picture.

As a dancer or athlete, when we execute a movement with our body, each of our muscle cells is analogous to one of the individual entertainers on the football field remembering and executing their individual movement to help create the big picture. However, in muscle memory, while the physical scale is much smaller than the stadium scale, the complexity is far, far greater—with many more individual players. The director/choreographer of the halftime show might be analogous to your brain—particularly the spatial right brain, which orchestrates the big picture so that the myriad impulses of the muscle memories—the individual players—orchestrate to gracefully execute the movement.

Thinking in Silence, Thinking in Space

Immediately, as I began to study modern dance and to develop muscle memory, I realized that I had to *silence that little voice* in the back of my head—the one that is constantly talking. The language I was listening to and speaking as a dancer was no longer verbal—it was spatial and kinetic.

Movement requires coordination—*integration*—of both body and brain. Specific locations in the brain are wired to specific locations in the muscles via the incredible network of the nervous system—the body's electrical system. It is through this neurological system that the body and the brain can talk and listen intimately to each other.

They carry on an electrical conversation that assembles into a dynamic electrical field. This electrical field is *spatial*—it occupies and exists within the nervous system of our body right now. *Feel is our ability to perceive the integrity, the entirety of the spatial electrical field of our body.* Our sense of balance is precisely this. From the moment we are born (and even before), we are *electrical* beings. We begin to interact through the spatial language of feel. You are conversing in the electrical language of *feel* right now. Close your eyes and listen inside.

Mind in Matter—Two Simple Techniques

The very first step toward developing and cultivating this sense of *feeling* is to silence that little voice in the back of your head. There are two very simple, yet powerfully effective ways to develop and cultivate a calm, still, silent, open, and empty space of deep inner listening and contemplation. First of all (how about *right now?*), rest the front of your tongue on the roof of your mouth—right behind your top front teeth, at the gum line. If you are not talking, eating, or breathing hard through your mouth, you can do this all the time—even when you are asleep. Since ancient times, the purest internal martial arts disciplines have used this practice. Practitioners have known that resting and relaxing the front of the tongue just behind the front teeth connects or engages the microcosmic orbit. It literally creates an electrical grounding of the brain into the body. This is the first step of mind *in* matter.

Energy rises from the base of our spine to the crown of our head along the back or dorsal side of the body. Practicing the tongue technique, we complete the orbit, grounding the energy down along the front of the body. Deep inner listening starts with consciously practicing this simple technique.

The second very simple, very profound way to develop and cultivate a calm state of inner silence is through mindful, conscious breathing—all the time, constantly. Using the tongue technique, breathe slowly and deeply through your nose. Throughout your day-to-day activities, from wakeup to dreamtime, be aware of your tongue and your breathing. Be *in* your body.

Deep inner listening can be a conscious state of awareness within the nervous system—the electrical field of the body. When we are listening deeply—intimately—our awareness *is* our electrical field. You are an electrical entity.

A Feeling Meditation

Here is a simple exercise you can use to develop that intimate, subtle inner listening: Lie comfortably on your back; arms at your sides, palms up, fingers naturally curled; legs uncrossed, hips and feet naturally turned out. Close and relax your eyes; let your visual focus relax. With your tongue in place, begin breathing consciously.

Explore and contemplate the mechanics of your breathing. Your lungs do not inflate and deflate on their own. They have no muscle tissue to expand or to contract them. Your lungs are suspended in an airtight chamber. As you expand your chest, you increase the volume of that airtight chamber to inflate your lungs. As you compress your chest, you decrease the volume. Feel how many different muscles work to achieve this expansion and contraction—the complex web of muscles that surround and connect the ribs as well as the wall of diaphragm or solar plexus muscles that seal off the upper chest from the lower abdomen. Strive to actually *feel* the shape and size of your lungs as you breathe.

The next step in this exercise is to *send* your breath through your body. Begin with your left foot. As you inhale slowly, send that breath to the toes and the bottom of your left foot. Feel each cell taking in that breath—as if each one had a small set of lungs. As you exhale, relax and release any tensions you are holding there. Feel those tensions exiting your body with your exhalation. With each breath continue to pull the energy up through your left leg and then your right leg—all the way to your hip sockets. Then begin at the base of your torso—at the perineum muscle, just in front of your anus. When you have filled your torso up to your shoulders, continue with each arm starting at your fingertips and finally conclude with your neck and head. Go through your face slowly and be aware of tensions you hold there. Also take the time to fill and permeate your brain, relaxing and dissolving your thoughts. Keep your tongue in place.

When you first try this exercise, it may take some effort to keep your focus. Keep working with it and build some consistency. It may take fifteen to twenty minutes or more at first. Eventually you will be able to do it in only a few minutes. Obviously in this exercise you are not actually inhaling and exhaling to each location in your body. The air is always going in and out of your lungs. This meditation of directing the breath is actually an exercise in directing awareness and consciousness to all areas of the body via the *nervous system.* This is a way to develop and strengthen conscious articulation of your nervous system and to develop *feel.* As you strengthen your nervous system—as you enhance and increase its functional capacity—your inner listening becomes subtler, more accurate, and more intimate.

The function of deep inner listening is to bring awareness and consciousness *into* the body via the electrical nervous system.

Tongue placement and conscious breathing are two effective techniques for bringing mind *into* matter.

Grounding

What is grounding? In electrical terms, grounding is a way of connecting an electrical system into a very large capacitor—namely, Earth. When we put our tongue in place, we are grounding our electrical brain more effectively to our electrical body—a *lowering* of consciousness. This practice helps us shift from mind *over* matter to mind *in* matter.

Grounding as a technique for developing and cultivating a calm, still, silent, open, and empty space of deep inner listening also includes grounding our body-being to Earth. We ground energetically into the Earth's surface and align with gravity. By grounding, we create an intimate relationship with Earth's gravitational and magnetic fields—between *our* energetic body-being and *Earth's* energetic body-being.

The tai chi wave walk—outlined in "Running—Aligning"—is an effective grounding practice. Using this exercise, we may begin to notice energy moving into and out of our feet. The ancient internal martial arts recognize that energy enters through the center of the ball of the foot and exits through the center of the heel. We can practice this energy flow by being conscious and articulating the inward and upward flow of energy as we inhale and bring weight to the ball of our foot. Then we articulate the downward and outward flow as we exhale and transfer the weight to the heel of our foot.

Relaxation is essential for grounding. In order to allow our weight to pass *through* our muscles and into the Earth, we must relax completely. Only then can our muscles compress without holding tension. Relaxation is also paramount in every aspect of developing and strengthening our neurological intelligence of feeling. We must strive to maintain a state of continuous physical, mental, and emotional relaxation. This allows us to naturally settle into our calm, still, silent, open, and empty space of deep inner listening and contemplation.

Centering

Earlier I mentioned the first of two distinctions I found between ballet and modern dance. The second distinction has to do with the *center of movement*—the location within the body where the movement is generated. In classical ballet the movement *appears* to come from the chest, shoulders, and upper back. This area of the body is held very still. In modern dance, however, all movement is generated from an area of the lower torso. This center is called the don tien in tai chi. It is the second chakra—also known as the pelvic chakra—located an inch or two below the navel in the center of the body, just in front of the spine. The color of this chakra is orange. (The spectrum ranges from red at the root chakra, to orange at the second, yellow at the solar plexus, green at the heart, blue at the throat, indigo at the third eye, and purple at the crown.)

Finding Our Center

A good meditation for centering is to lie down on your back and relax. Use the tongue and breathing techniques and go into your calm, still, silent, open, and empty space of deep inner listening and contemplation. Now feel your way to your *orange center* by breathing to this place. As you inhale, go closer and closer to the most minute center point of this energy vortex. As you exhale, see and feel the orange light and energy radiate outward in all directions. (You can actually do this exercise up and down the complete chakra system—patiently locating and energizing each one with your breath and *feel.*)

From your orange center, use your conscious breath and pull or draw the energy up through each leg to that center, then through each arm. This orange center is truly where each arm and each leg is rooted, where each originates. Feel the intimate connection between this center and all parts of your body—all the way out to your fingertips and toes. Finally, take a few minutes to *feel* the shape and form of your pelvic girdle—that big bowl of bone that skeletally connects your upper body to your lower body. *Feel* where your lower spine fuses to your pelvis. *Feel* where your hip sockets are located at the sides of your pelvis. *Feel* how this bowl wraps around and embraces your orange center. Get an intimate sense of the relationship between your pelvis and your orange center.

Power Center

This orange center is the physical location of your calm, still, silent, open, and empty space of deep inner listening and contemplation. The Hawaiians call this center *na'au* (nah-OW) and experience it to be the physical home of the soul. In *ka hana pono* (the practice of pono), there are three centers: *mana'o* (mah-NAHoh)—the mind and intellect; *pu'uwai* (poo-oo-VAI)—the heart and emotions; and the aforementioned na'au—the center of movement and gut instinct. Ancient Hawaiians trusted and depended on na'au for guidance and direction. It is the deepest part of the body, the physical *home* of the soul. (Take a moment to practice these pronunciations, by the way, because we will use these words throughout this book.)

We considered the importance of pelvic alignment in our running—an essential element for effortlessness and efficiency in our form. Likewise, when mana'o and pu'uwai are in alignment with na'au, we are in alignment with *'uhane*—we have perfect access to our *spirit* guidance. Centering in the na'au is therefore an essential and vital component of ka hana pono and of effortless power.

In Hindu practices, this same center is regarded as the point of death in the body. The Japanese call this center *hara*—it is the temple of the body, very similar to the Hawaiian regard for the na'au as the physical home of the soul. (In the honorable Japanese form of suicide known as hara kari, the knife is driven to this exact spot, and death is swift.)

All of these cultures recognize the *stillness* and *emptiness* at the very center of this place. Centering is not a new-age technique—it is an ancient and highly regarded artful practice. It is recognized throughout the world in myriad cultures.

In our zendurance training, we direct our feeling awareness to this center and find the *stillness* within. Out of this pelvic center of stillness, our efficient and effortless movement is generated.

Stretching

While some athletes, trainers, and exercise physiologists can give evangelical testimony about the wonders and merits of stretching, others scoff at it and avoid it like the plague. Why is there so much controversy?

There are many approaches and techniques for stretching—producing myriad results. Many people know that stretching can increase flexibility and suppleness in joints and muscle tissue. It has also been scientifically shown to stimulate the production of elastin and collagen in the muscle tissues—maintaining production that normally declines with age. Some believe it can reduce the incidence of injury while others consider stretching to *cause* injuries. This discrepancy has to do with the *approach* to stretching. With more than twenty-two years of experience, I find stretching to be a valuable practice. I approach it from a calm, still, silent, open, and empty space of deep inner listening and contemplation.

The movements of our bodies—athletic training or day-to-day chores—are simply an array of muscle cells contracting and releasing, or shortening and lengthening. We normally associate *strength* with our ability to contract and compress the muscles. Likewise, we associate *flexibility* with our ability to lengthen and relax the muscles. We emphasize muscular strength in our training and racing. However, in endurance athletics, it is *equally essential* that the muscles be capable of lengthening and relaxing. The endless repetition of contracting and releasing the muscles in long endurance events is incredibly demanding. If a particular muscle *and* its associated nerves do not have adequate training to contract *and to release* in an effective and timely manner, things just start to fall apart. We get a firsthand experience of hitting the wall, of bonking.

Go Home and Relax

Mindful, meditative stretch training improves the ability of the muscles *and the nerves* to return to a relaxed state—to return *home*. Consistent practice improves the memory of that relaxed state—of that home—for both the muscles and the nerves. In each cycle of the repetitive movement pattern that constitutes a specific endurance athletic activity, each muscle cell and its corresponding nerve ending has a period of relaxation—perhaps only a few tenths of a second. If the memory of home is very clear, the nerves and muscles find their way back to that relaxed state instantly. This homing is an essential aspect of efficiency. Inflexible and stiff muscles that cannot rapidly and completely release and relax work *against* their opposing muscle groups. This resistance makes our movements inefficient.

Stretching Basics

The two important components for stretching are a balanced set of stretches and a quiet, mindful, and relaxed approach. Choose a set of stretches that allow you to relax completely instead of stretches that require you to hold tension in one set of muscles to stretch another. It is best to start with a few minutes of relaxed breathing while lying on your back, as mentioned above.

Approach each stretch slowly and deliberately. Close your eyes and breathe into the muscles and nerves you are stretching and relaxing. Feel the tensions release, especially as you exhale. I like the image of the specific points of tension releasing in the muscle fibers like carbonation bubbles. Notice when and where you are holding tensions. Embrace each one with your breath—bring each one into your calm space of awareness. This conscious breathing will help you integrate body and mind together. *Stretching is a process of relaxation.*

Through conscious stretching meditation, you will calm the electrical activity of your neurological system and dilate your circulatory system. You will also lengthen and relax the muscle tissues. Remember, it is as much mindful as it is physical.

Your set of stretches should rotate through all the major muscle groups of the arms, legs and upper and lower torso and spine—stretching each group two to three times during the session. Advance very slowly and gently into each stretch, working each with the breath for a minimum of thirty seconds, with a pause after each one. A good session should take thirty to forty minutes or more. If you are a novice, it may help to explore some basic yoga classes. There are many, many forms of yoga, and each teacher has a slightly different approach and style. As a technique for cultivating and developing *feel*, look for classes that provide a quiet, relaxed atmosphere with a calm, slow, easy approach. Seek out classes that emphasize relaxed stretching and conscious breathing.

Feel and Meditation

Notice that all of the techniques and practices mentioned so far are *meditations*. Meditation forms, like yoga forms, are diverse. Certain forms and techniques are more effective than others—relative to each individual and to our varying skill and experience levels. Generally, all meditative practices cultivate and develop that calm, still, silent, open, and empty space of deep inner listening and contemplation. For our consideration, we can distinguish two basic types of meditation. The first is mindful, conscious *engagement*—engaging in some specific activity from our calm, still space of deep inner listening. The second type of meditation is mindful *disengagement*—being present in our calm, still space with *no* activity, *no* thoughts.

Our zendurance movement meditation is the mindful-engagement type. In developing *feel* and in gaining proficiency and mastery in endurance athletics, we aspire to mindfully engage—as intimately as possible—our neurological system. Through this practice we strive to accurately and intimately coordinate and integrate both body and mind through movement. Philip Maffetone states that—of the three main systems of the body: muscular, metabolic, and neurological—it is the *neurological* system that responds best to training, that learns and strengthens most readily through our training activity. So like it or not, the neurological system is the one that will most improve your athletic performance. That's how essential *feel* is.

The Ultimate Moving Meditation—Tai Chi

Many of us translate *thoroughly engage* and *mindfully engage* to mean engage as intensely as possible—in other words, "go real fast" and "work real hard." However, strengthening and training the nervous system and developing *feel* occur best at low levels of intensity. A great practice for developing *feel* and strengthening the nervous system is tai chi. In tai chi, the pace is *very* slow and allows our awareness to *rest* in the calm, still, silent, open, and empty space of inner listening as we move. The purpose of patiently practicing the slow-moving solo forms of tai chi is not to get faster or better than someone else—it is to cultivate chi energy and greater levels of *feel. Feel is the articulation of electrical chi energy.* We have already considered the value of this kind of approach to our zendurance athletic training during our low-intensity and recovery sessions—bike tai chi, for instance.

Tai chi is unquestionably the most powerful training method I have experienced for strengthening and educating the nervous system. Generally—with a calm and meditative approach—many of the internal martial arts and many forms of yoga are quite effective.

Making the choice to diligently practice tai chi or to approach *any* form of movement meditation very slowly and from a calm space of inner silence is a profound choice. It contrasts with our ingrained notion of power through effort. It is a choice to pursue *effortless* power. Effortless power happens through *feeling. Feel* occurs when we are present in our calm, still and empty space.

Feel and Athletic Training

We can apply this same meditative, effortless power approach to *all* our low-intensity and recovery training sessions. We conduct these training sessions specifically to cultivate *feel*—without concern for athletic performance. During these sessions, we can forget the watch, forget the distances, and forget all the numbers entirely. In these *feel* sessions we deliberately and thoroughly focus on training and educating our neurological system. We *feel* each and every stride or stroke as completely and intimately as possible throughout the entire session. Developing neurological strength and mental stamina through this approach becomes extremely valuable in maintaining our graceful and efficient form during our longest sessions and races. If our form falls apart, misery steps in. The repetitive circular nature of most endurance athletic activities is a great opportunity for developing and cultivating the meditative capacity for *feel*—especially at a slow pace.

Alas, for many of us, to train slowly—even occasionally—is a most difficult choice. To truly develop *feel* we must make the choice to regularly include *feel*-oriented sessions in our training program so that we can strengthen and educate our neurological system. During these sessions, it is helpful for us to affirm, *I am developing feel. I am developing effortless power.*

Feel And Alignment

When we see someone with good alignment, what are the visual cues? The most obvious one is good posture. We have already considered running as the endurance activity that most accurately reveals posture and alignment. We can actually see alignment *energetically*. We can see how smoothly energy flows through someone with good alignment.

In our zendurance approach to running we discover that alignment is a process of listening—where we are refining our relationship with Earth's gravity. Alignment occurs as we become more *intimate* in our relationship with gravity. In choosing to develop alignment and grounding, we begin to transform our relationship with gravity. It transforms from a cumbersome force that *acts upon* us into an asset—a potential energy resource that we have to interact with. For a playful analogy, as we develop and cultivate alignment, life takes on more of a *trampoline* quality. Get a little more *bounce* out of life through alignment!

Our Old Friend Professor Gravity

Alignment is not about overcoming or defying gravity. It is a practice of continuously choosing gravity as a teacher—a *guide*—as a continuous indicator. Alignment occurs when we are intimately feeling gravity from our calm, still, silent, open, and empty space of deep inner listening and contemplation. Earth's gravity is one of the most profound and powerful components of *feel*. It is with us *always*. Alignment is a lifetime process of feeling and listening to gravity. This process of continuously feeling and listening to gravity is paramount to maintaining efficient and effortless form.

Mirror Alignment

Dancers have another effective way of developing and cultivating alignment. Most dance studios have at least one mirrored wall. In the dance studio, I constantly engaged in a process of *feeling* the movement and *seeing* the movement—inner listening and outer listening simultaneously. The challenge was to match them up—to evaluate by sight how accurate my *feel* was. As an illustration, go stand sideways by a full-length mirror. Without looking in the mirror, stand up straight. Now look in the mirror and see if you are really *aligned*. What kind of curve does your spine have? How is your pelvis oriented? What is the position of your shoulders and upper back? Is your neck long and straight?

Let's begin to match up what we feel with what we see. If you have the opportunity, periodically ride on a stationary bicycle stand or run on a treadmill in front of a large mirror—and match up your inner listening with your outer listening. Try this out with both a side view and a front view. The mirror provides real-time instant comparison. Viewing videotape of our swimming, biking and running forms can also be valuable, although it is always a delayed response. Video is, however, far more practical for swimming and for actual running without the treadmill. Mirrors allow for instant perception and response—a most accurate "tuning."

Alignment improves as the matchup between the inner and outer listening becomes more accurate. In my study of dance—as I began to match up the *feeling* with the *seeing*—my body became more aligned muscularly, skeletally, and energetically. I literally morphed. This morphing process took years—in fact, I am still morphing now. So are you. It never stops. This metamorphic process occurs throughout our lives. It is through our neurological intelligence of *feeling* that we can *articulate* that metamorphic process. Using our *feel* of gravity and our inner and outer listening, we can align ourselves mindfully, muscularly, skeletally, and energetically. Alignment brings clarity and intelligence—it is a reawakening process.

Extending Feel

I worked frequently with a few other dancers for many years. Energetically, we knew each other very well. Occasionally, either in rehearsal or in performance, we would experience an incredible phenomenon: Together we could generate a *field* of energy—literally a *collective feel*. As we danced, we could accurately and intimately feel each other's presence in this field—we could feel each other's movements as well as our own. Each of us could *feel* both our individual bodies and our collective energy field.

As dancers, we rehearsed many times together—consistently and repeatedly moving through the space (the *field*) in exactly the same relationship to one another. The energetic field we developed through our many rehearsals was a conscious and articulate entity. Each of our individual electrical fields was part of this collective entity—as though all of our individual neurological systems merged together.

This same collective feeling is often a powerful part of our racing experience—especially at the starting line. We become part of a large, *highly amped* energetic entity. Yes, we do literally feel the *electricity* in the air at the starting line. We can close our eyes and *feel* it. We can embrace and tap into this tremendous electrical entity. We can open up to it and feel it intimately and still maintain our individual identity.

Begin to extend and expand your sense of *feeling*—your neurological awareness and intelligence. Extend it into the medium of water and into the swimmers around you when you swim. Extend your electrical intelligent sense of *feeling* into your bicycle, into the riding surface and the riders around you. Extend your intelligent sense of *feeling* through your shoes, into the terrain, and into the space and the runners around you.

Feel and the Cardiovascular System

As I began to study tai chi, and to develop a lucid and articulate experience of the electrical nature of *feeling*, I began to notice a distinct physiological change. My body and mind became very peaceful, calm, and keenly aware. The physiological change occurred not only in my electrical neurological system, but also in my cardiovascular system. My heart rate would slow down, and I could clearly feel my blood pressure lower. Changes in blood pressure are regulated by the constriction or dilation of the veins and arteries. By consciously training and educating the neurological system through conscious feeling, we have quite a bit of control over our own blood pressure.

As we practice yielding, blending, and aligning in our approach to movement and to the ordinary experiences of our lives, we give up our *resistance*. Resistance—mentally, emotionally, or physically—causes an increase in blood pressure. We respond to stress, anxiety, and tension physiologically by constricting our veins and arteries. This results in higher blood pressure and significantly more *resistance* and *tension* in our cardiovascular system. Consequently, our heart must work harder to circulate the blood at this higher pressure. Circulation of our blood—along with the oxygen, nutrients, and waste that it transports—diminishes at higher pressure. Obviously, so does performance.

Improving Circulation and the Flow of Traffic

As an analogy, consider the major highway "arteries" of traffic around any large city during morning rush hour. Want to create instant havoc? Begin to close down one or more lanes to traffic—*constrict* the flow. As the flow diminishes, backups and traffic jams buildup and commuters stress out. They start yelling and swearing at each other or diverting to their cell phones. Who's happy? Only the oil companies and the wireless communications companies.

Physiologically the same thing happens to many of the commuters. Not only are the arteries of traffic constricted, but so are their circulatory systems. (It's possible that consumption of coffee and nicotine—both vascular constrictors—plays a major role in creating traffic jams, especially in the morning.)

Continuing with our highway system analogy: If we invest time and energy toward widening and enlarging our highway arteries, we can improve the flow and circulation of traffic. It doesn't take a civil engineer to figure out the optimal time to add lanes and widen the roadways. The best time is *not* during the high-intensity flows of rush hour. It is during the low-intensity off-peak hours. The same is true for improving our own circulation systems. The most effective time to open up and widen the veins and arteries for improved and more effortless flow and circulation is during low intensity, calm training sessions. This is when we can most effectively train and educate our neurological system to relax and dilate our cardiovascular system. If we restrict all our training to high intensity rush-hour-type sessions, then our highway work will be slow and inefficient. There will be a lot of stressed-out, unhappy commuters in our cardiovascular system. (For a more detailed account and explanation of the physiological performance-

enhancing gains that can be realized through low-intensity training, refer to Maffetone's book *Training For Endurance*, Chapter 4.)

The circulation system and the nervous system are inextricably
linked—as are *all* the systems of the body. When the nervous system is relaxed and calm, the circulation system is relaxed (open
and dilated) and calm (low pulse rate).

Feel And Aerobic Base Training

Perhaps the most widely accepted tenet of endurance athletics is
the necessity to establish an aerobic base or foundation. What is a
base or a foundation? In endurance sports this is typically defined
as a *quantity*—usually a *distance* referred to as base miles. What
is occurring during those base miles? What kind of progression is
taking place as we build base miles?

As we develop aerobic base, we are strengthening and developing the muscular and cardiovascular systems *and* also strengthening and educating the neurological system. We are building a
more thorough and articulate electrical system, creating more and
better connections between our brain and our muscles. The same
is true for the circulation system: We are building more and better
vascular connections in our heart, lungs, and muscles.

The necessity to establish an aerobic base foundation may be
the most widely accepted tenet in endurance athletics. However,
there is little agreement about intensity levels of training in establishing that base.

Let's consider the muscular system: It is about 80 percent aerobic muscle tissue and only 20 percent anaerobic muscle tissue. In
the 80 percent aerobic tissue, there is a wide spectrum of different
response times—some of the muscle cells respond very slowly and
some respond much faster, with a continuous spread in between.

When we train slowly, we activate and develop the slower muscle cells *and* their corresponding nerves and capillaries. As we train
closer to our aerobic limit, we activate and develop the progressively faster muscle cells *and* their respective nerves and capillaries. Generally, not as many of the slow cells are activated when we
are training fast and not as many of the fast cells are working when
we are training slow. If we train a broad spectrum of these cells—
the slow and the fast—we literally strengthen and develop many
more nerves, capillaries, and muscle cells. This increases our neurological capacity and our cardiovascular capacity much more so
than if we train just the slower cells or only the faster ones at a con-

stant, unchanging level of intensity.

A stronger, more intelligent and intimate neurological system and a stronger, more developed and intimate circulation system equate to a stronger, more complete and intimate intelligence of *feel.* Building an aerobic base effectively develops and cultivates *feel* when the aerobic training includes a balanced spectrum of intensity levels.

There is another aspect of *feel* and aerobic base. Usually in training the slower muscles, the body's metabolic rate is lower and the blood pressure is low. It is much easier to keep our calm, still center when our metabolic system is relaxed. As we train calmly and slowly, our muscle memory will record the calm, relaxed experience. We will build a *base of calmness* as we build a base of aerobic fitness.

When it's time to race, our high density of nerves, capillaries, and fit, efficient slower muscles will *support* our high-intensity effort as a *foundation.* The muscles will also be recalling and generating a state of stillness and calmness as their cellular memories are activated. This calm condition enhances the efficiency of the metabolic and neurological systems and serves as a stable foundation for our mental and emotional state as well. We will race calmly and efficiently.

Rather than low-intensity recovery training sessions, we engage in low-intensity *feel* training from a calm, still, silent, open, and empty space of deep inner listening and contemplation. We can affirm to ourselves: "I am developing *feel.*" "I am cultivating effortless power."

Clearing Our Muscle Memory

By now, we can clearly see the direct correlation between developing and cultivating our *feel* for athletics as it corresponds to strengthening and developing a highly intelligent and functional nervous system. We can appreciate the merits of being in a calm, still, silent, open, and empty space of deep inner listening and contemplation as we train. This calm stillness also has a profound effect on the quality of our nerve-muscle memory. Each time a movement or feeling is recorded in this memory, all the mental and emotional reactions and responses are stored with it. These include judgments, emotional feelings, and the conditions and circumstances of our surrounding environment at the time the event was stored.

This nerve-muscle memory system is so effective that it can

retain those memories for the entire span of our lives. Even if we never consciously recall them, they still remain an integral part of our body-mind being and affect our functional capacity—either enhancing or diminishing it. Individuals spend considerable time and energy recalling and resolving past memories—particularly those events that were traumatic and extreme.

What happens when we recall and resolve or clear one of these traumatic and extreme memories? First of all, we recall the physical sensations as well as the thoughts, judgments and emotional responses/reactions associated with those sensations. When we truly resolve or clear that recollection, we *complete* our relationship with it. This completion requires that we *embrace* the entire nerve-muscle memory—its physical, mental, and emotional qualities—in a calm and still space. Then the traumatic nerve-muscle memory transforms—it is *cleared*. The fear, anger, guilt, negative judgments, and disempowering thoughts and patterns are cleared and replaced with calm inner silence and non-judgmental deep inner listening.

In the clearing process, our capacity to *feel* and to *endure* becomes stronger. Our body-mind being becomes more functional, articulate, and efficient when these traumatic memories are resolved. The nerve-muscle memory no longer stores or holds the *charge* that was there. It is free of the burden and the tension that held the charge—literally the *electrical* charge—in place. The energy channels within the nerve and muscle cells are freed up. The electrical system becomes calmer and more efficient.

Clearing Through Zendurance Training

As we strengthen our calm, still, silent, open, and empty space through our athletic training, we increase our potential to heal and to clear these traumatic memories. As we train from our calm space of deep inner listening and contemplation, this healing process will gradually occur without our actually being aware of it. Although we may not consciously recall these traumas, as we move and activate our body-mind being, fragments of past nerve-muscle memories will gradually surface in our calm inner space and dissolve. Our functional capacity to respond to the *present* circumstances of this moment will replace the triggered reactions to circumstances of the past. We get more proficient at "being here now." As we strengthen our calm inner space, our capacity to accurately perceive, embrace, and respond to our present experience improves.

In this clearing process, we will notice an increased capacity to *feel* pain and to *feel* pleasure without being at the effect of the sensation. We are able to remain calm and present with greater levels of *electrical activity* generated by our body-mind being. As our judgments and emotional ties fall away, pain and pleasure become very similar to one another. The distinction between them becomes subtler. We are free of our aversion to pain and our attachment to pleasure.

When our *feeling* sensations are experienced through a functional and intelligent neurological system and embraced in a calm, still, silent, open, and empty space, then our emotional *reactions* are cleared. Out of this clearing process arises the possibility for emotional *response* as a functional choice for expressing feelings.

An Illustration

As an illustration of this process, I will share with you an incident from my own life—my birth. The moment of birth—including the circumstances and conditions of the environment as well as the chemical, emotional, and energetic state of the mother—can be perhaps the most latent and profound experience of one's entire life. It is also one of the most difficult to recall and complete.

Two very traumatic events occurred during the process of my birth. First, as my mother went into labor, the woman in the bed next to her died giving birth. My birthing environment was in a state of chaotic emergency. My mother had previously arranged with her obstetrician that she be given no painkillers—in order to *feel* her labor—a rare request in the 1950s. However, in the ensuing pandemonium, the doctor injected her and she was numb to the process. Second, my father shot himself—either accidentally or intentionally—just before the labor.

I knew nothing of these circumstances on the "conscious" level until thirty-five to forty years later, when my grandmother and mother recalled the events for me. It certainly provided me with some explanation as to why I was often very frightened as a young child, even with no obvious threat in my immediate environment. I barely occupied my body as a child. I was afraid to *feel*. However, as I grew and engaged in all the kinetic experiences of youth—bicycling, swimming, and team sports—and then began to earnestly study dance, tai chi, and running, my experience of being *present* in my body began to clear. I remember the first time I rode a bike with no training wheels, the first time I danced to rock music. Kinetic activity was like a magic liberation for me.

My collegiate choice to study movement as a form of intelligence was an epiphany in many ways. Through my training and discipline, I *cleared* my nerve-muscle memories and began to occupy a body that was open and functional. By the time my mother and grandmother shared with me the trauma of my birth, I had embraced and completed the stored memories of that experience through *movement*—movement sourced from a calm, still, silent, open, and empty space of deep inner listening and contemplation. I had accomplished this without ever consciously recalling the event.

Our zendurance approach to aerobic training—through the cultivation of a calm, still, silent, open, and empty space of deep inner listening and contemplation—includes this *clearing*, this *liberation*.

Feel and Intelligence

Studying dance and tai chi has endowed me with more *intelligence* than any other form of study. The same can be said for any form of movement study—where there is an earnest intent on cultivating and developing the intelligence of *feel*. As a dancer, I spent six to ten hours a day in the dance studio developing my ability to listen and to speak the language of movement and the language of *feeling*.

At first, as I began to study dance, my initial challenge was just learning to move my body—to energetically align and to move with articulation, grace, and accuracy. But far more challenging than that was developing the ability to watch someone execute a phrase of movements and then to recall and repeat the same phrase. With lots of practice, I became more proficient at this process. Once I stumbled through the visual-to-muscular translation and got the *feeling* into my body, it was much easier to repeat the phrase and refine my articulation and accuracy of what I had seen. The mirrors were a big help. I was gaining proficiency in muscle memory and in the electrical language of movement and *feel*.

Even my eyesight was improving. I was exercising my spatial right brain, which really strengthened my peripheral vision. My approach to analyzing and problem solving transformed. In some odd way, I began to feel that I was actually *using my body to think*— not just in the dance studio, but also in everyday situations ranging from driving my car to my manual labor job at UPS and sensing *viscerally* the physics and engineering involved in some mechanical task. Now that my mind was occupying my body more and more—via the neurological system—I could use that intelligent internal electrical field to create spatial models within my body of what I perceived visually outside my body. This was the same visual-to-muscular translation I developed as a dancer. I was thinking with my body as well as my brain.

Does this process of *feeling what we are seeing* actually feel the same as reaching out and touching something with our hands? No. The visual-to-muscular translation process uses the nerve receptors connected to the muscles rather than the ones located at the surface of our fingertips and palms. We all have and use this ability to feel what we see, to some extent. Just backing a car into a garage requires that we *feel* what we are seeing. To avoid road debris while riding our bikes, we don't just visually aim our way around the obstacle; we *feel* our way around it.

Our neurological system—including our brain, nerves and receptors—is like a computer, a spatial array of on/off binary signals—storing and retrieving information. The physical location of consciousness is not limited to the brain—*every cell in the body is conscious and intelligent.* Kinetic articulation of that cellular consciousness and intelligence employs the integration of our nervous system with our muscular system.

Feel—as a form of intelligence—is the ability to consciously articulate the electrical field of the body with increasing accuracy and intimacy. This is a valuable asset in endurance athletics. It is also a valuable asset in day-to-day living and functioning in the body. Everyone has this electrical *field intelligence* and the potential ability to articulate that *field intelligence.* Don't think about it, *feel* it.

Feel And Intimacy

Throughout this discussion of *feel,* I have used the word *intimacy.* Intimate friends are usually close friends—open and honest friends we trust very much. Often we trust them enough to touch and to embrace—and in the case of lovers, to be very intimate.

As we strengthen our neurological system and cultivate our calm, still, silent, open, and empty space of inner listening, we begin to feel the same sense of intimate connection and presence in our endurance training. Ultimately we can experience this intimate connection with everything and everyone around us. This

does not mean that we will fall in love with everything and everyone around us. It means that our neurological intelligence endows
us with the infinite potential to connect our inner self with our
outer self. Through neurological intelligence, we have infinite experience potential. Our perceptions can be infinitely vivid and lucid.
Likewise, our expressions can be infinitely clear and concise.

Intimacy is infinity. Neurological intelligence is our experiential
conduit to infinity.

INTELLIGENCE OF TRI-ZEN

Introduction

Many spiritual paths recognize a system of energy centers that each of us embodies both physically and spiritually. We briefly considered these energy centers in "What Is Feel?"—both the seven-chakra energy system developed in ancient Asia and India, and the Hawaiian system of the three centers: mana'o (brain), pu'uwai (heart), and na'au (body).

In our zendurance athletic practice, we focus primarily on our na'au center—associated with the pelvic chakra, located just below the navel. As mentioned earlier, this is the center where our movement and action originate and is considered by many spiritually evolved cultures to be the physical residence of our soul, the source of our chi—our life energy.

In the next section, "HeartCore Zendurance," we will expand our practice of zendurance beyond just our zendurance approach to athletic training. We will begin to *integrate* the health and happiness, along with the quality of presence and awareness that we have developed through zendurance training into our daily lives. We will address questions like: *How can I be absolutely present and practice zendurance all the time—whether I am training or helping my kids with their homework? How can I be completely present at my job and with my family with the same peaceful, extraordinary awareness I am developing as an endurance athlete?*

A key component of this process of integration lies in a clear, experiential understanding of the energetic nature of *intelligence*. Each of our three energy centers—mana'o, pu'uwai, and na'au—is a unique *source of intelligence*. As endurance athletes—specifically as triathletes—we enjoy a broad base of overall fitness from swimming, biking, and running. Likewise, as human beings, we can enjoy a broad base of life fitness by training and engaging all *three* of our intelligent energy centers. Three sports and three energetic centers!

MANA'O

The past is history and the future is a mystery. This very moment is all we have—it is our gift. That's why we call it the present.

Introduction

Our brain is most often regarded as our source of intelligence. The sacred Hawaiians call this energetic center mana'o. Oriental cultures identify this as the third-eye chakra—located in the core of the brain, behind the forehead. Our mana'o center is the source of our thoughts. We usually regard our thought process as our primary intelligence. Through this emphasis on our mana'o as the *sole source* of intelligence, we have evolved as humans to regard our thoughts, considerations, and judgments to be our true essence, to be our true *identity*.

In our zendurance approach to athletic training, however, we are cultivating a new experience of intelligence and identity. Through our neurological system, we are developing the intelligence of *feel*. Our sense of identity is evolving to be more energetic and less concrete. Our experience of intelligence is expanding beyond just our ability to produce thoughts in our brain.

The Power Of Observation

We are using our sense of *feeling* to cultivate that calm, still, silent, open, and empty Zen space. As we become more familiar with this Zen presence *here and now*, we are discovering the intelligent ability to quietly observe our own thoughts. We are learning how to disengage from that little voice in the back of our heads. This intelligent capacity to disengage and observe our thoughts is profoundly liberating and empowers us to use our mana'o as an effective tool—rather than allowing our thinking mind to dominate and run the show of our lives.

Chainsaw Metaphor

Let's look at a simple metaphor that illustrates this profound distinction between our mana'o intelligence as a valuable tool versus our mana'o as the director of the show—as our sole source of intelligence. Imagine that our thinking mind is a chainsaw. (This may seem like a crude comparison, but bear with me.) A chainsaw is an indispensable tool in the hands of an experienced operator who operates with a clear intention and well-defined objectives. However, in the hands of a novice, that same tool becomes quite dangerous—not only to all surrounding life and property, but to the operator as well.

In our global culture, we suffer from a terrible affliction: We are unable to disengage from the thinking mind, unable to control or to silence its unceasing and relentless commentary. The result of this rampant thinking is truly as violent as if we were blindfolded and flailing that chainsaw around in front of us at full throttle.

Spiritual Fitness—Be Here Now

With an undisciplined thinking mind, we are usually dwelling in the past, projecting into the future, or judging, resisting or attempting to manipulate the present moment. All of our experiences in life occur only in *this* present moment. If we perpetually violate the present by dwelling in the past, projecting into the future, or attempting to control and manipulate the present (always for some future gain), then we effectively *cut off* our life energy in this moment.

Our zendurance training is a practice to strengthen not only our physical fitness—but our *spiritual fitness* as well. Spiritual fitness is our ability to remain steadfast and source our awareness and our intelligence from a calm, still, silent open and empty space of Zen presence. With spiritual fitness, we can *observe* our thoughts from this place of stillness and silence. We can watch them arise and watch them dissolve.

For many of us, this practice of continuously observing our thinking mind without slipping into thought identity—without being swept away by the drama of our fears, desires, and judgments—is far more difficult and daunting than it is for us to be calm, still, and present as we engage in our zendurance training. That is because the movements and feelings that comprise our athletic activity happen only in this present moment—*right now!*

Movement does not know past or future, only the present moment. This is why many of us, with undisciplined thinking minds, can find our first foothold toward true consciousness and intelligence through endurance athletics and other kinetic activities. Conscious and focused movement is our first discovery of thinking in something other than words. We source our kinetic activity from our na'au intelligence—our chi center—and this source of intelligence is always present *now*.

As we hone our spiritual fitness, we stay centered and remain detached from our thinking. We keenly observe and embrace our thinking minds rather than *being* our thoughts. We begin to observe the *nature* of our mana'o intelligence. We observe its behavior—how our mana'o manufactures thoughts, including the patterns we use to create thoughts in response to various circumstances and stimuli.

Eckhart Tolle has written a brilliant and very effective book about cultivating this specific aspect of spiritual fitness—detaching, observing, and eventually *mastering* the thinking mind as an articulate tool rather than living our lives as *slaves* to a relentless, blundering and ignorant thinking mind. His book is titled *The Power of Now*. It is one of the most empowering books I have read as an athlete and as a human spiritual being. In a clear and practical way, he guides us through the profoundly simple, yet tedious and difficult practice of being present in *this* moment. As soon as we slip into the past or trip into the future, we have lost our handle on this tool—our mana'o intelligence. Tolle offers brilliant, insightful guidance in transforming our day-to-day *thinking* existence.

Operating the Chainsaw

Returning to our chainsaw analogy, as we gain the ability to stand back and *observe* our thoughts, it is as though we have removed the blindfold so that we can actually see the cuts we are making with the chainsaw. We still do not actually *see* the chainsaw itself—but we can observe what it does. We still don't know how it is that we hold or operate it.

It is only when we begin to observe the *nature* of our mana'o—*how* our thoughts and our patterns of behavior are formed—that we can, for the first time, *see* the chainsaw itself and observe it in operation. We can see how we make those cuts and how the chainsaw behaves in various situations and circumstances. With spiritual fitness—with the steadfast strength to stay present here and now—we can begin to use our thinking mind effectively as a tool. We learn how to hold and operate the "chainsaw of reason."

Cutting with the Chainsaw

In our thinking mind/chainsaw analogy, the mind produces thoughts just as the chainsaw produces cuts. Is *thinking* similar to *cutting?* With a chainsaw, we are separating, cutting apart. Similarly, our thinking mind also makes *distinctions*—which are also separations. The most basic separation each of us makes is the separation or distinction between self and others—between *me* and *you.*

This distinction creates the possibility for observation, perception, and thought. We cannot observe things that we are not separate from. It is through our separate and distinct identities as human beings that we are able to create unique and individual experiences. This distinction as an individual also allows for the possibility of communication, expression, and contribution.

Hawaiian Wisdom

The Hawaiian word for our thinking mind is *mana'o.* This word begins with *mana*—life energy. This is followed by *'o.* In grammatical terms *'o* is a particle used to mark a subject—to *distinguish* it. This describes perfectly the nature and function of our thinking mind. In order for thought to occur, there must be an individual observer or thinker. To be individual is to be isolated—distinct from some other event, thing or being. *Mana'o* literally means "a distinct, separate entity of mana." This is precisely how the thinking mind operates—by creating the condition of separation.

Skillful Means

In traditional Buddhist teachings, a well-disciplined, pure, and clear-thinking mind endows us with the functional intelligence of *skillful means.* Skillful means begins with keen observation of things or events and their interrelationships. This keen observation can only happen *now,* in the present moment, and it is most lucid and functional when unencumbered by the compulsion to judge, resist, or change what is being observed. As we develop our spiritual fitness, we are able to remain steadfast in our calm, still, silent, open, and empty Zen presence in order to be keen and accurate in our observations.

Through skillful means, our mana'o intelligently observes things and events and then instantly compares these present experiences to similar ones stored in memory. From that comparison, our mana'o can consider all the functional laws and principles relevant to the present experience in formulating an appropriate response. With skillful means, we can integrate and adapt to this present moment. This functional process of skillful means is essential in our harmonious and effortless relationship with Universe.

Our skillful means can function brilliantly *only* in this present moment—as we hone our ability to be keen, detached observers.

Accurate perception can only occur when we witness our mana'o intelligence from our calm, still, silent, open, and empty Zen center. From our Zen center, we *do not mistake* mana'o intelligence as being our true, essential nature.

Ego

What happens when we *do* occupy the thinking mind as our sole source of intelligence and identity—when we are *absent* from our Zen space? What is the opposite of skillful means? Ego! *E.G.O.* translates to Edging God Out. Edging mana out. Ego is when we mistake our mana'o intelligence—with its condition of separation and distinction—as being our true spirit nature. Ego is *'o* without *mana*—a powerless "particle" with no life force.

Throughout this discussion of mana'o intelligence, we can clearly see that the transformation from ego to skillful means is contingent upon our spiritual fitness. Spiritual fitness is our ability to remain steadfastly *present* here and now in our calm, still, silent, open, and empty space of deep inner listening and contemplation. Spiritual fitness allows us to intelligently access the past without dwelling in it. This detachment empowers us with the skillful means to recognize the principles and laws that are at work in this present moment and imbues us with the functional intelligence of adaptation. *Brilliance* begins with our ability to be detached yet *completely present* in this moment. Brilliance also includes our competence and mastery at using the tool of *distinction* effectively.

Mana'o Intelligence and Athletic Training

In our diligent pursuit to athletically train and race more effectively, we have the opportunity to transform our thinking mind into a tool of skillful means for designing and implementing an optimal training program. Through an appropriate, comprehensive athletic training program, we are capable of remarkable endurance achievements and performances. When this happens, we create a perfect blend of mana'o and na'au intelligences. We experience mind *in* matter.

Conversely, when the thinking mind is in *ego mode*, it is attempting to control and to run the show as our sole source of intelligence and identity. In this mind-*over*-matter approach to training, we usually experience injury, burnout, or stagnation. Overtraining is not the fault of a weak body. It is the result of a blindly operated mana'o (like the chainsaw) projecting to the future and attempting to ignore or manipulate what is true right now. Our na'au intelligence is *always present here and now*—we can always trust it. Overtraining results from our thinking mind attempting to run the show and ignoring the clear distress signals from our body.

This simple pair of scenarios illustrates the infinite possibilities and synergy of integrating our mana'o and na'au intelligences versus the agony and disempowering limitations of disconnecting our mana'o and na'au intelligences. These scenarios play out not only in our endurance training and racing but also in each and every moment of our lives.

First Step to Spiritual Fitness

The very first step toward true spiritual fitness is to develop our ability to be steadfast and completely present here and now. With spiritual fitness, we skillfully operate our mana'o intelligence from our calm, still, silent, open, and empty Zen space of being. This first step is when we pull off the blindfold of mistaken identity and begin to operate that chainsaw of reason with wisdom and discernment—transforming it into a tool of skillful means.

PU'UWAI

Hawaiian Wisdom

In the Hawaiian culture, *pu'uwai* refers to the intelligence of the heart. The translation of *pu'uwai* reveals much about this energetic center of intelligence. *Pu'u* means a mass, such as a hill or point of land, or any round area of the body. *Wai* (pronounced vai) means "fresh water"—distinct from *kai*, which means "ocean water." *Wai* can also refer generally to bodily fluids, though each fluid has its own specific name. So, *wai* can refer to blood—although the specific word for "blood" is *koko*. In a literal translation, Hawaiians identify our heart as a "mass of fresh water"—fresh water being the precious cradle of life. Hawaiians value and appreciate fresh water so much that the word for "wealth" is *wai-wai*—water-water.

Just as fresh water is the cradle of life for all the Earth, our blood is the circulation of life in our body. *Pu'uwai* identifies our heart as the circulator of life in our body. As endurance athletes, we can certainly appreciate the essential ability of our hearts to circulate "wealth" in our bodies. Heart fitness is a fundamental part of our overall aerobic fitness. In training, we often use a heart rate monitor to listen to our pulse rate, and we may even base our fitness training programs around target heart rates.

Heart Intelligence—Obscured by Science

How is this "pump," this "mass of precious water" essential to our spiritual fitness as well as our physical intelligence? What is the nature of our energetic heart center? Why do we consider it as a source of intelligence?

Even from a scientific perspective, there is now mounting evidence that concurs with what the romantic in each of us has known since the beginning of time—that our pu'uwai is our *transmitter* and our *receiver* for mana, our life energy. Let's take a moment to look a little closer at mana and how it is similar to light. We know through conventional modern science that light can behave as both a particle and a wave. Light seems to have one foot firmly planted in the solid physical realm of objects, where it behaves as a particle—a tangible irreducible piece of matter. Light has its other foot just as firmly planted in the nebulous, metaphysical realm of energy, where it behaves as a wave—an intangible, immaterial force. Mana functions in the same way. In our physical universe, it is a measurable electrical current. In our metaphysical universe, it is the mysterious phenomenon of love. Our pu'uwai is the transmitter and receiver of mana as love. As it pumps, our heart also generates the highest electrical voltage in our body.

Modern science and biomedicine give little credence or attention to this mana life energy as an essential and primary element of our composition and our daily lives. However, many advanced ancient civilizations and religious systems recognize mana as fundamental in the existence of all life. There are more than a hundred names for "mana" from myriad cultures. These advanced ancient cultures base their healing systems and spiritual practices on mana. Our modern biomedical science is just beginning to reluctantly refer to mana as the fifth force. While Hawaiians refer to it as mana, the Chinese refer to it as chi. These terms do not refer just to the emotional aspects we associate with love—they also recognize the energetic and informational *intelligence* of this universal life energy.

Our scientifically based endurance training programs consider the physical aspect of our heart—like our pulse rate and blood pressure—yet exclude any notion of mana. In fact, our "highly advanced" systems of science have little, if any, regard for the dualistic love/life energetic nature of mana. Why? As we know, conventional science is based on our mana'o intelligence and its ability to *separate* and to *distinguish*. Mana is essentially the opposite. It is universally integrating, permeating, and circulating. The natural tendency of mana'o intelligence is to distinguish itself through isolation and separation. When we slip into thought identity, we put on the blindfold of ignorance and allow the chainsaw of reason to run the show.

Complete Opposites

One of the first connections the chainsaw of reason will sever is the connection to pu'uwai intelligence. After all, the respective natures of mana'o and pu'uwai are completely opposite each other. Paul Pearsall, in his book *The Heart's Code: Tapping the Wisdom and Power of Our Heart Energy*, calls this disconnection of the mana'o from the pu'uwai the "lethal covenant." In this lethal covenant, the isolating, cutting, and thinking mana'o intelligence drags the body around on its unbridled binge through life, refusing to honor and listen to the connective, networking brilliance of the pu'uwai intelligence.

At this point, the isolationist mana'o is saying, *This pu'uwai stuff is a waste of time. It's not going to improve my performance as an athlete or my potential for success, reward, and recognition.* We must remember however the plain irrefutable truth: no circulation, no life. The major cause of heart-related illness and death may appear to be cholesterol, high blood pressure, and other tangible, measurable conditions. However, the deeper underlying cause is a type A brain trying to run the show—refusing to heed the *intelligence* of the heart. It is the unbridled, blindly operated mana'o chainsaw that kills the heart. Remember, the mana'o isolates and distinguishes; the pu'uwai circulates and integrates. In a harmonious and synergetic relationship, the two are capable of miracles—especially healing.

Intelligence of Circulation

We identified the spiritual Zen function of our mana'o intelligence as skillful means.

The spiritual function of our pu'uwai intelligence is the same as its physical function—circulation and integration. On the spiritual level, that circulation of mana—in the intelligent waveform of love—is a shared, collective circulation. All our heart centers are intelligently circulating the same wai—the same "precious cradle of life." Our hearts are all connected to the same collective intelligence—through a shared, common circulation system of love. This is the essence of *integrity*—a circulating, collective intelligence of love.

As athletes and even more essentially as human beings, we are well aware of the need to keep our circulatory systems and heart pumps clean and unimpeded. This is equally true in the emotional and spiritual realm. Built-up, dysfunctional and parasitic emotions are the cholesterol of our pu'uwai circulatory intelligence.

The Power and Cholesterol of Emotions

Let's look a little deeper into this notion of "emotional cholesterol." First, let's look briefly into the nature and function of our emotions. How do our emotions function as part of our pu'uwai *intelligence*—the intelligence of circulation and integration? Physiologically, emotions can be detected and measured as chemical and electrical changes in our bodies—including, of course, our brain and heart. This energetic, electrical nature of emotions makes them part of our spatial-matrix language of *feel*. Emotions are part of our intelligence as electrical beings. As energetic electrical states, emotions help to power our heart's transmissions and receptions with others—in much the same way we use electricity to power radio transmitters and receivers. Emotions are energetic components of our circulating, connective intelligence.

These powerful energetic emotional states become plaque buildup when an unheeding and ignorant thinking mind insists on isolating itself—dwelling in the past, projecting into the future, or manipulating the present. By violating the present moment, the isolating, thinking mind effectively prevents the pu'uwai intelligence from networking and connecting to the here-and-now. The energetic, emotional states of the heart are *sealed* into the body, left to echo within and to harden and collect as plaque. This plaque adds to the *reactive dysfunction*—rather than the responsive function—of our thinking mind as it operates in the backward-flowing victim scenario. In this situation, our mana'o can only see that *the world is doing it to me.*

Healthy emotional states—those that respond to the present moment—are powerful fields or systems of energy that facilitate the transmission and reception of mana. They help keep us energetically connected with all life around us. Our connection to others is vital to our *physical* health as well as our emotional health. In Israel, researchers followed ten thousand men with angina. The single most important health improvement factor was each man's perception of how much his partner loved and supported him. This was more important than diet, exercise, or anything else. At Duke University, researchers surveyed thirteen hundred patients who were suffering from serious heart disease. The researchers found a strong correlation between the patients' survival rate and their connection to other humans whom they could confide in. Fifty percent of the "loners" died within five years, compared to 17 percent of those who had a trusting and loving connection with someone. Marriage and life expectancy has been another area of intense research. Marriage cuts a woman's chances of dying young by 50 percent. For men the results are even more astounding—married men are five times more likely to live longer than their unmarried counterparts.

Pu'uwai Intelligence

A healthy heart center is just as vital to our energy and information exchange as it is to our physical health and endurance fitness. This exchange is essential to our *collective* intelligence—an intelligence that is incomprehensible to our *isolationist* mana'o. Our mana'o intelligence needs the aid of phones and computers to create a network with others. Our pu'uwai intelligence however is our true link to the *real* "worldwide web." Think of it as "www.pu'uwai.net." Our pu'uwai intelligence is completely wireless, mobile and unencumbered by the hardware of technology.

Just how *intelligent* is our pu'uwai? Paul Pearsall has written almost three hundred pages on the nature of this intelligence in his aforementioned book *The Heart's Code*. Dr. Pearsall is a psychoneuroimmunologist who survived stage IV lymphoma. As well as authoring several books, he has made more than five thousand national and international presentations. He is highly regarded by many Fortune 500 companies as well as medical schools and societies. In the acknowledgements, at the very beginning of his book, Pearsall writes:

"The possibilities suggested in this book, that the heart thinks and feels, that our cells remember, and that there is a subtle yet very powerful and pervasive form of energy that connects every thing and every person, are suggested by the creative and careful research of many scientists." (p. xv)

Pearsall addresses some intriguing questions in his book. He explores the functional nature of the heart's intelligence and how that intelligence connects us together—how the energy *and information* of our hearts is transmitted and received. He explores this heart connection not only among humans, but also between humans and nonhuman life-forms and even machines. All his explorations are scientifically supported. He relates a very powerful true-life story in the beginning of the book as a clear example of the heart's intelligence—titled "The Heart That Found Its Body's Killer."

Supporting Evidence

Pearsall was speaking to an international group of psychologists, psychiatrists, and social workers at a meeting in Houston, Texas. He lectured about his convictions that our heart serves a vital and essential role in our psychological and spiritual life. When he concluded his presentation, there was a question-and-answer session. A psychiatrist came to the microphone to relate her experience with one of her patients—a heart transplant recipient—whose experience supported his ideas about heart intelligence and cellular memory. This medical professional was in tears as she related her patient's powerful story.

Her patient was an eight-year-old girl who had received the heart of a murdered ten-year-old girl. The little girl's mother brought her to the psychiatrist because she would wake up screaming at night. In her dreams she repeatedly saw the man who had murdered her donor. The girl's mother told the psychiatrist that her daughter knew who the murderer was from these dreams. After several sessions, the psychiatrist could no longer deny the reality of what this child was telling her. Together, they decided to call the police. With descriptions provided by the little girl, they found the murderer. He was easily convicted with evidence that the little girl's donated heart provided to her through its *cellular memory*, revealed through her dreams. "The time, the weapon, the place, the clothes he wore, what the little girl he killed had said to him . . . everything the little heart transplant recipient reported was completely accurate." (p. 7, *The Heart's Code*)

Compelling enough?

Our Weak Sport

Those of us who are triathletes all have our *least* favorite athletic activity—the sport that offers us our greatest opportunity for growth and experience—what we call our weakest sport. Likewise, we each have that least favorite, least familiar *intelligence*. For most of us type A, competitive over-achievers, our pu'uwai is the weakest energetic intelligence—it is our weak sport so to speak. This is the one where we are lacking most in experience and training. The elites and type A's among us have much to learn about our pu'uwai intelligence from those of us who might be back-of-the-pack athletes but are generally more balanced and functional as human beings—thanks to our heart-based intelligence of circulation, integration, and connection.

Sharing Intelligence

The *integrity* of our pu'uwai is a *mutually shared* and *collective* intelligence that needs no additional hardware in order to link up and go online with others. Through our pu'uwai intelligence, such integrity and connection are available to us instantly and continuously. We need only develop our ability to tap into our heart's intelligence from our calm, still, silent, open, and empty space of deep inner listening.

Conclusion

Pu'uwai integrity constantly provides us with essential guidance and valuable wisdom on our Zen path—guidance and wisdom that are beyond the comprehension and the capacity of our thinking mind-mana'o. The pu'uwai intelligence of integrity is so central and indispensable to our path that the next section of this book is titled "HeartCore Zendurance." Those of us who are type A's (yes, that includes me) can benefit greatly from reading Pearsall's *Heart's Code*. It is essential that we develop a deliberate practice of listening to our hearts and exercising our pu'uwai intelligence. Pearsall explores such terms as *cardio-sensitivity* and *cardio contemplation* in his book.

Throughout this book I have chosen as much as possible to use the term *we* rather than *you* and *me*. This is a simple way of continuously recognizing and honoring the vital and essential wisdom of pu'uwai—the wisdom of connection, of *we* and *us*.

Our mana'o provides us with skillful means, a very valuable tool for effective training. Our pu'uwai provides us with integrity, an

equally valuable asset as athletes—especially in racing. We will
consider the valuable function of pu'uwai intelligence in our
endurance racing in the section, "Zendurance Racing and
Performance." Great race performances begin with skillfully craft-
ed training programs. However, the true inspiration on race day is
born through the integrity of open, connected, and intelligent
hearts and is fueled by the race itself as a *living entity* of collective
energy and intelligence.

NA'AU

Introduction

We started our discussion of the three energetic intelligences
with mana'o, the energetic center associated with our brain.
Biologically, we perceive the brain as the source of thought. On
a *spiritual* parallel, we honor our mana'o intelligence as our
source of *skillful means*. Next we explored our pu'uwai intelligence, associated with the heart. *Biologically*, we recognize the
heart as the pump for the circulation of blood. Spiritually, we
honor pu'uwai intelligence as our source of *integrity* and connection with one another—our transmitter and receiver of love and
collective intelligence.

Biologically we associate our na'au with our abdomen—our
intestines, liver, kidneys, stomach, pancreas, and so forth. We
know that these vital organs provide and regulate the energy supply for our body, heart, and brain. In the seven-chakra system,
we associate na'au with the second or pelvic chakra, known as
the chi center. *Spiritually*, our na'au mirrors its biological function as a power supply. It is our mana power supply. The first
chakra, in close proximity to the na'au, is also part of this mana
supply. This is our sexual energy chakra—the fire of creation.
Our na'au sits just above and is heated by this fire of creation.

In "What Is Feel?" we considered at length our na'au as the
intelligent source of movement and action—as the intelligent and
articulate center of feeling. We are beginning to think spatially
through our electrical neurological matrix of feeling—truly a form
of intelligence.

Hawaiian Wisdom

In the *New Pocket Hawaiian Dictionary*, we find the following definition for *na'au*: "Intestines, bowels; mind, heart; of the heart or mind." While the most common usage for *na'au* is "intestines," it also pertains to heart or mind. If we look in the same dictionary for the Hawaiian translation for "intelligence," we find the word *na'auao* (pronounced nah-ow-WOW). The last syllable *ao* translates to "daylight." Therefore *na'auao* translates to "daylight intestines" or "daylight mind." Similarly, the translation for "ignorance" is *na'aupo*. *Po* means "night" or "darkness." The ancient Hawaiians gave precedence to their gut instinct of their na'au intelligence over the mana'o or pu'uwai intelligences.

Our Second Brain

We considered material from *The Heart's Code* that provides strong supportive evidence for a unique intelligence of the heart—much different from the brain's intelligence. Likewise, Dr. Michael Gershon summarizes research that reveals the biological intelligence of the gut in *The Second Brain*. The nervous system of the gut, known as the enteric nervous system, continuously monitors conditions of the rest of the body's systems. All thirty classes of neurotransmitters found in the brain are also present in the enteric nervous system. In our abdomen, we find twenty hormones and 70 to 80 percent of the body's immune cells. Gershon's research shows that nine times more messages flow from the abdomen to the brain than brain to abdomen.

Regulated Power Supply

As endurance athletes, we often take for granted the consistent and precisely regulated energy production and distribution that is essential to our aerobic activity. Such a reliable source of energy requires true intelligence—as does our immune system's ability to maintain and regulate health throughout the body and to cope with stress. This regulated energy production and immunological maintenance is a continuous birth-to-death intelligence, as is the heart's circulatory intelligence.

We can summarize the nature and function of our na'au intelligence—both biologically and metaphysically—as the intelligence of *activity*. Biologically, we know that our activities can only be generated by the energy that our enteric system intelligently provides in a regulated and consistent manner. Metaphysically, we experience our na'au as our origin and center of kinetic activity. We experience a place of *stillness* deep in the core of our na'au from which our movement and sense of feeling are sourced and orchestrated.

Grounding and Spiritual Fitness

In "What Is Feel?" we considered the electrical and gravitational aspects of *grounding*. In the context of our three energetic intelligences—skillful means, integrity, and activity—the na'au intelligence of activity becomes the grounding into the physical universe for the intelligences of skillful means and integrity. Activity strongly and firmly grounds our skillful means and our integrity into *this* present moment.

As mentioned in our discussion of mana'o intelligence, for many of us kinetic activity provides our very first experiences of a source of intelligence and an identity beyond our day-to-day mundane thoughts and judgments. It is the *grounding* of activity that provides us with our first foothold in cultivating and strengthening *spiritual fitness*—our calm, still, and steadfast presence *here* and *now*. It is the *grounding* of activity in our na'au that functions as the physical home of the soul.

In our consideration of mana'o intelligence, we considered the unhealthy dysfunction of ego-fixated thinking—where we slip into thought identity. We also considered the unhealthy dysfunction of our pu'uwai as emotional plaque—where our energetic emotional states have no grounded connection to the present moment.

As endurance athletes, we are acutely aware of our physical health since our rigorous training activities provide us with rapid and clear feedback on our body's condition. Inactivity and physical illness can diminish our grounded presence here and now. Through our zendurance approach to our athletic training, we engage the grounding intelligence of activity to develop and strengthen our spiritual fitness. With spiritual fitness, we can *navigate* each present moment in our lives as it unfolds—from our calm, still, silent, open, and empty space of awareness. In view of this enlightened approach to activity, we can forgo any further discussion of physical illness and ungrounded, unintelligent activity.

More Ancient Hawaiian Wisdom

To conclude our discussion of na'au intelligence, let's return to the underlying wisdom of the Hawaiian culture and language. Let's break down *na'au* into *na* and *au* and consider the meanings for these as separate words. We look again to the *New Pocket Hawaiian Dictionary: na* translates to "by," "for," "of" and "belonging to." *Au* can mean "1) A period of time, era or age, the passing of time. 2) Current (of water). 3) Movement, eddy, tide." Using these meanings, we can construct a translation of *na'au* as: "Of, or belonging to a current, for a period of time." In this translation, we can consider the "current" to be our current of mana—life force. Our souls inhabit our na'au centers for a period of time—the span of our lives—to channel and flow this life force.

While our na'au center is the source or home for our mana, it is our pu'uwai center that transmits and receives mana—that connects and integrates our life force with that of others. Our mana'o provides the skillful means for cultivation and articulation of our mana.

Another pronunciation of *au*—written as *'au*—means "to swim." It also means "staff" or "handle." As the physical home of the soul, na'au provides a grip or handle for the soul to ground to as we swim through our journey of life.

THE ENERGETIC NATURE OF INTELLIGENCE

Essentially, we are endowed with three energetic intelligences— skillful means, integrity and activity. What makes these three intelligences *energetic?* Each is a unique form of intelligence that functions dynamically in an energetic medium, rather than in an apparently solid and concrete reality. Through the phenomenon of *feeling*, we are already beginning to cultivate a *tangible* and articulate relationship with this energetic medium in our own bodies. We are beginning to experience an energetic, electrical intelligence and to perceive our own bodies as energetic fields or matrixes.

Skillful means, integrity, and activity are the three *intelligent aspects* of mana. Each of these unique intelligences is infinite in potential—infinitely *articulate* in the energetic field of mana. These sources of intelligence have no constraints with regard to size, distance, duration, or the like.

Free-Flowing Natural Springs

We can imagine each energetic intelligence as a natural spring that has been sourcing and flowing water since the beginning of time. Like natural springs of water, we share each of these intelligences. We can *each* drink from any one of these infinitely abundant springs at *any* time. We can drink as much as we want—there is enough water flowing from each spring for *all* sentient beings. No one can possibly own or control the flow of these three springs. All of us—*all sentient beings*—share these three energetic intelligences mutually. Each of us has ample, unlimited access to these three intelligences, *and* we can support and assist each other in navigating that access.

As intelligent aspects of mana, these energetic intelligences have no distinct parameters, no boundaries. They permeate all things. They exist together and occupy the same space simultaneously—like three sources of water mixing together. As we develop the spiritual fitness to be steadfastly present here and now in our calm, still, silent, open, and empty space of deep inner listening and contemplation, we gain infinite access to these three intelligences. Our potential for intelligence is infinite. Our connection with each form of intelligence is intimate.

The Energetic Intelligence Triangle

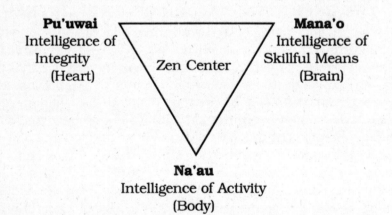

Pu'uwai
Intelligence of
Integrity
(Heart)

Zen Center

Mana'o
Intelligence of
Skillful Means
(Brain)

Na'au
Intelligence of Activity
(Body)

Our three energetic intelligences—mana'o, pu'uwai, and na'au—form a triangle, which we shall herein refer to as the *energetic intelligence triangle*. Our calm, still, silent, open, and empty *space* of being present here and now *is located in the center of our energetic intelligence triangle*. Spiritual fitness is our ability to remain steadfast and present in that center without slipping into our mistaken ego identity as the mana'o intelligence. From the center of our triangle, we have balanced and equal access to all three forms of intelligence.

Let's return to the analogy of the three natural springs that source and flow from these energetic intelligences. As we develop spiritual fitness, we remain calm, still and centered. In this state of peace, we stop agitating these natural springs and we allow them to clear, purify and distill. The sparkling waters of our three springs of intelligence become sweeter and more vibrant. Eventually—through the steadfast and peaceful centeredness of our spiritual fitness—the waters of all three springs converge and flow together. It is in this state that we truly experience effortless power and brilliance.

Improving Our Water Quality

As endurance athletes, our most effective approach to training is to focus on improving our weaknesses while maintaining our strengths. Creating an effective training program begins with honest self-assessment in identifying our strengths and weaknesses.

Building spiritual fitness also begins with honest self-assessment: *How clear and unimpeded is my connection and access to each of the three sources of intelligence? How familiar am I with navigating each of these connections? How clear and pure is the "water" of each and how much am I agitating and polluting each intelligence?* The books I mentioned—*The Power of Now* and *The Heart's Code*—can be quite valuable in improving our navigational skills and assisting with any restoration work that is necessary to improve the water quality of our mana'o and pu'uwai intelligences. A wise and sensible zendurance approach to our athletic training is already improving the access and water quality of our na'au intelligence.

Tangible Intelligence

Let's begin to quietly observe the *presence* and *feeling* of each of these intelligences within us. We can begin to notice which of the three intelligences is/are operative in specific moments of our day-to-day lives. Which of these intelligences do we enthusiastically and effortlessly engage? Which intelligence(s) is/are we less adept at and less inclined to engage? It requires tremendous discipline and tenacity to keep these questions—these inquiries—in our awareness each moment of our day. Our intention is to become tangibly familiar with the *landscape* of our relationship to these intelligences and our *navigational skills* in accessing them.

When we are training, which of these intelligence(s) is/are most prominent and which most dormant? How about when we are at home with our families? At work? Racing? We can observe the energetic presence and activity of each of these three unique intelligences in all our familiar daily routines. This exercise will enhance our awareness and the quality of our presence in each familiar activity.

Here are a few more questions to investigate: How does each form of intelligence *function* in our lives? How is each intelligence an articulate aspect of our mana? How do we engage the intelligence of skillful means in our lives? How do we engage the intelligence of integrity in our lives? How do we engage the intelligence of activity in our lives? These are not the kinds of questions we can simply write a brief reply to. These are questions that require deep contemplation, deep inner listening. In contemplating such questions, we begin to open up—to explore and navigate the *metaphysical landscape* of our experiential and spiritual wilderness. These are questions—*investigations*—we choose to live with, just as we live with the *quest* of endurance athletics.

Strength of the Triangle

It is not just incidental that there are *three* energetic intelligent aspects of mana. A triangle is the strongest and most stable system. In addition to its unsurpassed strength and stability, the triangle is also the simplest system. Those of us who are triathletes have a clear physical experience of this triangular strength and stability. Triathlon provides us with aerobic ability and endurance versatility that surpasses single- or even dual-sport training. The *synergetic* result of triangular training is undeniable. For example, very few single-sport runners could adequately train to *race* a marathon on thirty miles of running a week—yet a thirty-mile running base, when combined with biking and swimming, is quite adequate for racing a marathon gracefully and with minimal physical duress.

Triangulation

The process of *triangulation* is used to precisely determine the location of a specific place. This process is used for aviation and marine navigation and in land surveying. It is the basis for global positioning systems (GPS) as well. Synchronized signals from *three* known locations—satellites or beacons—are compared at the fourth point to determine the specific distance from each of the three sources. From these three pieces of data, the location of the fourth point can be precisely determined. We use a similar process of triangulation to develop our spiritual fitness—to locate and remain steadfast in our calm, still, silent, open, and empty center.

We can enjoy the synergetic strength and stability of both our endurance triangle and our intelligence triangle. We can benefit from the precision of triangulation in developing our endurance fitness and our spiritual fitness. To do so, we must equally maintain all three events of the triangle—be they endurance activities like swimming, biking, and running, or the intelligent activities of our mana'o, pu'uwai, and na'au. Our fluency in all three must be equally developed. This indicates the essential importance in contemplating the questions and conducting the honest self-assessment and investigations mentioned above. A triangle with a weak or missing point is no longer a strong and stable system. A triathlete who is highly deficient in one of the three endurance activities may never experience a great race performance. Likewise, if we are deficient in any of our three intelligences, we may never truly experience the effortless power of spiritual fitness.

T-1: TRANSITION ONE

Terminology

Some of the terms and expressions we are using—as well as the contexts in which we are using them—may seem new and unfamiliar to you. We have considered a *spatial and electrical language*. We have introduced the possibility of *spiritual fitness* and a *metaphysical landscape*. We have talked of exploring and navigating that metaphysical landscape. For those of us who are loyal to the world of solid and stable matter with its concrete landscapes, all of this may sound new age and fantastical. Yet terms like *navigation, browsing, surfing,* and *web sites, addresses and pages* are becoming more familiar and accepted every day.

Computers have introduced us to the *tangibility* of cyberspace—another *energetic* landscape complete with locations that we can return to again and again. The metaphysical landscape of cyberspace is rapidly becoming a commonly accepted, familiar, and tangible reality for our global culture. The metaphysical landscape of spiritual awareness and activity—including our three energetic intelligences—has actually been an integral part of our experiential and spiritual wilderness since the beginning of time—although it is often ignored in our contemporary society. However, the advent of computers and cyberspace is just a very recent blip on the big screen of time and human civilization. We are entering, expanding and becoming familiar with the landscape of cyberspace very quickly. Our ability to explore and to navigate the infinite metaphysical landscape of spiritual awareness—beginning with the three pristine springs of energetic intelligence—is an inherent and natural ability for each of us individually and for all of us collectively. *It is indelibly encoded in our cellular memory.*

Opening the Metaphysical Map

"What Is Feel?" and "The Intelligence of Tri-Zen" are the initial layout of a *metaphysical map* that reveals some of the geography of this infinite landscape of spiritual fitness. In choosing to enter, explore, and navigate this metaphysical landscape, we are not required to accept any religious doctrines or practices; nor are we required to eschew any.

In the next section, "HeartCore Zendurance," we will build on this metaphysical map and explore further the geography of this landscape in our pursuit of spiritual fitness and effortless power in *all* areas of our lives—including endurance athletics. We will continue to develop and refine our navigational skills—based on the energetic intelligence triangle that is comprised of the *skillful means* of distinction, the *integrity* of circulation, and the *activity* of here and now.

Our mana'o, pu'uwai, and na'au intelligences are wonderful gifts and powerful tools in our lives as athletes and as ordinary human beings.

2

HEARTCORE ZENDURANCE

ZEN PENTATHLON

LEG STRENGTH FOR FITNESS AND INTELLIGENCE

ZEN PENTATHLON: INTEGRATION: THE MAIN EVENT

HEARTCORE INTEGRATION: FIRST LEG

HEARTCORE INTEGRATION: SECOND LEG

HEARTCORE INTEGRATION: THIRD LEG

HEARTCORE INTEGRATION: SUMMARY

ZEN PENTATHLON: CONTRIBUTION: THE FINAL EVENT

PRACTICAL NAVIGATION

T-2: TRANSITION TWO

LIVE SIMPLY SO THAT OTHERS CAN SIMPLY LIVE

ZEN PENTATHLON

From Athletic Triathlon to Spiritual Pentathlon

As triathletes we must blend and coordinate three unique endurance activities to create an effective and comprehensive training program. This endurance triad enhances and improves our overall aerobic fitness beyond the capacity of a single-sport training program. Similarly, in our day-to-day lives, we blend and coordinate *five* activities to develop and cultivate our overall *spiritual* fitness. Together these five activities make up what we will call the *Zen pentathlon*. Through this Zen pentathlon, we engage and exercise all three of our energetic intelligences—mana'o, pu'uwai and na'au—to *triangulate* and strengthen our spiritual fitness.

The five activities in the Zen pentathlon are: 1) contemplation, 2) approach, 3) practice, 4) integration and 5) contribution. While these five activities may not be as physical—as obvious or as tangible—as swimming, biking, or running, they are sequential steps that lead to true spiritual fitness. We will consider each of these five steps/activities and how we can apply each of them to successfully transform our athletic training into zendurance. We will explore some of the functional mechanics and dynamics of each one—as we did with swimming, biking, and running—so that we can develop effective techniques and become more proficient as Zen pentathletes. A key part of our proficiency comes from understanding how each of these five activities enhances our connection to our three energetic intelligences.

CONTEMPLATION

What Is Contemplation?

Swimming is the first event of a conventional triathlon. *Contemplation* is the first event of the Zen pentathlon. While swimming is easy to define as a tangible activity, contemplation is not so easy to define or to recognize as a tangible activity. What is contemplation? What does it mean to contemplate something? Close your eyes for a moment and see yourself in the activity of contemplation. Perhaps the most common similarity that we find in our unique individual visions is that we see ourselves in a state of *stillness*—probably sitting.

Each of us might make some reference toward being open and toward keen observation. In contemplation we become physically still and mentally quiet. We cease to act upon things or to make decisions. Our na'au intelligence grounds us in the "activity" of being still. That physical stillness supports us in being quiet mentally so that we can be present here and now. This stillness can really help our mana'o intelligence become calm, open and keenly perceptive. It enhances our curiosity and inquisitiveness.

As athletes, our process of transforming endurance training into zendurance practice actually begins with the stillness of contemplation. We soon discover that *graceful* movement originates from the stillness of our pelvic center—our na'au intelligence. Our mana'o intelligence gradually ceases its chatter about the past, the future, and controlling the present. In this still and quiet Zen space, we can enter the language and intelligence of *feel.*

Contemplation and Mana'o Intelligence

As we engage in contemplation, we are first turning off the noisy chainsaw of reason so that we can actually listen. We know already that our mana'o intelligence is usually the loudest of the three. To be more specific, it is not the energetic intelligence of mana'o that is noisy; it is our *ego relationship* with it that creates the noise. When we turn *off* that chainsaw of reason and let the dust settle, it is much easier to access pu'uwai and na'au. Contemplation is the silence and openness of our mana'o intelligence linked with the stillness and the here-and-now-ness of our na'au. *Contemplation is the process of locating and moving to our calm, still, silent, open, and empty space of being—the Zen center of our intelligence triangle.*

Contemplation requires patience, discipline, and the willingness to be open and present without any attachment to immediately finding answers, making decisions, or taking action. You may recall our discussion about *questions* back in "Starting Line." The activity of contemplation moves us into the Zen center of our intelligence triangle, where we can be completely open and present to questions and to the true *quest* of endurance athletics.

Simple Geometry of Contemplation

When we engage in contemplation, the appearance that we are doing nothing seems to clash with our associations of productivity and value. Therefore it requires great courage and conviction to *turn off the chainsaw of reason* and just *be*. Through contemplation, we move away from the mana'o apex of our intelligence triangle into the *Zen center* of the triangle. In the Zen center, our access and connection to all three intelligences is equal and balanced—giving us the power of triangulation. This is the *essential* first event in our Zen pentathlon—turn off the chainsaw and return to the Zen center of the triangle—very simple, yet very subtle.

With consistent practice we can develop a *feel* for contemplation, just as we develop a *feel* for swimming. While swimming seems far more real than contemplation—more tangible and obvious—we know from our training that effective swimming technique is actually very subtle—there is more to it than just what meets the eye. Through swim training, we are already developing a deep and subtle sense of feeling and intelligent discernment that we can apply to the less tangible activity of contemplation.

APPROACH

Choosing a Path

The second event of the Zen pentathlon is *approach*. In our day-to-day lives, where productivity and efficiency are our measures of value and worth, we usually choose to *approach* the tasks and activities of our lives in the most direct way, taking the shortest and straightest path. Yet any skilled hunter can tell you that the shortest and most direct pursuit will not often result in successfully capturing the prey. Likewise, during the morning rush hour, the most direct route to work or school may take a good deal longer than a less direct and less congested route.

Even the methodology of our endurance training program is not a direct approach, particularly with running. We do not effectively train for a sub-3:30 marathon by attempting to run 26.2 miles in 3:29 once a week. Our skillful approach is much more circuitous— a mixture of long, slow runs and shorter tempo runs, along with recovery runs and cross-training. We build endurance and speed one step at a time.

Approaching Relationships

Suppose that we are initiating our first contact with a potential new client at work. The fast, efficient get-down-to-business approach with all our pressing agendas may not actually support us in being genuinely present and intelligent with that person and establishing a relationship based on honesty, trust, and caring. We may overlook several fairly obvious qualities in the person because we are so eager to make the sale. Likewise, the direct get-down-to-business approach may compromise our personal relationships, since we often cloud our perceptions of others with our own agendas, overlooking the obvious. This is especially crucial in our relationships with our children.

Setting Our Attitude and Intent

Our *approach* to any given athletic training session, situation, task, or relationship includes the degree of openness, sensitivity and perceptive ability we bring into the moment—and this is largely determined by our *attitude*. If we are patient, open, and inquisitive—Zen centered—we can effectively engage and coordinate *all three* of our energetic intelligences as we approach each training session, task, situation, or relationship.

In this empowered state, we can approach each experience as an opportunity to practice our spiritual fitness. Our approach can transform any experience into an empowering opportunity or into a dismal lockout. For example, our approach can diminish any training session into a laborious and exhausting ordeal or transform it into a graceful zendurance meditation. An effective and empowered approach is directed by clear intent.

One-Two

The first event of our Zen pentathlon—*contemplation*—lays the foundation and sets the intent for the second step—*approach.* Through contemplation, we move away from our ego-based noisy relationship with our mana'o—bent on controlling each moment or relationship—into the Zen center of our triangle—our space of clear and open intent. From that calm, still center we open up equal and balanced access to our three energetic intelligences and approach each moment and each experience of our lives with openness and sensitivity, with our skills of yielding, blending, and aligning.

Bowing

Jack Kornfield begins his book *After the Ecstasy, the Laundry* with an entry titled "An Opening Bow." More than thirty years ago,

Jack went to Thailand to become a Buddhist monk in a traditional forest monastery. As is the custom, every time he entered the
meditation hall or took his seat for training with the master, he
would *bow*. Bowing at the monastery entails dropping to your
knees and placing your forehead and palms on the stone floor
three times. This diligent and conscious gesture is a humble and
reverent act of respect that expresses the monk's commitment to
the path of simplicity, humility, compassion, and awareness.

In addition, Jack was told that the bowing custom was also to
be observed every time he met an elder monk—even in passing.
This meant that he had to bow to any other monk ordained before
him—regardless of age. He found himself bowing to the cocky
younger monks and to the retired rice farmers—those who had little experience or appreciation for spiritual practices or for the wisdom that could be cultivated in the traditional monastic ways.
Eventually he began to find and honor some worthy characteristic
in each individual he bowed to. The activity of bowing became his
diligent *approach* to each individual and each experience. He began
to realize the transformative power that this simple, humble gesture held.

If we approach our lives with a humble sense of bowing, we are
more willing to embrace and to greet *all* the experiences that life
offers us with openness, patience, and curiosity. We are ready and
willing to effectively use our skills of yielding, blending, and aligning. With a humble, open, and patient bowing approach, we can
embrace the beauty *and* the suffering, our successes *and* our fail-
ures, our clarity *and* our confusions. Jack Kornfield writes: "To
bow to what is rather than to some ideal is not necessarily easy,
but however difficult, it is one of the most useful and honorable
practices." (p. xi)

Bowing is a humble gesture. Whether standing or kneeling, we
bend at the waist, lowering our heads and leveling our spines hor-
izontally. This humbling gesture lowers the mana'o center and levels the playing field for all three intelligences. Humbleness and
humility are honorable qualities of spiritually intelligent beings—
those who build their awareness and fitness equally from the pure
waters of all three energetic intelligences. In considering the gesture of bowing, we begin to regard our *approach* to any given situation as the attitude we assume when we greet each moment and
each experience—both the good ones and the bad ones. This attitude reflects the *position* we occupy—either the Zen center of our

intelligence triangle or the ego.

How we *approach* our relationships, tasks and work, training and racing, playing, eating and even sleeping largely determines the quality of our experiences and how they nourish our well-being.

Preparation and Observation

As endurance athletes, our *preparation* for each training session and each race is a great place to start looking at our approach. We can begin to keenly observe how we prepare for each training session: How does your body feel today as you are driving to your staging area? Are you nervous and tense or calm and relaxed? What thoughts and visions do you have about this session? Are you mentally preoccupied with some other matters? Are you eager, vibrant, and feeling alive? As you dress and set up your equipment, are you preparing to settle into the stillness of a moving meditation or will this be a tortuous ordeal? Are you patient or agitated as you set up your bike and check the tires? Do you take a moment to look up and around you—to truly experience the weather and surroundings?

Keen, *nonjudgmental* observation is paramount in both preparation and approach. In observing how we prepare for our training sessions, it is important not to judge or criticize ourselves, or to try to correct anything. We are simply becoming more aware of our preparation process and how that impacts the quality of our training. We are learning how to observe from our calm, still, silent, open, and empty Zen center. Judgment and criticism come from our ego, rather than from our Zen center. Don't forget, keen observation starts with *contemplation*—openness, stillness and emptiness.

As we transform our preparation for athletic training and racing into a Zen *approach*, we can take time to bow in some way. We can humbly bow in honor and in gratitude for the health, wealth, education, nourishment, and freedom that make this moment, this training session, or this race possible. *Very few human beings on this Earth are endowed with all these assets.* Our fortune is very worthy of a bow of gratitude and appreciation.

We may bow also with humility and respect for the tenacity, strength, and temperance we patiently develop through training and racing. We choose to include in this humble gesture a simple prayer for guidance and safe deliverance and to express our gratitude. We may pause for a moment to recollect an ancestor or to think of a loved one. We can even offer and dedicate each session or race to someone. In whatever way we choose to bow, we lower our ego-based mana'o and align equally with all three intelligences.

Zen Approach

Zen, as an approach, is open and without attachment to a desired result. This does not mean that we must train mindlessly, with no clear objectives. Our Zen approach is embracing, flexible and responsive in this moment. We work with the clear objectives of our training program in a diligent manner that is appropriate and harmonious to the present circumstances—both internal and external. Our zendurance approach is humble and respectful of the infinite possibility and opportunity inherent in this moment. In our humble, bowing, Zen approach, we literally bend down to open the window for effortless power.

Going Beyond Preparation

Unlike our *preparation* for a training session or race—which is complete when we actually start—our *approach continues* moment by moment throughout our *entire* training session and throughout our lives. Approach includes not only how we prepare for a specific activity, but also our openness and willingness in each moment to receive and perceive what each moment and each experience has to offer. It includes our openness and willingness to yield, blend, and align with each moment and each experience.

Through contemplation, the first event of our pentathlon, we move to the Zen center of our intelligence triangle—a place of openness and stillness, equally situated among our three energetic intelligences. In our Zen center, we are intimately present in this moment. From the Zen center, endowed with access to all three energetic intelligences, we can approach each moment and each experience as an opportunity to develop and cultivate spiritual fitness.

PRACTICE

Introduction

As the third event of our Zen pentathlon, *practice* is the center step of our spiritual fitness training. The main purpose of most traditional spiritual communities is to provide an environment and a community network that is supportive and conducive to specific forms of spiritual practice. Unlike contemplation and approach, practice is real—it has an *external appearance* and is often the focal point of a spiritual path. It is the formal training activity that leads us toward our spiritual fitness.

What Do We Practice?

Many different activities are recognized as formal practices for spiritual fitness—traditional forms like yoga, meditation, and prayer and nontraditional ones such as our endurance athletics. As Zen or spiritual practitioners—regardless of the activity—what is it that we actually practice? Very simply, we practice being calm, still, open, empty, and silent—qualities that help us to be completely present here and now, in this moment. Regardless of the activity we use—from meditation to running—our practice begins when we move to the Zen center of our intelligence triangle, by letting go of our noisy egoic relationship to our mana'o intelligence through *contemplation*.

We *practice* absolute presence in the moment—building spiritual fitness moment by moment. In the long hours of our endurance training, we have ample opportunity to become skilled Zen practitioners—to train and race from our calm, still, and open Zen center, and to balance and engage all three of our energetic intelligences, so that we are brilliant during each moment of our activity.

It's the Real Thing

Practice is a lot more tangible and easier to identify than contemplation or approach. Practice has definable, measurable parameters, such as duration, location, and a specific form of activity. This is certainly true with our endurance athletic training. We train for a measurable period of time and cover a measurable distance, engaging in a specific form of activity at specific rates of intensity. For instance, we might define a training session as a 120-minute bike ride on a moderately hilly course, keeping our heart rate within a given range. In this way, our practice has a tangible and measurable format that contemplation and approach seem to evade.

We establish this tangible format by intentionally setting the parameters and committing to the activity from start to finish on a consistent basis—perhaps daily. Without such tangibility—without the specific intention and the clear and deliberate commitment to practice some tangible form of activity—it is difficult to consistently progress along the path of spiritual fitness.

As we consciously *prepare* for a practice session—in our case, an athletic workout—and clearly define our objectives, intensity levels, duration, and so forth, we are calmly engaging in contemplation and clarifying our approach. It is the *tangibility* of formal, defined practice that inspires us to be *clear* in our approach, and it is our approach that largely determines the quality of our experiences in life and the success of our intentions.

Endurance Training as Practice

Each of us has a unique approach to our endurance training, with a unique intent and vision of what we are training toward. Some of us approach our training with the intent to simply improve our overall health and fitness, to reduce stress and to have fun. Our ego-driven agendas about our training are few and simple. This simplicity of intent—virtually free of our ego's desires and expectations—allows for a flexibility and responsiveness in the present moment and current circumstances. This can make the transformation of our endurance training into spiritual zendurance practice relatively easy and clear. Yet, without specific objectives—without a delicious and tangible "carrot" dangling in front of us (okay, how about a chocolate morsel?)—our motivation and discipline may be diluted and inconsistent.

At the other end of the spectrum are those of us who carefully construct our yearly training programs around specific goal races with well-defined results that we hope to achieve. The clear objectives and parameters of these meticulously designed training programs give us a very clear vision of what we intend to accomplish and realize—they provide measurable goals and indicators of our progress. As we know from our discussion on discipline, both clear vision and focused intent support us well in being motivated and diligent disciples. However, this goal-oriented approach to training and racing can be a dangerous undertaking, with well-hidden pitfalls and obsessions—courtesy of our friend the ego!

The Real Challenge

When we undertake goal-oriented training as a viable Zen practice, we are challenged to clearly distinguish between true zendurance training—as a joyful practice toward both endurance fitness *and* spiritual fitness—and obsessive endurance training solely as an attempt to climb the ego ladder. Goal-oriented training and racing can offer tremendous motivation and may enhance the clarity and purpose of our training, but it also challenges our discretion each moment and in each circumstance—to distinguish between the swift and silent sword of true skillful means and the noisy chainsaw of egoic mind.

Truly skillful and effective goal-oriented training, in its purest essence, requires a diamond-like clarity, transparency, and brilliance of skillful means—mana'o intelligence—in a balanced integration with our na'au and pu'uwai intelligences. If our mana'o is clouded by ego, we are certain to fall not only from the ego ladder, but from the endurance ladder as well—through injury and overtraining. Transforming our goal-race training into a viable practice of spiritual fitness offers us the challenging opportunity to walk the razor-sharp line between the humble brilliance of skillful means and the desires, delusions, distractions, dramas, and disasters of our ego.

The ability to distinguish between true brilliance and egoic desire begins with our ability to move to and remain in the Zen center of our intelligence triangle—disengaging from our ego, so that we approach each moment equally endowed with all three energetic intelligences.

So what is practice? It is the deliberate and conscious choice to approach each moment, each circumstance, and each relationship from the Zen center of our intelligence triangle—seamlessly and continuously.

Skipping Dinner for Dessert?

Because *contemplation* and *approach* seem quite subtle—less tangible and harder to grasp as activities or events in our Zen pentathlon than *practice*—it is tempting as endurance athletes to just skip over them and focus directly on our endurance athletic training. Drawing on our experience as triathletes, that would be similar to skipping over our swim and bike training if running was our favorite sport. We might become great runners that way. However, when we participate in a triathlon race, chances are that our ineptitude in swimming and cycling will leave us completely wasted by the time we get to the running event. Even our running performance will be disappointing. This is like skipping over dinner so we can load up on dessert. It may taste good, but it probably won't support and sustain our overall health or improve our athletic ability.

In contrast, a balanced zendurance approach to all three sports—where we hone the effortless form of each one—will set us up well for an effortless running performance. In conclusion, we do not want to underestimate the power and impact of the first two *subtle* events in our Zen pentathlon—contemplation and approach. They are essential for transforming our athletic training into zendurance practice.

Before we transition to the fourth and fifth events of our Zen pentathlon—*integration* and *contribution*—we are going to look at traditional forms of spiritual *practice*. These are forms of practice that have been a part of many different spiritual paths for hundreds and perhaps thousands of years.

LEG STRENGTH FOR FITNESS AND INTELLIGENCE

Introduction

It may assist us in transforming our endurance training into a rewarding and effective spiritual practice of zendurance if we entertain a brief overview of traditional spiritual practices and consider the mechanics of these practices. I have limited experience with traditional forms of practice and spiritual communities; therefore, I do not profess any extensive knowledge or formal training in these traditional forms. What I offer here is based on my simple observations and experience.

A Little More Spiritual Geometry

Most conventional spiritual practices belong to one of these six branches: *meditation, yoga, service, diet, prayer,* and *devotion. Each* of these six branches of practice has a *unique relationship* to our three energetic intelligences. (See diagram.) First, you will notice that the six branches of practice are grouped into three pairs. These three pairs of practices comprise what we will call the three practice legs of our intelligence triangle.

The two practices of each practice leg connect and integrate the two energetic intelligences that are located at each end of that leg. Through each specific form of practice, we build specific aspects of spiritual fitness. We do this by exercising and strengthening those two energetic intelligences. This is what we mean by leg strength for fitness and intelligence. What leg of the triangle is our zendurance training located on? Which intelligences do we exercise and strengthen during our training? Stay present with and *contemplate* these questions as we continue.

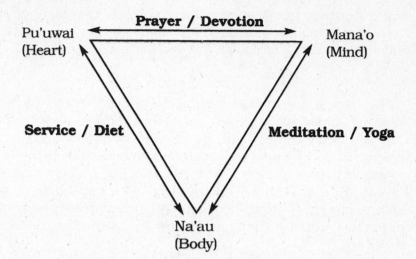

Intelligence Triangle—With Practice Legs

THE MEDITATION AND YOGA LEG

Mind and Body

Yoga and meditation are the two traditional forms of practice that engage and join together our mana'o (mind) and na'au (body) intelligences. Of the three pairs of traditional practices, our zendurance training most resembles the meditation/yoga leg of the triangle. After all, the most apparent purpose of endurance training is to build endurance fitness by strengthening our na'au intelligence of activity through a training program designed by the skillful means of our mana'o intelligence.

Breath

The most basic component of this practice leg of the intelligence triangle is *breath*. Our breath serves as the most fundamental connection between body and mind. We can either breathe through consciously articulated volition, or let go and allow our breath to occur from a more latent and sub-conscious will—while we sleep, for instance. Breath is a *vehicle* that allows us to explore the vast continuum of consciousness existing between our metaphysical mind and our physical body. Breath is quite literally the lifeline that holds the two together. We have already considered the importance of breath in our zendurance approach to athletic training. Conscious breathing keeps us present during our repetitious endurance training and is an integral part of our *feel.*

Meditation

There are many diverse meditation techniques and postures—some are simple and some are quite advanced and complex. In traditional forms of meditation, we usually sit quietly and train our awareness to be present with each breath, in each moment. In stillness and silence, we are able to *witness* our thoughts arise into form and then dissolve. Our intention with meditation is not to leave the body; it is to *witness*—to become completely present and aware beyond our judgments, desires, fears and the commentary of our ego.

As we engage in meditation, we are not escaping from our fears, judgments, desires, and so forth. We are not stopping or preventing them. We are *embracing* them and observing them—without adding to them or acting upon them. In meditation, we simply remain present with our fears, desires and judgments as they arise—we are no longer *taken* by them, no longer kidnapped and possessed by them.

Finding a Handle

We are able to disengage from our thoughts by using the physical stillness of our body as a *handle* for our awareness so that we no longer act like a mental tumbleweed blowing aimlessly and randomly across the landscape of thoughts. The grounded physical nature of our body is one of complete presence and awareness right here and right now—with every breath, from birth to death. The intelligent na'au activity of *stillness* grounds our mana'o intelligence here and now.

Transforming the Chainsaw into the Sword

Meditation is essentially the formal practice of *contemplation*—that's the first event of our pentathlon. When we engage in meditation, we *deliberately practice* contemplation. We practice moving away from our noisy ego-driven chainsaw into our calm, still Zen center of the intelligence triangle. We practice this over and over again, each time our ego commentary of fear, desire, and judgment surfaces. By practicing this centering process of contemplation, our mana'o intelligence will gradually transform into the *swift and silent sword of skillful means*—intelligent presence and sharp keen awareness here and now. Sharp awareness and keen observation are powerful tools for endurance athletes. They are essential for developing efficiency, grace, and speed.

The First Step

Meditation is the formal practice of *contemplation*—it is the *first step* in the pentathlon of spiritual fitness. Perhaps this is why simple sitting meditation is the most popular and widely accepted form of practice among traditional Eastern spiritual paths. *Simple* sitting meditation is one of the subtlest and most difficult of all activities to engage in with complete presence, yet the rewards from consistent and diligent practice are profound and can be applied to every area of life.

Yoga

Yoga is a word derived from the ancient Sanskrit language. It is similar to *yoke* and it means "union." If we consider this in relation to the six branches of spiritual practice diagrammed above, then each of these branches is yogic in nature—each serves to unite two of our energetic intelligences. For the sake of clarity, we shall regard yoga as the form of practice that engages the skillful means of our mana'o intelligence to strengthen and enhance our mana and our conscious presence in our bodies. It is the practice of mind *in* matter.

Traditional forms of yoga exercise are comprised of postures or movements fused with specific breathing techniques and sometimes visual imagery. Yoga can be very simple, gentle, and relaxing, or it can be rigorous, demanding and intense. Some of the esoteric advanced forms require a great deal of training and instruction. Through some of these esoteric forms, practitioners have accomplished feats that defy our modern scientific explanations of human possibility. These extraordinary feats include the ability to voluntarily stop the heartbeat and breath for some length of time.

The common thread that links all the forms of yoga together is the use of skillful means and conscious breathing to enhance and strengthen our physical health and quality of energy—to develop and enhance the intelligence of our body and our spiritual mana strength in physical form through mind *in* matter. Does this sound familiar? Our zendurance training closely parallels yoga.

THE SERVICE AND DIET LEG

Heart and Body

Service and diet are the two traditional forms of practice paired together to link our pu'uwai (heart) intelligence of connection and integrity with our na'au (body) intelligence of activity. It's easy to see why meditation and yoga are complementary in their pairing—sometimes they are indistinguishable from one another. Breath is their medium. Service and diet may seem a bit more peculiar as a pair—the "odd couple." Do they have a common thread or medium, such as breath? Their relationship will clear up later on. Sit with this one in contemplation for now . . .

Service

Service is a key practice of many traditional spiritual paths *and* many modern cultures. Service is physical activity guided by and sourced from the heart. In the practice of service, we allow the integrative and collective intelligence of our pu'uwai to guide the intelligence of our activity. It is our physically active way of connecting and circulating with the mana life force outside our individual selves. Typically service is a pragmatic and practical activity that enhances someone else's health and quality of life, or the health and quality of life of our environment.

Value of Service

Through service, we are discovering, demonstrating and actualizing our mana integrity—our connection with all life. At its highest resonance, service requires no recognition or reward. Through the intelligence of our pu'uwai, we clearly experience our inextricable mana connection and integration with *all* life. When we serve others, we are simply serving *ourself*—our shared intelligence of integrity. Through sincere service, we experience not only the giving but the receiving as well.

Service is the vital and essential practice of putting our connective intelligence into tangible physical form. Without service, our activities are generated only from our skillful means of distinction and isolation. In this scenario, our connective pu'uwai intelligence fades in our physical reality. We become lonely and isolated—no matter how many people we surround ourselves with.

Acts of Service

Service is practiced within the traditional spiritual community through activities like the day-to-day chores of cleaning, cooking, gardening, and maintenance; and through teaching, counseling, and assisting others. As a traditional practice, charitable acts of service may also be performed outside the spiritual community. Many of our modern-day relief funds, charitable organizations and nonprofit foundations are established to provide service to others. In their purest form, these charitable acts do not require that the recipients join up or subscribe to the programs or tenets of the organization. These acts of charity are performed in recognition and acknowledgment that we are all one integrated community of life with myriad unique connections to our shared energetic intelligences and mana.

Diet

Many traditional spiritual paths adhere to some kind of dietary guidelines—ranging from simple, bland foods to extravagant feasts. As endurance athletes, we are well aware of the beneficial or detrimental consequences that our diet can have on our physical and mental health. Our well-tuned bodies are often quick to respond to dietary changes—providing accurate and immediate feedback. What we eat affects our mental and emotional health as much as our physical health. As the old adage goes, "We are what we eat."

Sharing

In many traditional spiritual communities, preparing and sharing food is an important focal activity of the community as a whole. Sharing food is one of the most basic bonding and communal activities throughout our human evolution. If *service* is how we engage our bodies to nurture and connect with our surrounding universe, then it is through *diet* that we complete the cycle as we nurture our bodies from our surrounding universe. Both service and diet are practices of integrating and circulating with our universal life energy—our mana. Simply put, service and diet are the formal practices of *giving* and *receiving*.

Feeling Left Out

This practice leg of our triangle links together and engages our pu'uwai (heart) and na'au (body) intelligences. Our mana'o intelligence may question the value and validity of altruistic service and healthy diet, since it is somewhat excluded from this practice leg. The discipline to practice service and diet requires a clear vision and commitment sourced from the Zen center of our intelligence triangle. Likewise, when we are engaged in the solitude of yoga and meditation—directly linking mana'o and na'au intelligences—our excluded pu'uwai may yearn to break the solitude and head for the nearest party to celebrate our connectivity. Here again, the key to our discipline is clear vision and commitment held at the Zen center of the intelligence triangle.

THE PRAYER AND DEVOTION LEG

Heart and Mind

This is the pair of practices that connect our pu'uwai (heart) and mana'o (mind) intelligences. Of the three practice legs of our triangle, this one does not directly challenge or engage our na'au intelligence of activity—so it is the pair of practices that seem to be the most immaterial and nonphysical. With the absence of na'au, these practices appear to have the least amount of bearing on our physical here-and-now existence. For those of us who are activity oriented, who are pragmatic realists, this pair of practices may appear even superstitious.

In our modern cultures, prayer and devotion are often the focal practices of our organized religious programs or services. How do prayer and devotion function to integrate our pu'uwai with our mana'o? What are the dynamics of prayer and devotion in the energetic intelligence triangle? If *breath* is the thread that connects our mind and body together—providing our mana'o-to-na'au connection—what is the thread that connects our mind and heart together—providing our mana'o-to-pu'uwai connection? These are more questions for us to sit with and contemplate for now.

Approach

In our discussions so far, the words *prayer* and *devotion* have briefly surfaced in association with *approach*. We looked at offering a prayer or devoting our training session or race as a way of *bowing*—of humbly approaching our endurance athletics and effectively transforming our quest into a practice of zendurance. We have examined how our approach to each training session, each task, circumstance, and relationship, can determine the quality of our experiences and the clarity and success of our intentions.

With prayer and devotion we can transform each moment into a precious opportunity to practice spiritual fitness and tap into effortless power. *Prayer and devotion are the formal and deliberate practices of approach.* Now we begin to see how valid and powerful these practices can be. Even without directly engaging the na'au intelligence of activity, prayer and devotion can have a strong bearing on the quality and outcome of our physical activities.

Prayer

Through prayer, we allow our loving pu'uwai heart connection with all life to operate and to speak through the voice of our skillful means. Our mana'o intelligence becomes an expressive instrument for our intelligence of integrity.

In traditional spiritual paths, prayer forms are as diverse and unique as are forms of yoga and meditation. There are prayer vigils where people congregate and pray silently—a collective of quiet individual voices. The Native American sweat lodge ceremony blends prayer and singing with the fire of purification. In churches and temples people pray and sing hymns collectively from prayer books and hymnals.

Speaking with Our Heart

In all its myriad forms—from individual to mass congregation—prayer is founded in our pu'uwai collective awareness and intelligence. Pu'uwai thinks and speaks of our loving mana connection with others. If service is the practice that connects and integrates us with others through our *activities*, then prayer is the practice that connects us with others through our *thoughts* and *speech*. *The Heart's Code* offers scientific validity even to prayer. Our thoughts and attitudes—how we hold and regard each moment and each other—largely determines the quality of our experiences and our relationships. It's all in the approach! Prayer offers us the opportunity to make our approach more deliberate and articulate.

Who Hears Our Prayers?

For those of us who are unaccustomed to prayer, we may ask, *What or whom do we pray to?* Our concern for an audience is not necessary. Pu'uwai is a collective intelligence—a living network, beyond our individuality. Pu'uwai keeps us continually connected to an infinite audience. As a practice, we need only focus on giving voice to our heart in order to articulate our approach through the intelligence of connection. Our heart always knows to whom or to what we must direct our prayers.

Devotion

Often we associate devotion with loyalty. If two people remain married for a lifetime, they are devoted to one another. What is it in loyalty and devotion that keeps these two together—sheer luck? A lifetime marriage is a test of true commitment and discipline. To what are they committed? What are they loyal and devoted to? In traditional spiritual paths, our devotion can be for a saint, a prophet, a deity, or a teacher. Like a true and lasting marriage, this may also be lifetime devotion.

Honorable Qualities

In a spiritual context, we devote ourselves to the *honorable* qualities we perceive in others. These are qualities that reveal *spiritual fitness*—qualities such as humility, kindness, tolerance, integrity, forgiveness, generosity, patience, brilliance, and grace. (What honorable qualities are you devoted to?) These qualities of spiritual fitness are unique abilities derived from the brilliant and effective integration of our three energetic intelligences. *Devotion is the practice of assimilating and integrating these honorable qualities into our own spiritual fitness.*

Devotion—Our Metaphysical Diet

Devotion is similar to diet. Both are practices of assimilating and integrating with the world around us—diet physically and devotion metaphysically. We know that a diet of healthy, whole foods results in a foundation of good physical health and well-being. Likewise, conscientious and deliberate devotion to honorable and beneficial qualities results in good mental and emotional health and well-being. Devotion *does* also enhance our physical health, just as diet enhances our mental and emotional health.

The qualities we choose to devote ourselves to may be qualities we recognize in our spouses, parents, or children, in our friends, teachers, coworkers, athletic mentors, strangers, our ancestors, notable people in history, entertainers, holy people, prophets—even our pets.

Discernment

Devotion goes beyond our attraction to certain qualities—beyond our egoic judgments of good or bad. We may find certain people annoying because they respond to situations and to people differently than we do. From our Zen center of the intelligence triangle, we can wisely discern between ego-charged qualities—those that attract or repel our ego—and honorable qualities—those that truly originate in and express spiritual fitness. Devotion requires discernment, just as diet does.

Devotion is the practice of recognizing, honoring, and nurturing these honorable qualities in ourselves and in others. *Just as equally*, devotion is the practice of recognizing, honoring and nurturing those qualities in ourselves and others *even when they are latent and obscured by their opposites*—fear, ignorance, and greed, for instance. This level of devotion is far more challenging to our spiritual fitness. It is not to be confused with attempting to change or reprogram someone else with "my way." This is the kind of devotion that lifetime marriages are made of. This high level of practice is ultimately a devotion to *tolerance and compassion*. It is a diligent practice of approaching each moment, each person as a reflection of our own being.

SUMMARY

Six Unique Paths

Very briefly we have considered the six general branches of traditional practice and how each one develops leg strength in our intelligence triangle. Each branch of practice functions in a unique way to integrate our energetic intelligences and to strengthen our triangle. Each one of these branches of practice is like a unique path in the metaphysical landscape between two of our energetic intelligence springs—those natural flowing sources of wisdom. There are hundreds, if not thousands, of books about the specialized practices within these branches. In these few pages, our focus has simply been to explore their functions in developing the leg strength for our spiritual fitness.

The Endurance Training Question

Now that we have considered all six branches of traditional spiritual practice—paired up to comprise the three legs of our intelligence triangle—how does our endurance training relate to these six traditional types—meditation, yoga, service, diet, prayer and devotion?

It is easy to see the similarity of zendurance to *yoga*—our union of body and mind with conscious breath, keen observation and graceful movement. Transforming our athletic training into zendurance practice first begins with contemplation, with moving to our Zen center. So our endurance training is initially transformed into zendurance when it becomes moving *meditation*.

Through skillful endurance training, we maintain our health and enhance the quality of our own lives and those around us. Many of our races raise money and awareness for charitable causes, especially diseases. Here is a great opportunity to serve others through our vibrant health. Even the inspiration others receive from our healthy endeavors and accomplishments is a *service*. And did someone say *diet*? Healthy diet and healthy endurance training are one of those lifetime marriages.

Many of us pause to *pray* and to dedicate or to offer our training session or race to others, as we carry our thoughts and love for them throughout our activity. We may also pray for guidance, strength, and safekeeping. Prayer is a pause to allow the heart to speak. Many of the world's greatest races include a moment of prayer before the start. Finally, as a discipline, our zendurance training and racing is a *devotion* to the honorable qualities of health, diligence, honesty, discipline, patience, grace, and more.

Balancing Our Practice

Each traditional form of spiritual practice focuses on exercising and integrating two of our energetic intelligences. Each unique branch of practice uses the nature or essence of one form of intelligence to strengthen and expand the other. Often, when we really enjoy a specific type of practice, we will conduct that single form of practice to the virtual exclusion of any other form. This can certainly be the case with our endurance training as a form of practice.

This diligent, singular focus may eventually lead to great achievements, recognition, and to a profound, ecstatic moment of clarity and enlightenment—of "Aha!" In this precious moment—known as *satori* in various forms of Buddhism—we briefly and vividly experience a very clear and brilliant glimpse of our true, infinite, boundless, and powerful nature; our infinite spiritual fitness.

This is a valuable and astonishing discovery—the ecstasy so to speak.

After this ecstasy, we are left with the laundry—the practicality of *integrating* this truly infinite, boundless, and powerful spirit nature into our day-to-day existence as healthy and ordinary human beings. *Integration* is the fourth event of our Zen pentathlon. Now that we have a clearer sense of how the third event, *practice*, functions as the leg strength of our intelligence and spiritual fitness, we can return to the Zen pentathlon, for *integration*, the most challenging event—the big one.

ZEN PENTATHLON
INTEGRATION: THE MAIN EVENT

Short-Term Enlightenment—Quality Athletics

As endurance athletes, most of us have experienced those unforgettable moments of ecstasy as we cross the finish line of a significant goal race. It is not just the supreme satisfaction of our physical accomplishments that make these experiences so powerful and life changing. It is also the clarity of our awareness and the *tangible* spirit presence that we feel deep inside ourselves and in those around us. We feel a deep and heartfelt gratitude for this tangible loving spirit connection with all life.

This enlightening moment of finish-line satori—in which all the pieces of our lives fit together to reveal a clear overall picture and balance—can have a lasting and transforming impact on our lives. We are often so inspired that we immediately return to our endurance training with an even greater level of commitment, passion, and enthusiasm, ready to take it to the next level of mastery.

For a time, this growing intensity of passion and focus in our endurance athletics—even to the exclusion of other areas of our lives—may bring great insight, joy, and supreme satisfaction. Eventually and inevitably, each of us will begin to experience an imbalance. We may become skillful enough to transform our athletic training into pure zendurance and effortless power so that we become successful world-class iron-distance triathletes. However, if our masterful approach and practice of zendurance excludes our family, community, and loved ones, or compromises our overall health, our spiritual intelligence and fitness, then we may begin to experience a deep and undeniable emptiness, despair and longing.

Long-Term Enlightenment—Quality of Life

If we truly intend to take it to the next level and live the zendurance life of spiritual fitness and effortless power, then we must *integrate* the zendurance approach and practice of our athletic training with our day-to-day lives as human beings. Zendurance requires that we exercise and strengthen, balance and coordinate *all three* of our energetic intelligences in order to develop true spiritual fitness. In our quest so far, we have focused on using our athletic training to develop our zendurance skills of yielding, blending, and aligning and to gain experience in the first three events of the Zen pentathlon—contemplation, approach, and practice. Now it is time to begin the fourth event of the Zen pentathlon—*integration*. This is the real challenge for spiritual fitness.

As we gain spiritual fitness in each and every moment and circumstance of our lives, we begin to significantly enhance the quality of our lives *and* those around us. Through Event 4—*integration*—we expand our ability to remain steadfast in our calm, still silent, open, and empty Zen center to include each moment of our mundane and ordinary lives. The open and mindful presence and the graceful skills of yielding, blending, and aligning that we have discovered and developed through our zendurance athletic training become even more tangible and familiar as we integrate them into our daily lives.

Honest Assessment

Let's examine some of the ways that we can *approach* the activity of integration—which is the realization of *true* zendurance. We must begin by taking an honest look at our lives as a whole—as complete human beings. Is your family life as rich and rewarding as your athletic endeavors? Do you derive real satisfaction in your work? Does your overall lifestyle follow the same healthy guidelines as your endurance training program—with the same awareness and management of stress?

Is your social circle supportive and appreciative of your quest to integrate a Zen approach to life? (Remember that your most intimate and cherished friends and family need not be as aerobically fit and as avidly ambitious of endurance athletics as you are in order to be supportive and instrumental in your endeavor to live the zendurance life.) Begin to notice how those around you intelligently integrate spiritual fitness and effortless power into *their* lives—regardless of whether they are athletically inclined or not.

Devote yourself to those around you. What can each individual teach you in her or his unique approach to the circumstances of day-to-day life? How does each individual relate to and embrace situations and circumstances differently than you? How does each individual uniquely engage and integrate the three energetic intelligences of mana'o, pu'uwai, and na'au? Our closest relations serve as our best teachers.

Just as each and every moment of our athletic training sessions is a valuable opportunity to develop aerobic fitness, each and every moment of our daily lives presents us with a unique and infinite opportunity to cultivate spiritual fitness. In your day-to-day life, begin to be attentive and mindful to these opportunities *as they arise each moment.* This is an incredibly challenging practice. Begin by honestly assessing your individual relationship, familiarity, and fluency with each of your three energetic intelligences. The situations that appear most difficult—the ones we resist the most—will require us to engage the intelligence we are least familiar and connected with.

Assisting others with patience and sincerity, regardless of any reward, requires clear and ready access to the connective heart intelligence. From our calm, still Zen center we can access and engage the crystalline waters of our pu'uwai intelligence so that we can circulate and integrate with all life around us.

Another scenario that can challenge our spiritual fitness is when we are experiencing mental stress and agitation—especially in those situations when we feel overwhelmed, where our ego mind is absolutely convinced that we are the victim, that the world is screwing us over. Being clearheaded—with the ability to accurately distinguish between what is true and what is actually our own resistance, our own judgments, and our own reactions to the truth—requires that we move to our calm, silent Zen center.

From our calm Zen center of the intelligence triangle, we can allow the waters of our mana'o intelligence to distill and purify. When these waters are clear and pristine, then our observations are keen and our communication is clear. We can approach each and every moment of our lives—even the most difficult ones—with our skills of yielding, blending, and aligning, as a unique and infinite opportunity to cultivate and develop spiritual fitness.

These are just two simple illustrations of how the ability to effectively shift our predominance among our three energetic intelligences from our Zen center can greatly empower our lives in each moment. This fluid transition among our intelligences is most enabled when we abide in the Zen center of our triangle.

Welcome the Challenges

Make a conscious choice to gravitate toward and attend to those areas of your life that are the most difficult and challenging. As experienced endurance athletes, we are already aware of the value and benefit that can be realized by using training techniques to address the weakest aspects of our athletic abilities. Our weaknesses offer us the greatest potential and opportunity for growth and improvement. If we focus only on our strongest abilities and avoid our weaknesses, we limit and narrow our potential as athletes and as human beings.

Transition

One way of viewing the integration and smooth transition among mana'o, pu'uwai and na'au intelligences is to compare it to transitioning among swimming, biking, and running. Flowing gracefully, effortlessly and swiftly from one activity to another is a very valuable and highly regarded skill in triathlon. Likewise the ability to transition among our three energetic intelligences gracefully, effortlessly and swiftly is a very valuable and highly regarded skill—one that we have endless opportunities to practice each and every day.

As triathletes, we diligently train in all three activities. Each of us is unique in our strengths and weaknesses, our likes and dislikes, and our familiarity with swimming, biking, and running. This is also true for each of us regarding our unique strengths and weaknesses, our likes and dislikes, and familiarity with our energetic intelligences of skillful means, integrity, and activity. Just as we consciously balance our athletic competence among all three endurance activities, we must consciously balance our spiritual competence among all three energetic intelligences.

Triangular Training

In his book *The Triathlete's Training Bible* Joe Friel has developed a "triangular" training system for triathlon fitness that is similar to the triangular training system we are developing for spiritual fitness. In chapter 6, "Building Fitness," Joe presents six elements of triathlon fitness: endurance, force, speed, muscular endurance, anaerobic endurance, and power. These six elements are wisely considered in developing training programs for three sports—constituting overall triathlon fitness. Likewise, we wisely consider *all six* forms of spiritual practice for our three energetic intelligences to develop our overall spiritual fitness. We can be just as intelligent, skillful, and creative in conducting our spiritual fitness training as we are in conducting our triathlon fitness training.

A well-designed triathlon training program is an effective tool that can enable us to produce remarkable results with the least amount of time and energy. The most effective strategy in training is to maintain and enhance our strengths while we focus on improving our weaknesses.

No Juggling Required

Our intention in HeartCore Zendurance is very similar—to implement a spiritual fitness training program that will enable us to produce remarkable results with the least amount of time and energy. As with our optimal endurance fitness program, we want to maintain and enhance our strengths while we focus on our weaknesses. Our strategy in HeartCore Zendurance is simply to transform our ordinary daily activities and obligations into spiritual practice—just as we transform our ordinary daily athletic training into the practice of zendurance. HeartCore Zendurance is *not* about taking on more activities or practices in life. It is *not* about increasing our time commitments or workloads. This is *not* a juggling act. HeartCore is about transforming the *quality* of our daily lives as they are right now.

We are already initiating the first step of this HeartCore Zendurance quest—by transforming our athletic training into zendurance. On the surface, our athletic training looks just about the same as it did before. We have not increased our athletic training load in order to practice zendurance. It is not necessary for us to train at higher intensity levels or for longer duration in order to transform our training into zendurance. This transformation happens one moment at a time, through our clear and conscious intent and *approach* to athletic training. It all starts with the clear awareness of contemplation.

Likewise, much of our success with integrating spiritual fitness training into our daily lives—through the practice of HeartCore Zendurance—has to do with diligently following the steps of the Zen pentathlon—contribution, approach, and practice—in each experience, in each moment of our ordinary lives. We begin this whole process by consciously moving to the Zen center of our intelligence triangle.

Let's look now a little more into the six forms of practice and how we can *integrate* them into of our daily lives as a path toward spiritual fitness without adding any more balls to the juggling act. This process of *integration* is the fourth event of our Zen pentathlon, and it is the most significant event—the big one. This is the one that ties it all together—that makes us complete, happy, healthy, and balanced human beings.

HEARTCORE INTEGRATION: FIRST LEG

MEDITATION

The Gateway

Contemplation is the *only* gateway for transforming our athletic training into zendurance practice and for transforming the experiences of our daily lives into the practice of HeartCore Zendurance. We must begin with contemplation.

Sitting daily in meditation for at least twenty minutes is the most effective and direct practice of contemplation. We sit with the deliberate and clear intention to relax and release that ego grip on our mana'o intelligence and to return home to our Zen center of awareness and deep inner listening. From this Zen center, we can ask the most basic and powerful questions: *What is the nature, the essence of these thoughts? What is the nature, the essence of these physical sensations? What is the nature, the essence of these emotional feelings? Where do these thoughts, sensations, and feelings originate from? Who is perceiving them? Who am I really?*

In meditation, we sit *with* these questions; we contemplate them and investigate them with genuine curiosity, patience, and inquisitiveness. What makes these questions so powerful is not the answers we might construct. These questions are powerful in the way that they open us up and expand our awareness. To sit in contemplation and to be present with such questions requires great skill in concentrating and steadying our awareness—our ability to *witness*.

As we train and strengthen our attention, it begins to shine like a laser from our calm, still, silent, open, and empty Zen center. The skills we acquire through meditation enable us to then direct this laserlike attention to each moment of our everyday lives, including our endurance training. Through the strength of our Zen centered attention, we can begin to engage all three of our energetic intelligences and skillfully navigate through our lives—rather than being swept away by the powerful currents of our thoughts, our bodily sensations, and our emotional feelings.

Meditation and Stretching

Here is an analogy that illustrates how our athletic performance
and the quality of our daily experiences can improve through sitting meditation: In "What is Feel?" we looked at the value of *stretching* and how it improves our muscular and neurological efficiency.
When we approach stretching calmly and breathe consciously, we
distill and enhance each muscle cell's memory of home—of that
state of rest and relaxation. Consistent and regular stretching facilitates each muscle cell's ability to quickly, easily, and naturally
return home—even for a brief moment. Overall, both in our
endurance activities and in our daily lives, our bodies are more
open, at ease, and relaxed.

On a biological level, we can consider traditional meditation to
be a similar stretching process for the brain cells. Through meditation, we strengthen and enhance each brain cell's memory of
home—that state of rest and relaxation. We breathe consciously
and let go of our thoughts, just as we breathe consciously and
release muscular tensions through stretching. As thoughts arise in
our consciousness, we release our hold, our attachment to them—
we return to our Zen center of the triangle—to here and now. We
return to our conscious and centered breathing and our brain cells
return to home. Just as we experience greater efficiency in our
endurance training through relaxed movement and minimal resistance, we also realize greater efficiency and clarity in our consciousness through relaxed and open awareness and minimal
resistance in our thought.

This brain cell memory of home happens as we let go of the noisy
ego chainsaw and move to the Zen center of our intelligence triangle. From our Zen center home, we are no longer taken and possessed by the ego-derived manipulations of our mana'o intelligence. In each moment, we simply disengage and return home.
The true home for both our muscle cells and our brain cells *is* our
Zen center. *Meditation is contemplation*, the pure practice of moving to the Zen center.

I encourage you to seek out formal instruction for sitting meditation. It is also essential to have a clear sense of the purpose for
meditation—why we choose to meditate and our intention in
doing so. We have only briefly touched upon these issues. There
are several books that provide excellent guidance for the practice
of meditation.

Basic Insight Meditation Technique

Here is a very basic format you may wish to start with. Most of the basic instructions presented here are derived from *Seeking the Heart of Wisdom: The Path of Insight Meditation,* by Joseph Goldstein and Jack Kornfield. Sit upright in a chair or preferably sit on a mat on the floor with your legs crossed. If you choose to sit cross-legged, place a firm cushion or pillow under your buttocks. This will help keep your lower spine aligned by tilting your pelvis slightly forward and prevent you from slouching. Place your tongue up on the gum line behind your front teeth. Rest your hands on your knees with the palms up and fingers relaxed or place them in your lap with your fingers laced together.

With your eyes closed, bring your awareness to the base of your spine and slowly move your feeling consciousness up your spine to the top of your head. Feel your spine lengthen and align. Quiet your thoughts so that you can feel your whole spine as one *feeling,* as one energetic intelligence. Your awareness and your alignment are one and the same.

Now you can reverse the direction of your feeling consciousness. Begin at your crown chakra. Open and activate your spine's core intelligence, passing through each chakra center. Use your slow deep breath as a *vehicle* for your directed awareness and fill your body from head to toe with your breath awareness. Be patient and take your time. With consistent practice you will eventually be able to move through and fill your body in just a minute or so. When you have completed this process, the mental monologue should have subsided—thanks to the immediate presence of the body and breath, which helps to bring the mana'o into the *now.*

Breathe

Relax the focus of your closed or half-opened eyes and attentively follow each inhale and each exhale, no longer using your breath as a vehicle to specifically navigate through the body. As you inhale, feel your abdomen expand slightly. Then, as the inhalation rises, feel your chest expand and rise. As you exhale, feel your upper chest fall and your abdomen contract slightly. *Allow* your breath to find a relaxed, calm rhythm.

Train every ounce of your clear and concentrated attention on the sensations and feeling of each inhale and each exhale. Be completely and clearly present with the *feel* of your breath in your body—in either your abdomen, your chest, or your nose. Follow your breath continuously. Your intention here is not to breathe perfectly—it is to thoroughly witness the breath happening in each moment.

Drifting Away, Returning Home

Inevitably your attention will gradually drift or abruptly shift to something else—a bodily sensation, a sound, thought, image, emotion, or mind state. When you become aware of this shift, simply observe and note where your attention has shifted and be just as thoroughly present with that occurrence. Bring every ounce of your clear attention to this new occurrence—absorbing it completely, without analysis. This practice is one of gentle receptivity—always settling back to the Zen center of our intelligence triangle. Be curious and inquisitive; yet refrain from judgment, commentary, interpretation, analysis, or evaluation. True attention occurs from a ground of inner silence.

When this new occurrence has passed, return your attention to your breath again. During this practice of meditation, you may realized that your clear attention has disappeared—that you have temporarily been swept away into the sensation, the sound, thought, image, emotion, or mind state. Simply notice the distinction between focused attention and unconscious wandering. Without any self-criticism or judgment, gently return to that state of soft, open observation—to the Zen center—and begin again to train your clear and concentrated awareness on your breath.

Five Hindrances

There are five hindrances to meditation: desire, aversion, sleepiness, restlessness, and doubt. It is very easy to get lost in one of these five mind states. These five hindrances will pull us most strongly away from our Zen center or prevent us from moving there. The sooner we recognize and *witness* them during our meditation, the less powerful they will be and the sooner we will return to our Zen center.

Staying Present at Home

Our intention in the practice of insight meditation is not to accomplish anything—it is not to reach some significant elevated state of awareness, or to make anything special happen. Insight meditation is a simple practice of being absolutely present with what is actually happening in the moment *without* trying to control it. It is the constant and seamless practice of returning to and abiding at the source of our awareness at each moment—the calm, still, silent, open, and empty Zen center of our intelligence triangle.

Transition Meditation Exercise

Here is a simple meditative exercise to improve our tangible access to our three energetic intelligences. This exercise is *not* a substitute for traditional insight meditation, as outlined above. You can try this simple exercise for a few minutes or more at the conclusion of your insight meditation practice.

Bring your feeling awareness to your mana'o intelligence center—located at the third-eye chakra—and begin to hear the sound *mana'o* as you inhale—a long, drawn-out *maaah-naaah-oohh.* Allow the sound to fill, to clear and expand your mana'o intelligence. As you exhale, hear the mantra in the same long, slow way. From your Zen center, use the breath and the mantra to access and connect with your mana'o intelligence. Fill your third eye chakra with light consciousness—as though you were cleaning and polishing it.

Spend a few minutes here and then transition to your pu'uwai intelligence center—located at the heart chakra. Access and connect with this energetic intelligence as you slowly breathe and sound *pu'uwai—puuu-uuu-vaiii* at the heart center. Clean and polish your pu'uwai center with light consciousness, using your breath and mantra. Repeat this same process for your na'au intelligence—located at your pelvic second chakra—sounding *naaah-auuw.*

Throughout this exercise, use your sense of *feeling*—really locate precisely and feel each energetic center. Feel the mantra, the breath, and the light consciousness within each center. You may notice that your eyes focus on different points as you connect with each—even though they are closed. Allow your eyes to find these points naturally.

This exercise can help improve our access to each energetic intelligence from the Zen center by increasing the *tangibility* of each one. One of the most powerful techniques throughout our zendurance quest is that of increasing our *tangibility*—our sensitivity to the metaphysical levels of awareness and existence.

We can call this exercise a transition meditation. It can be instrumental in improving our transitional skills among our energetic intelligences. During those moments of our lives when things are falling apart, we might actually remember to pause, to discern which energetic intelligence we need clear access to at that moment, and to successfully execute the transition and access. In that moment, we can use our breath and the respective mantra. This process might help us become "tri-spiritualists."

Practical Applications

Through our insight meditation, we are developing the skills of concentration and steadying our awareness. Eventually we will be proficient enough to consciously apply these skills during even the difficult moments of our lives. We will be able to return to the Zen center of our intelligence triangle and ask those most powerful questions: *What is the nature, the essence of these physical sensations, thoughts and emotions? Where are they coming from? Who is perceiving them? Who am I really?* This is indeed the very first step toward effortless power—the ability to *witness* what is happening in the present moment without judgment, commentary, evaluation, or the compulsion to change anything.

Building a Base

As with endurance training, a consistent and gradual base building of insight meditation practice will yield the best results. By including a daily sitting practice, our zendurance training and racing will become more clear and vivid as moving meditation. We will adapt the same calm, centered, and still state of contemplation and the skill of witnessing in our daily lives. We begin to familiarize ourselves with the energetic landscape of contemplative witnessing. We start to gradually access and engage all three energetic intelligences in a conscious and articulate manner. Through traditional sitting meditation and zendurance training, we find ourselves progressively calmer in our day-to-day lives.

Did I Keep My Promise?

Just a short while ago, I promised that we would not increase our time commitments and activities. Already now I am suggesting that we add twenty minutes or more of sitting meditation. Is this a contradiction? Twenty minutes of sitting meditation is infinitely more beneficial than twenty minutes of TV time. (My all-time favorite bumper sticker says, KILL YOUR TELEVISION.) The benefits we can realize from this practice will more than make up for the loss of sleep time if giving up TV time is not a plausible alternative.

The Essential Gateway

How essential is meditation to zendurance? The word *Zen* is the Japanese pronunciation of the Chinese word *ch'an* which is the Chinese pronunciation of the Sanskrit word *dhyana*. Guess what *dhyana* means? *Meditation!*

YOGA

Pure and Simple

Our zendurance approach to athletic training provides us with experience that is similar to yoga, although not in a traditional context. Traditional forms of yoga focus on enhancing and strengthening our mana life force through specific physical exercises combined with conscious breathing techniques. This is similar to our zendurance approach to aerobic training. Unlike our endurance training, however, traditional yoga is not cluttered with the agendas of training schedules, mileage quotas, performance goals, and *pursuits of the ego*. In traditional yoga, there is no competition, and no distractions—simply the union of breath and body for the sake of mind *in* matter.

The experience we gain from traditional yoga, tai chi, or stretching—the intimate union of body and mind—can really help us refine and develop our Zen approach to endurance training. This experience endows us with the discernment to recognize our ego's attempts of mind *over* matter and gives us the ability to return to the spiritual fitness of mind *in* matter.

It is worthwhile to learn at least an introductory form of traditional yoga from a qualified teacher. Practicing a traditional form of yoga can substantially increase our ability to stay Zen centered, to feel relaxed, calm, and present *in our bodies* during our endurance training *and* in our daily lives. As mentioned in "What is Feel?" this ability is essential for clearing our nerve-muscle memories. With even a basic level of instruction and some self-discipline (clear vision), we can easily maintain a twice-weekly practice of relaxed, yogic breathing and stretching on our own or—even better—with a group of friends.

Go Easy

Hatha yoga is an ideal traditional yoga form that combines relaxed, deep breathing with slow and gentle stretching through *asanas*—postures we assume for a minute or so. These *asanas* are usually practiced in a particular sequence that facilitates our union of body and mind—na'au and mana'o—through progressively deeper levels of relaxation using conscious, articulated breathing. This peaceful approach highly complements our zendurance approach to athletic training.

For those of us who maintain a challenging and demanding athletic training schedule, the more rigorous forms of yoga—such as Ashtanga—may be too much of the same thing. Initially, our emphasis is better placed on the gentler forms of yoga that promote deep relaxation through breathing and stretching. Our purpose is to use our breath to gently draw our consciousness into our bodies. This process of feeling our conscious breath in our bodies is the primary technique of mind *in* matter. Conscious breath in harmony with relaxed and graceful movement is the essence of transforming our athletic training into zendurance. In view of this intimate connection of breath and movement, even the casual study and practice of a traditional form of yoga can strengthen and advance our skills.

HEARTCORE INTEGRATION: SECOND LEG

RELATIONSHIPS

Giving and Receiving

The complementary nature and relationship between yoga and meditation is easy to see. On the surface, diet and service don't appear to have that much in common, yet they are paired together as the practice leg that links our pu'uwai and na'au intelligences. If we regard *service* as "giving" and *diet* as "receiving," they become inseparable—a complete cycle. When we serve, we are giving. When we eat, we are receiving in the most basic way. The very first thing we each do as infants is to suckle—receive milk. From there we can expand our diet to include not just food but also clothing, shelter, advice, knowledge, inspiration—all those things we receive and consume, both material and immaterial.

Family—A True Practice of Service and Diet

In our daily lives, *family* is the most immediate, familiar, and intimate practice of service and diet—of giving and receiving. This function of giving and receiving expands outward to include community. Family and community provide our most immediate day-to-day opportunities to engage in the traditional spiritual practices of service and diet—of giving and receiving. Instead of unconsciously going through the motions of "having" a family, we can begin to consciously engage all three of our energetic intelligences in the *practice* of family. Rather than "belonging" to a community, we can begin to *practice* community.

We can be just as deliberate, just as brilliant and creative in our practice of family and community as we are in our practice of zendurance. We have learned to deliberately and intentionally approach our endurance training as a practice toward spiritual fitness and effortless power. Now we can start to deliberately approach our relationships with family and community as opportunities to practice spiritual fitness and effortless power. In our Zen pentathlon, intentional *approach*—the second event—is the step that can transform *any* of our activities into a practice of spiritual fitness and effortless power.

Occupation

In our global culture, money has become our most common and widely accepted material means of "accounting" for wealth and for the balance of giving and receiving—although there are certainly other means as well. We invest much of our time and energy into this monetary system of accounting for wealth through our jobs and occupations. Herein lies another powerful opportunity to consciously and deliberately practice giving and receiving. Again, instead of having an occupation, we are endowed with a formal commitment of time and responsibility to *practice* occupation. After all, most of our jobs are considered to be in the service industry. *The Diamond Cutter,* a book by Geshe Michael Roach, is an excellent guide to the spiritual practice of occupation.

What is the common element among family, community, and occupation? *Relationship.* Our relationships with one another—and with all forms of life—constitute our primary arena for service and diet—for giving and receiving. Returning to an earlier question: If the common element between yoga and meditation is *breath,* what is the common element between service and diet? The *interaction of relationship* is the medium for integrating our pu'uwai intelligence of circulation and integrity with our na'au intelligence of activity. The practice of service and diet—of giving and receiving—includes sharing material wealth as well as experience, skills and abilities, wisdom, insight, and love. We each share our own unique blending and integration of all three energetic intelligences.

THE INCREDIBLE POWER OF IMPRINTS

The Cosmic Mirror

Let's look a little deeper into the interaction of relationship as an opportunity for spiritual fitness. In the very beginning of this book, we considered a principal tenet of many spiritual paths: Our *outer* universe reflects and mirrors what is true of our *inner* universe. Our universe operates from the inside outward.

It can be quite difficult to grasp and to accept responsibility for this inside-to-outside flow of our universe in our interactions and relationships with one another. When we are experiencing frustration, anger, exasperation, or the like in our relationship with someone else, it is easy to convince ourselves that the source of resistance and negativity is not within *us*—that it is most certainly coming from the other person. Let's take a moment to examine how it is that we actually *create* our universe and how this is based on the *mental imprints* we ourselves generate, as explained by author Michael Roach.

Mental Imprints—Ancient Tibetan Wisdom

Michael Roach was born and raised in the United States. In addition to graduating from Princeton University with honors, he was the first American to complete a twenty-year study of Tibetan Buddhism and receive the ancient degree of "*Geshe*"—master of Buddhism. In 1981 he helped start Andin International Diamond Corporation. What started with a capital outlay of fifty thousand dollars has today exceeded annual sales of over one hundred million. Michael's conscientious spiritual practice of business is firmly rooted in Buddhist wisdom based on the ancient Tibetan texts.

Throughout his book *The Diamond Cutter*, he speaks of imprints that we plant in our minds through each thought, word, and action. These imprints are like seeds that we would plant in a garden. Once these imprints are planted in our *subconscious* mind—as a result of our thoughts, words, and actions—they germinate, take root, grow, and strengthen. We can associate our subconscious mind with the soil in a garden. Like the seeds we plant in a garden, the imprints planted in our subconscious remain hidden beneath the surface until they break through and emerge sometime later. The imprints we plant in our subconscious minds—through our thoughts, words and actions—surface and play back to us through the universe around us when a similar situation arises.

This imprinting phenomenon is the underlying operating process of our cosmic mirror—it is how and why our outer universe can accurately reflect our inner universe. Imprinting demonstrates the mechanics of this inside-to-outside flow—also known as the Law Of Karma.

Roach illustrates this powerful operating principle with his experiences in the diamond business. He has determined that the real cause of a business failure is the accumulated effect from many seemingly insignificant thoughts, words and actions. As an example, these can include small, deliberately inaccurate communications—those little white lies—and negative emotionally charged actions—selfishness and stinginess, for example—sourced from our fears, as well as anger and impatience.

Taking Care of Our Garden

Michael emphasizes that this imprinting phenomenon is a functional and operating dynamic of consciousness—*beyond our issues of judgment and morality.* The seeds we plant in the garden of our consciousness determine what we will harvest through our experiences in the future. If we recklessly and indiscriminately broadcast weed seeds through negative thoughts, words, and actions; then, in time, weeds will grow in our consciousness garden and emerge or flower through our outer universe.

On the other hand, if we carefully choose and plant our imprint seeds—through our positive and constructive thoughts, words and actions—with patience, diligence, and deliberate intention, then we will experience a diverse, well-balanced, and nourishing harvest in our lives as these imprints flower in our consciousness and emerge through our outer universe.

This principle of planting imprints in our consciousness—the principle of karma—clearly demonstrates how it is that each one of us *creates* our universe from the inside out. This is not a fairy tale, it is based on *cognitive truths* derived from the experiences and wisdom of great spiritual masters of many faiths who have investigated and applied this principle for more than twenty-five hundred years.

When we consciously embrace and adhere to this principle of imprinting, we can profoundly transform and empower our relationship and integration with the universe around us. We can begin to experience the universe as our garden—as the present moment garden where we are harvesting the results of imprint seeds we planted in the past.

Athletic Illustration

In our quest toward mastery as endurance athletes and as human beings—toward athletic and spiritual fitness and the path of effortless power—it is essential that we constantly observe and honor this powerful principle. Let's look at the relationship between our endurance training and our race performances as an example. As athletes, we know that the quality of our training and our *approach* to training largely determines the quality of our racing performance. We know that our training includes our attitudes, emotions, and mental clarity as well as the mechanical process of training. *All* of these have a tremendous impact on our race performance.

The principle of imprints is quite similar to the relationship between training and racing—however, it is much more comprehensive. We are planting these imprints into our subconscious continually—with *every* thought, word, and action. In addition, we are experiencing in any and every given moment the results of imprints we planted in the past. We are simultaneously planting new imprints *and* harvesting the results of old ones *all the time*.

Michael Roach offers many examples of imprint seeds and the results that they produce—all based on ancient wisdom. For example, if we wish to experience prosperity and abundance in our lives we must "plant imprints for this in our subconscious mind by maintaining a generous state of mind." By living an ethical life, we are planting imprints that will manifest our world as being a happy and harmonious place to live. If we avoid reacting with anger, we are planting imprints that ensure physical health.

Relationships and Imprints

The arena of relationship—as an opportunity for spiritual practice—is possibly the richest, most complex and challenging arena of all. Our human relationships provide the most accurate mirror into our own being. Accepting and embracing the imprints that emerge through our relationships with others requires tenacity, humility, honesty, and a certain consciously held trust that what is being revealed and presented to us through another person is completely appropriate and accurate. Our relationships with others—our day-to-day interactions with *all* human beings—family, friends, community, coworkers, and even strangers—may be the most common and frequent activity of our lives. Hence the *medium* of interaction and relationship offers us vast opportunities for spiritual practice.

In his book *Journey of the Heart*, Jonathan Wellwood explores the spiritual practice of our intimate relationships—those with our spouse or close companion. These *intimate* relationships reveal our most *intimate* and deepest imprints—both desirable and undesirable. It can be pretty difficult and challenging sometimes to accept and embrace what our closest relations reveal to us. We may be tempted to "go out for a run" rather than stay present in the moment with the truth of our imprint as it is being revealed to us. The urge to run away can be very strong when that imprint is not something we really want to accept *as our own*.

We started out looking at the formal practices of service and diet and now we have jumped into the vast pool of relationship. If we are transforming family, community and occupation into spiritual *practice*, what is it that we are really practicing? If the medium of service and diet is the interaction and sharing of relationship, does this mean that we must agree with everything that everyone says? Do we give away all that we have in order to attain sainthood? If we literally create those around us acting and responding as they do because of imprints we planted in the past that are just now flowering into consciousness, then what is the use of *practicing* relationship *now*?

CLEARING IMPRINTS

Review of Muscle Memory

In "What Is Feel?" we actually looked at this same imprint phenomenon, but we examined it as *muscle memory*. We considered how those memories—held and stored in our muscle and nerve cells—can be reactivated and experienced again, how they can shape our present reality. In our zendurance approach to movement and *feel*, we have considered the process of clearing—the process of completing and dissolving those old muscle memories and replacing them with a state of calm, still, silent, open emptiness that enables and empowers us to clearly perceive and respond to the present moment without the entanglement of the past.

When we complete and clear these nerve-muscle memories, we no longer hold the tension of the electrical charge within the cells. We are free to respond—not from the imprisonment of the past, but from the clear and infinite opportunity of the present moment. This clearing occurs when we are genuinely present—in our movements and in the conscious occupation of our bodies—from the Zen center of our intelligence triangle. This same process of clearing can also occur in our relationships.

Clearing Imprints in Our Relationships

To truly *practice* relationship as an endeavor toward spiritual fitness and effortless power with our friends, family, community and coworkers—we must begin with the first event of our Zen pentathlon. We must move away from our ego-driven chainsaw relationship with our mana'o intelligence and return to the Zen center of our intelligence triangle. From our Zen center, we are free from our ego-based desires to control and manipulate. No longer do we plant the seeds of negative imprints that flower into our consciousness in the future as negativity and resistance.

When we first begin to consistently reside in our Zen center as we *practice* relationship, we will continue to witness our own negative imprints—those planted in the past. We know this is just as true in our Zen approach to endurance athletics—first we must clear our old painful nerve-muscle memories before we begin to experience harmony and effortless power in our movements.

During these experiences—especially in our relationships—it will require tremendous diligence and tenacity to remain steadfast in our Zen center and not slip back into our ego-based reactions and thought identity. We must consciously and deliberately *approach* each relationship and each moment as an opportunity to plant imprints of harmony and mutual support. If we are impeccably consistent in this *practice* of relationship—remaining Zen centered and present—then gradually we will begin to experience profound shifts in our relationships. These shifts will literally manifest *through* those around us—it will appear as if *they* are the ones who have changed! This experience is astounding.

This is how we transform family, friendship, community, and occupation into spiritual practice. We practice Zen centeredness and presence in all our relationships with as much impeccability and diligence as we do in our zendurance training. Through tireless and devoted awareness in our endurance training, we have already begun to develop a *clear discernment* of when we are Zen centered and present in our endurance training. This is when we experience harmony, efficiency, and effortlessness in our training and racing. We can develop the same clear discernment in our relationships as well. We can experience the same harmony, effortlessness, and satisfaction.

Getting a Feel for Relationships

The *medium* of relationship and interaction is vastly different from the medium of breath and movement. However, the clear discerning awareness and the Zen centeredness and presence *is the same*. Each medium has its unique *feel*—just as swimming, biking, and running each has a unique *feel*. We develop *feel* through the experience of contemplation, approach, and practice.

In our endurance training, when we are experiencing resistance, fatigue, or frustration, we can relax, slow down, find our form and get centered. This process in our relationships is essentially the same process—being present, calm, still, and centered. In our bodies, it even *feels the same*. If we are really at home in our Zen center when we experience a negative imprint that flowers into our consciousness—through someone else's behavior toward us—we can stay consciously present with the negative imprint in a neutral, relaxed, calm and open way and begin to clear that imprint.

Through our zendurance training, we have trained our bodies to be at home—to be in that calm, relaxed, open state. Our muscle memory of that home—which is our body's ability to remain centered and relaxed—can support us profoundly in our practice of relationship. When things get difficult in our relationships and we feel that urge to fight or flee, our ability to stay present in our calm, still bodies is invaluable.

Including Relationships in Zendurance

If we limit our pursuit of spiritual fitness solely to the individual practices of meditation and yoga—working only with mana'o and na'au intelligences—and simply seclude ourselves or go on vacation in our relationships, we are left with a large and empty void— *an absence of pu'uwai intelligence*. While we may highly tune and develop our mana'o and na'au intelligences to become great and accomplished athletes, we severely limit our connection with our surrounding universe. As an illustration, consider this scenario:

Choice 1: You train diligently for Hawaii Ironman. You put in eight to twelve hours a day training—including yoga, meditation, and massage—following your training program to the letter. You eat a perfect diet and get adequate rest. You divorced your spouse and separated from your family so that you could live in seclusion and get serious about training and racing. When you show up at the pier in Kailua for the start of the race, there are *no* other competitors, *no* water patrol, *no* spectators, *no* volunteers—just you and the clock. You cross the finish line with a new overall record. At the finish line you find your finisher's medal, your trophy, a $70,000 check, and your brand new Isuzu. *No* people—Kailua is empty. You drive your Isuzu back to the vacant hotel and take a hot bath.

Choice 2: You train adequately for Hawaii Ironman after winning a lottery spot. Your training program balances a healthy family life and a satisfying occupation. Your diet is pretty sound—a little ice cream here, a little pizza there. Your Hawaii Ironman race begins— after kissing your spouse and hugging the kids—with the classic fiftten hundred pairs of flailing arms making white water in Kailua

Bay. More than five thousand volunteers are there to support you and witness this 140.6-mile pilgrimage. You feed off the ecstatic energy from the thousands of spectators, especially on the run. The last quarter mile down Ali'i Drive is completely electric as you run into the brilliant light of the finish line with your spouse and children—tears streaming down all your faces. In their own unique ways, they have all done this race and all of the training with you. As you cross the finish line with them, you bow down first to receive your traditional Hawaiian ti-leaf lei, then your finisher's medal. Ah, and then there is the healing touch of your masseuse and the hugs from your family and friends. Your really didn't notice your finish time—thirteen hours and something—you were too dazzled by the electrical energy of the finish.

The Glory of Companionship

Which experience seems more fulfilling, more satisfying? Behind each Ironman finisher, there is the connective heart energy of hundreds or thousands of people. What really nourishes each of us—athletes, volunteers, family, and spectators alike—is our incredible collective energy, our connectivity and integrity, which is so tangibly present throughout the race. That race experience of tangible connectivity and integrity is simply a condensed and concentrated version of our everyday lives and relationships.

THE PRACTICE OF DIET

Communion Through Food

Of all human activities, preparing, serving, sharing, and eating food is perhaps our most fundamental practice of giving and receiving. No wonder this is a formal practice of many spiritual traditions. In our day-to-day lives, eating meals together may be the most consistent and frequent way in which we gather as families. There are even sociological studies showing that families that gather and share at least one meal together are healthier, more functional families. Mealtime is one of the greatest opportunities in which to *practice* relationship and connection. This includes both eating *and* *preparing* food.

Preparing Food

How much time do we actually spend *preparing* food? In our fast food culture, we expect food *now* with a minimal investment toward preparation. Instead of whole, real foods, our emphasis is on eating foods that are processed to be ready now—with little preparation. Can we even recognize the real foods that our processed and packaged substances are derived from? Not too often—not unless we read the ingredients, wading through a list of chemicals and additives.

Processed and fast foods have lost most of their mana—their connection to our Earth and to the life that surrounds us and nurtures us. However, diet, as a traditional spiritual practice, is intended to nurture and strengthen our connection with our surrounding universe. Fast food is a result of our overactive and stressed ego-driven mana'o intelligence isolating and distinguishing itself. It is 'o without *mana*. We eat fast food at the expense of disconnecting from our na'au and pu'uwai intelligences. After all, most fast food is not healthy for our bodies or our hearts. With all that packaging to discard, it's not healthy for our planet, either.

As a spiritual practice, diet *connects* us to our planet and to our ultimate physical power source—our sun. Real, whole foods—which *do* require time and energy to prepare—are our closest physical connection to our universe. Even our most advanced, expensive and exotic supplements cannot substitute for this connection. They simply do not have the mana. A conscious approach to the practice of *preparing* food is a *vital part* of this connection. As mentioned earlier, the formal practice of diet in traditional spiritual communities emphasizes both conscientious preparation and cleanup as well as the communal activity of eating.

Gardening

Many of these traditional spiritual communities go even one step farther—gardening, farming, and/or livestock rearing. As someone who has gardened for years, I feel that gardening is an essential practice of diet—of connecting with the Earth through my food source. I garden year-round here in Kona—even when I am in peak training for iron distance. My approach to gardening is simple—I grow leafy greens for cooking, a variety of herbs, green beans, and a few varieties of peppers. This is what grows easily in our environment with a minimum of care. We eat from our garden every day.

The Time Element

Are food preparation and gardening really all that time consuming? Yes, to a narrowly focused mana'o intelligence, most certainly. However, a *simple* organic garden appropriate to your environment—once established—is a minimal time commitment. It can be a great family activity—especially building and starting your garden. Even eating herbs from a simple indoor window herb garden provides significant health benefits. In many areas now, there are local organic farming cooperatives that you can subscribe to—paying a weekly or monthly fee—that reliably provide you with seasonal produce on a regular basis. Real, whole foods actually cost less than fast foods and keep us healthier—which adds up to low food and medical bills. That means less time working and more time really practicing diet with our family and friends. I recommend Philip Maffetone's books—particularly *Eating for Endurance* —as comprehensive and informative guides to diet, specifically for endurance athletes.

Food and Family

In Hawaii, we are known for the cultural emphasis we place on *o'hana*—our families, often large and extended families of both blood relations and close friends and neighbors. There seems to be little distinction between them. Preparing and sharing food, especially local food, is our most significant connection—our most frequent activity together. Nowhere else in the world do I hear so many popular songs on the radio every day about food.

Preparing and sharing *real* food is perhaps our most powerful affirmation of connectivity with one another and with our Earth. The inclusion of diet as one of the six formal branches of spiritual practice is not arbitrary.

THE PRACTICE OF RELATIONSHIP AS A SERVICE

A New Look at Volunteering

We have discussed the practice of relationship as a process of clearing negative imprints when they flower. We have considered how the process of clearing and completing those imprints will appear to us *through* those around us—as if they are the ones who have changed. How is this so-called practice of relationship relevant to the traditional spiritual practice of *service*?

In a conventional sense, we regard service as altruistically performing good deeds for others—volunteering to assist others—even when it is not our responsibility to do so. When we choose to participate in relationships from our Zen center, when we compassionately embrace our own negative imprints—as they appear through others—and replace them with seeds or imprints that will flower as harmonious, supportive, and empowering experiences in our future, we are actually *volunteering*. We are consciously and diligently choosing to do so.

We may not view this practice of being Zen centered and present as our obligation or responsibility. No one is going to issue us a citation if we choose to get angry with someone who is reflecting for us a negative imprint—yet our bursts of negative emotion affect everyone's health detrimentally. So while it is not our legal obligation, this *practice of relationship* is a fundamental and viable path toward health, harmony and happiness.

Serving Others Through Ourselves

We actually benefit *all* beings immeasurably as we clean up our own acts. In fact, our own "act"—including *all* of our thoughts, words, and actions—is the only one we can really clean up. It's not that we don't make a positive difference in our community by volunteering for the kids' school fund-raiser, for instance. We *do* make a positive difference. On the immediate material level, the school's funds increase. On the long-term deeper spiritual level, when we pitch in with the fundraiser and practice generosity, we plant the seeds of positive imprints in our consciousness that will—in time— flower as generosity and abundance in our universe.

Volunteer service does grant us the opportunity to set down our obsessive mirror of self-reflection and connect with those around us—without the focused attention of personal gain. This context of volunteer service can really strengthen and clarify our practice of volunteering or choosing to clean up our own acts. By temporarily setting down the mirror of self-reflection for a time, when we return and pick up that mirror again, we see ourselves more truthfully and accurately.

Volunteering All the Time

In the quest to integrate spiritual fitness into our daily lives, we do not need to set aside more of our time for the formal practice of volunteer service—although, as we have just considered, it can help us refine our practice of cleaning up our own acts. Ultimately, we make a commitment to the practice of spiritual fitness through service and diet—in the medium of interaction and relationship—

all the time, moment to moment, in all of our interactions.

When we are present and at home in our Zen center, *all* our relationships transform effortlessly into appropriate, spontaneous and empowering experiences of spiritual fitness—both for ourselves and for our relations. Recognizing, experiencing, and acknowledging the true spiritual essence and infinite potential of each other is the greatest and most empowering *service* of all. It is a service that requires commitment, diligence, compassion, tolerance and self-honesty. In HeartCore Zendurance, we strive to practice this service during every moment of every interaction and relationship.

Blending

In our zendurance approach to athletics, we refine our training into a spiritual practice. Our *feel* for the medium of breath and movement as a union of our mana'o and na'au intelligences becomes more refined and articulate. The delineation between yoga and meditation disappears. This is also true in our relationships—family, community, and occupation. As we purify and refine our thoughts, words, and actions, we transform our day-to-day interactions into the *practice* of relationship. Our *feel* for the medium of interaction and relationship as a union of our pu'uwai and na'au intelligences becomes more refined and articulate. The delineation between giving and receiving disappears. The practices of service and diet are practices of sharing and circulating our health, wealth, intelligence, ability, and spiritual fitness and love.

This entry on service and diet very briefly indicates the vast and challenging opportunities for spiritual practice in the infinite medium of interaction and relationship. Many books have been written about this rich and promising resource. To truly undertake the spiritual practice of relationship, I highly recommend that you read some of these books—such as *Journey of the Heart* and *The Diamond Cutter*.

HEARTCORE INTEGRATION:
THIRD LEG

The Vital Heart-Brain Connection

As we considered earlier, prayer and devotion link our mana'o and pu'uwai intelligences. These two intelligences are very different from one another in their essence and can be quite contrary. Our mana'o intelligence functions to isolate and distinguish. Our pu'uwai intelligence functions to circulate and integrate. Without some kind of practice that blends these two powerful intelligences together, we can experience much inner tension and conflict. Life can become a constant and grueling tug-of-war.

Without a heart-brain connection, the mana'o becomes that cold ruthless chainsaw of reason and the pu'uwai becomes an uncontained, undirected flood of emotion. In this struggle, neither intelligence has any discernment. *Literally*, the separation of and opposition between our collective mana'o intelligence and our collective pu'uwai intelligence have caused the great wars of our world.

No matter how pure and how extensive our endurance training might be, without some form of prayer and devotion, this powerful opposition will not cease. Prayer and devotion are the *only* two forms of practice that can meld our skillful means with our integrity and shape them into an astounding and powerful constructive force that can permeate our lives in remarkable ways.

Practicing prayer and devotion does not mean that we have to be active members of a religious congregation or that we must subscribe to some particular doctrine. As unique as each of us is in our approach and technique regarding our practice of endurance training, so we are with our practice of prayer and devotion.

For those of us with a strong na'au-to-mana'o connection—who really enjoy practicing meditation and yoga, either traditionally or through zendurance training—prayer and devotion may be low on our priority list. For us, this practice leg of our intelligence triangle represents our weak sport, so to speak. Keep in mind that the great wars—with all their tragedy, misery, and destruction—have been generated by a complete absence of this leg of the intelligence triangle—a failure to integrate our mana'o and pu'uwai. Peace is not just a lofty spiritual ideal—it is a very practical, healthy, and essential condition of life. Our individual inner peace is inextricably connected with our collective global peace.

Compassion

When we link our skillful means with our integrity, we experience *compassion*. Compassion is the *medium* that links heart and brain through prayer and devotion—just as breath is the *medium* that links body and brain through yoga and meditation—just as relationship is the *medium* that links heart and body through service and diet.

Through the medium of compassion, we develop the wise discernment to recognize and choose the principles and tenets that guide us gracefully through our lives and relationships. Through prayer and devotion, we develop a *feel* for operating in this medium of compassion. As we develop and strengthen our compassion, we begin to experience a much greater capacity for tolerance in our everyday interactions. This capacity for *tolerance* is similar to our capacity for tolerating the physical sensations of pain, as we considered in "What is Feel?" Compassion and tolerance enable us to remain calmly present and steadfast with emotional and mental pain, frustration, and anguish. Compassion and tolerance are essential in our ability to clear the negative imprints that flower in our consciousness during our interactions and relationships.

CREATING A SHRINE

Real and Tangible

Here is a fun and creative way to develop the seemingly immaterial practices of prayer and devotion: We can ground them and make them more tangible in the physical here-and-now by creating a *shrine*. For many of us this may seem like a strange or unfamiliar activity: *Gee, this is like bringing church into my home.* There are many cultures in the world that include shrines as an essential element and a primary focal point in the home. You need not be embarrassed or uncomfortable about having a shrine. For the majority of our global population, this is a common and fundamental practice. A shrine simply serves as a *physical conduit* to link our two immaterial intelligences. It does not have to be a heavy statement about your beliefs. Yet as a physical link between pu'uwai and mana'o, as an expression of compassion, it can be quite powerful.

How powerful can a shrine be in generating and inspiring compassion? My wife, Fatima, diligently practices spiritual fitness through prayer and devotion—although she has no interest or aspiration toward endurance athletics or physical prowess. Our simple home, in its entirety, is a temple, a shrine—every room, including the kitchen and bathroom. Fatima thoroughly attends to our temple-home daily—cleaning, renewing the flowers that adorn our temple, and maintaining the objects and sparse furnishings. Every person who enters our temple is transformed—all experience their own tangible compassion—the *harmony* of their pu'uwai and mana'o. Even our daughter Erin's high school graduation party— more than one hundred and fifty young people partying in and around our temple-home—was an experience of genuine harmony and peace, with no energy whatsoever toward "enforcement." There were no wild teenagers, just spiritually intelligent young people.

The Other Shrine

There is one more significant element in our temple home—or the *absence* of one significant element. *We have no television.* Especially in the cultures of the Western world, television has replaced the shrine as a conduit for devotion. Many of us *devote* ourselves daily, for an hour or more, to the television. Remember that spiritual devotion is a practice of honoring, assimilating, and integrating the noble and honorable qualities that strengthen spiritual fitness. Honestly, how much of what is broadcast on television—both programs and commercials—truly promotes and energizes the noble and honorable qualities of spiritual fitness— humbleness, grace, generosity, and tolerance, for instance? Does television really manifest *compassion*? With a great deal of discernment and tenacious channel surfing, we may find some quality programming, but is it really worth our precious time and energy?

Warning: Television *is* a devotional conduit. We *do* assimilate and integrate the qualities we see on TV.

Getting Started

So how about we give *this* a try? Let's give up just two hours of television time for two hours of creating a shrine. The two hours do not have to be consecutive—maybe thirty minutes to an hour in a day spread over a week. Heck, let's make it easier—let's pick a recovery week or a taper week in our training schedule, when our endurance training is minimal.

Where should our shrine be? Let's choose a place in our house where we can be at peace—a place that we *feel* will support and enhance our compassion. Let's choose a place that is quiet, where we can be still and calm for fifteen to thirty minutes a day—a place where we can sit and practice our meditation. It may be the living room (not too close to the TV), a space in the bedroom, or even a corner in the basement. *Feel* it out. Eventually we might end up putting it where the TV *used* to be. How about that?

Let's start with a small table or a shelf or mantel. What can we include on our shrine? We allow the balanced dialogue between our heart and our brain—our *compassion*—to guide us. For those of us who are new to this, we may initiate our shrine with mementos of endurance athletics—finish-line photos, awards, and so on. This is very appropriate if we regard our athletic endeavors as a valuable practice toward spiritual fitness. We may start with a beautiful piece of cloth and include crystals, gems, feathers, stones, cut flowers, plants, or other gifts of natural beauty. We can also include pictures of those we love and are devoted to—family, friends, ancestors, mentors, saints, prophets, or sacred deities. We may include some of our artwork and creative expressions, or those of our children. It is also nice to have a box where we can place money, jewelry, and papers that we want to honor and bless—a race application before mailing, our child's report card, or a meaningful letter.

Offerings

Our shrine is a place for offerings—physical, devotional offerings to nurture and express our compassion—the peace and harmony between our pu'uwai and mana'o. Incense and candles have always been popular traditional offerings. By burning candles and incense, we are literally transforming the material (incense and candles) into the immaterial (scent, smoke and light). We are transforming matter into energy.

Maintaining the order and cleanliness of our shrine—as well as renewing our offerings of water, fruit, candy, money, flowers, candles, and incense—can be quite effective in maintaining the order and cleanliness of our mana'o-to-pu'uwai connection. While we devote anywhere from thirty minutes to several hours maintaining our na'au-to-mana'o connection through zendurance training every day, a simple five to ten minutes a day can go a long way toward our "compassion and tolerance fitness." Maintaining our shrine is also a form of offering.

Expressing and Experiencing Compassion

Our intention is to harmoniously engage both our mana'o and pu'uwai intelligences in the *creative* process of a shrine. Our shrine reveals and expresses the honorable qualities we are devoted to—that we are assimilating, integrating, and developing. It expresses and broadcasts those qualities through the offerings, objects, and images of people and deities and through the beautiful and balanced arrangement of all of them. The cleanliness and arrangement of our shrine is an essential element in its broadcasting strength. In its totality—its *synergy*—our shrine reflects the harmony and poetic balance of our mana'o and pu'uwai. It is our compassion in tangible form.

As we create, develop, and live with our shrine, let's be creative and playful—let's take a few minutes regularly and frequently to enjoy the process of expressing and broadcasting our compassionate inner beauty. We might be pleasantly surprised by how our friends and family respond as they experience and recognize their own compassion within. Often children will be inspired to create their own shrines—through their instinctual feeling and comprehension of what a shrine expresses—without any need for explanation. Our athletic friends may be awakened and inspired to see some of our racing and training mementos alongside holy or sacred objects. Our shrine may inspire us to see the orderliness, cleanliness, health and balance of our homes and workplaces in a new way—as we begin to *feel* the tangibility of compassion and sacredness.

Courage

Creating, maintaining, and living with our shrine is a profound and *courageous* practice of recognizing, acknowledging, and honoring the *sacredness* within us, the *sacredness* of our day-to-day lives, our surroundings and our relationships. What is so courageous about this practice? It is like standing up in the middle of the battlefield—amid the bullets, bombs, and bloodshed—to wave a flag of peace, to sing a song of serenity. Our mana'o—in its fear and terror of isolation—and our pu'uwai—in its remorse and resentment—require such courage to put down the weapons of hostility and embrace one another with compassion.

SACREDNESS AND APPROACH

What Is Sacredness?

Sacredness is our divine essence and intelligence. It permeates and resonates through each of us and throughout our universe. The courageous practice of recognizing and honoring our sacredness—both within us and around us—helps us develop a much keener awareness of the infinite opportunities in our day-to-day lives to engage and exercise our spiritual fitness. As we cultivate and develop the tangibility of our compassion and tolerance, we begin to *feel* our sacredness—our mana essence.

This compassionate and tolerant awareness—this *feeling* of sacredness—is the essence of the second event in our Zen pentathlon—*approach*. We begin to consciously approach each and every moment of our lives with diligence and clarity when we are in touch with compassion and tolerance. What were once insurmountable obstacles, circumstances, and problems—our *negative imprints*—either quickly or gradually become clear opportunities to exercise, strengthen, and express our spiritual fitness. When we regard each moment, each opportunity as being sacred, we are clearly connecting to our spiritual essence—we are abiding in our Zen center.

The Most Important Element of Zendurance

Now read this paragraph very carefully, because this is *really important material* for all of us HeartCore Zendurance folks: Our attitude and our approach to any event or relationship—*and to the imprints that we ourselves color and animate that event or relationship with*—will largely determine how we choose to respond to that event or relationship. Our approach and our attitude in the beginning determine our response in the end. That is to say, our approach to our *own* imprints—as they are being replayed or mirrored back to us through the people and events around us—sets up our response to them.

Our response includes our actions, our words, our thoughts, feelings, emotions, and energetic states. These, in turn, *create the imprint seeds* that will be replayed back to us sometime in the future—through similar events or relationships. This is how we construct the patterns in our lives—good or bad. Whether we are conscious of it or not, this is how we *literally design our own futures! How we respond now determines what we will be respond-*

ing to in the future. We're talking family, friends, health, wealth, endurance athletics—the whole candy store. We are determining our destiny *right now.* Our *approach right now* is an antenna that transmits to the future.

We see indications of this tenet in our endurance training. How we *approach* our endurance training—whether we choose to be diligently conscious of our approach or blissfully ignorant—largely determines the quality of our experience and the way in which we will perform in the future. It *ain't* just genetics after all!

Compassion and Approach

So what does all this "approach as an antenna to the future" stuff have to do with prayer and devotion and our shrine? The quality of our approach to each moment *is determined by how harmonious or conflicting our pu'uwai-to-mana'o connection is.* We can be either compassionate or confused. If our mana'o and pu'uwai are in harmony *right now*—no matter how rough our playback is treating us—we are transmitting harmony and effortless power into our future. Earlier we considered that our shrine *broadcasts* the noble and honorable qualities that we choose to honor. Our shrine is broadcasting these qualities for all who gaze upon it—giving tangibility to our compassion. Does our shrine also transmit to the future? Yes, it can if we activate it that way.

Approaching Each Day

Here is a simple practice that we can engage in to develop our ability to consciously articulate our approach to each moment of our day—a short meditation practice with our shrine. It is adapted from chapter 9 of *The Diamond Cutter*—titled "Setting the Day With Silent Time." The best time to do this practice is at the conclusion of your meditation, preferably in the morning. Before sitting to meditate, clean your shrine and the space around it. This cleansing process gently gets your body moving and helps to clear not only the physical space, but also the access to your Zen center and your connections to the energetic intelligences as well. Light some incense or candles.

When everything *feels* in order and you have closed out any noise and activity, gently sit down and get still. Spend about twenty minutes in meditation, as described earlier. As you complete your meditation, begin this practice of approaching your day.

Reception

One by one, you can bring your family, friends, and ancestors into your Zen center. Imagine a golden beam of light flowing between your heart and each of them as you bless, honor, and wish each of them well. You don't have to exhaustively connect with every single acquaintance. Rather, spend a moment being truly present with each person you do bring in—feeling their presence, their qualities, and your connection with them. Different people may show up in your Zen center on different days. This process will help you connect with your pu'uwai intelligence from your Zen center. *Feel* your heart connection with each person.

Staging Your Imprints

When you have completed the Zen center morning reception and all is clear again, you are ready to move to the core of this practice. Are you grappling with some nagging problem—an issue with your spouse or a coworker, some resistance with your training, a circumstance in your life that seems unfair or frustrating? What's been distracting you lately? Is there a problem you anticipate today? Use your Zen center of the intelligence triangle as a kind of stage. Re-create the scenario as accurately as possible.

Examine how this relationship or situation is a problem for you. Examine how *your playback of an imprint* from a past experience fills, colors, and animates the relationship or situation and makes it a problem for you. This staging process is not going to be easy at first. It requires that you stay firmly grounded in your Zen center without slipping back into ego-drive. Be aware that this practice is *not* a brain exercise to logically figure out why this is an issue or what went wrong.

As an example, let's say you are experiencing some form of rejection—your son refuses to help you with the yard work, your spouse won't travel with you to your next race or the boss is favoring a coworker unfairly. On your Zen center stage, recreate the scenario and experience the problem that it is for you. Keenly observe your anger or frustration—*while staying centered*. Now observe the scenario with the full knowledge and discernment of how you filled, colored, and animated the relationship or situation through your own playback of an imprint. Can you discern how—sometime in the past, either once or repeatedly—you planted the imprint seeds of that rejection imprint, by rejecting someone's request of you or by unjustly ignoring or favoring someone else?

Now see yourself being supportive, helpful, fair and just with your family, friends, or coworkers—planting the imprint seeds that will play back positively, that will diminish this problem and filter it out of your future. Try to create specific scenarios based on situations where you planted the seeds of these problem imprints and where you now respond in an honorable way, planting positive seeds. And finally, create a scenario of how you anticipate this problem arising or flowering again—possibly in the upcoming day. Imagine the problem arising for you again—and how you *used* to respond. This time allow the rejection experience to occur and simply stay in your Zen center without resisting or adding to the problem. Stay centered and neutral. Be intelligent and creative.

The next time this problem does flower again, the spiritual fitness you have gained through this staging practice will enable you to remain much more centered. From your Zen center, you will *approach* and respond from a place of sacred intelligence, transmitting harmony and effortless power into your future.

Envision Yourself

If you are not in touch with some specific problem or issue—or if you have completed the practice—you may choose to envision yourself going through the activities and experiences of the upcoming day—including your relationships and family time, work, training, and so on. See and feel yourself being centered, present, intelligent, happy, brilliant, gentle, humble, relaxed, compassionate, tolerant, generous, patient and discerning. Finally, see yourself *being* the person you aspire to be in the future, clearly emanating those honorable qualities that you are *devoted* to. Be generous and creative in these visions of yourself.

As you complete this practice of approaching the day, take a moment to appreciate the beauty of your shrine—the tangibility of your compassion. Now go forth into the splendor of your day and be brilliant!

Consistency and Creativity

Consistency and attentiveness will yield quality results in this practice of approaching the day. The time spent in this practice of approach will enhance every part of your life. Treat this practice with respect and diligence, as you do your endurance training. Your approach to both training and your daily life are inseparable from one another. Who knows? You might enjoy the benefits and results of this practice more than sitting in front of that other "devotional box"—TV.

The process and guidelines we have considered here are just a suggested format. Each of us, with consistent practice, will develop a specific and unique practice of approaching the day as we become familiar and articulate in that tangible medium of compassion. This will progress as the integration of our pu'uwai and mana'o becomes more intimate and articulate. Eventually we may easily combine our meditation with this practice. When we can realize this blend, we may not need to conduct such a detailed process of approaching the day. As first, it is beneficial to go through this process gently and deliberately, as we become familiar with the medium of compassion.

Completing Each Day

In addition or as an alternative to this morning practice of approach, you may choose to sit quietly in the evening in front of your shrine. You can review your day from your neutral, intelligent Zen center. Specifically, you can choose the three most difficult and challenging experiences of your day—when you experienced the most resistance, frustration, or anger. As in the morning practice, use your Zen center as a stage to experience and acknowledge your responsibility in creating these situations and envision yourself responding to them in a more harmonious, intelligent and centered manner the next time you play back these kinds of imprints.

You can also pick out three experiences from the day where you most clearly planted beneficial imprint seeds through your thoughts, words and actions—experiences that will transmit harmony and effortless power into your future. Take a moment to experience the happiness, joy and compassion of these three experiences.

The three negative and three positive experiences you choose to review may be significant, well-planned events in your life, or they may be brief, spontaneous, and seemingly insignificant moments. The compassionate dialogue between pu'uwai and mana'o will guide your choices here.

Next, you can envision and appreciate what you are grateful for—your health, family, wealth, intelligence, freedom, and friends. You don't have to be exhaustive and cite every single blessing. Just take a moment to feel gratitude and appreciation for these gifts. You may conclude by simply being calmly present in your Zen center without any agendas or thoughts—just your slow, relaxed breathing—returning to the activity of simple meditation.

Summary of Approach

These practices of approaching and completing our day are not cast in stone any more than our athletic training program is. There is not a single best process or method. *All* of our practices—our zendurance athletics, our practice of family, our meditations, and our prayer and devotional practices—continually evolve and grow. As traditional Zen practitioners say, "Everything changes." It is important to *allow* all of our practices—as well as our growth and development as human spiritual beings—to *gracefully* unfold, just as a flower unfolds.

We have concentrated here on adapting aspects of the traditional practices of prayer and devotion to create a practice of approaching and completing each day. This is a powerful and effective way of developing our ability to be present and Zen centered in our day-to-day lives *and* to transmit harmony and effortless power into our future. We can see clearly how this diligent practice of approach can truly transform our lives in sacred ways that our zendurance training alone cannot. Let's move on now to a few more image techniques that can supplement our conscious and compassionate approach to the sacredness of each moment and each experience.

Sacred Voice

In the traditional seven-chakra system, the throat chakra is situated between the heart and the brain. It is the energetic source of our voice. Voice is a vital link between our mana'o and pu'uwai intelligences. We know that our thoughts and speech—along with our actions—constitute our response to events and circumstances. They determine what imprint seeds we plant in our subconscious that will flower or surface in our future. To repeat: "Whether we are conscious of it or not, this is how we design our own future. *How* we respond now determines *what* we will be responding to in the future."

We equate voice with both speech and thought. Sometimes we voice only our rational mana'o intelligence. Sometimes we voice only our emotional pu'uwai. When our voice is positioned equally and harmoniously between our mana'o and pu'uwai, we voice our *compassion*. Prayer is an activity of thought and speech that is sourced from a voice positioned *equally between* mana'o and pu'uwai. Prayer is the activity of *voicing our intent* to experience the sacred nature of some event or relationship. It is our way of acknowledging the sacredness of our experiences and our relations.

We can begin to approach every thought and every spoken word as an opportunity for prayer—an opportunity to *activate* sacredness. We do not have to include any sophisticated religious terms or vernacular in our thoughts and speech. We simply begin with the diligent practice of observing and intentionally setting our voice position. *Am I forming my thoughts and speaking from a voice of compassionate intelligence—from a voice that is equally positioned between mana'o and pu'uwai?* This conscious practice of voice positioning can help us establish a strong and lasting connection with our sacredness. Just like our shrine, a centered voice position gives our compassion a tangibility that we can *feel* at any time, in any circumstance.

> *Aia i ka 'olelo no ke ala*
> *Aia i ka 'olelo no ke make*
> (In the word there is life
> In the word there is death)

Essentially, this ancient Hawaiian saying summarizes, in a concise and simple way, the very same tenet of Buddhism that we have been examining—the tenet of *planting imprint seeds* through our thoughts, words, and actions. *All* of the sacred cultures of the world recognize, honor, and practice this same tenet. It is an infinitely powerful and fundamental operating principle of our universe. This phenomenon of *imprinting* is fundamental to our *sacred approach* and *practice* in each moment of our lives. Recognizing and honoring the sacredness of each and every moment is the essence of integration.

Tonglen

In Buddhism, there is a conscious breathing practice called *tonglen.* As athletes, we already practice conscious breathing as part of the practice of zendurance. In tonglen we use our conscious breathing to relieve the burden of pain and suffering we perceive in ourselves and in others. As we inhale, we feel the hot, thick, and claustrophobic qualities of that pain. As we exhale, we transform that suffering into a light, cool spaciousness. We transform our resistance, aversion, and fear into serenity, ease, and peace. This is a practice we can do during our zendurance training and at any time that we are conscious of the opportunity—through conscious approach.

This traditional practice of tonglen, as well as our practice of voice positioning, can greatly enhance our ability to be Zen centered and present in our moment-to-moment approach to each event, circumstance, and relationship in our lives.

Tonglen and Breath Positioning

The primary mechanism for breathing is our solar plexus or diaphragm muscle—associated with our third chakra. Just as our voice source—throat chakra—is located equally between our mana'o and pu'uwai intelligences, so our breath source—solar plexus chakra—is located equally between our pu'uwai and na'au. We are aware that the traditional practice of *service* connects these two intelligences, so tonglen can be regarded as a simple and basic breathing form of service.

Does the practice of tonglen *really* relieve suffering? From the perspective of the isolating and logical mana'o intelligence, no it does not appear to. As a practice of consciously and deliberately linking our pu'uwai and na'au intelligences, *yes*, it does. Our pu'uwai intelligence energetically connects us all together in ways that are far beyond the scope of our isolating and logical mana'o intelligence. Through a *conscious choice* to practice tonglen, our mana'o intelligence must concede that our pu'uwai *does* have the functional intelligence to connect us together—to transmit and receive *mana*.

Remember that our na'au intelligence is our power supply—our source of mana—and our intelligence of activity. This practice of breath positioning links our na'au-based mana source to the transmitting and receiving intelligence of pu'uwai to create the breathing equivalent of prayer.

We plant imprint seeds of generosity, loving-kindness, and compassion through tonglen. Our precious mana—life energy—is a great potential source of wealth and health. The generous and compassionate practice of tonglen allows us to open up to suffering and to share that abundance and wealth—and in no way does it drain or deplete us. Tonglen is a win-win situation.

Compassion and Loving-Kindness

In her book *The Places That Scare You*, Pema Chodron offers valuable, simple guidance and instruction for cultivating and developing Zen centered compassion and loving-kindness—the very essence of planting beneficial seeds. *Compassion and loving kindness are our very strongest assets in gently confronting and embracing the experiences in our lives that scare us.* Creating and maintaining our shrine, consciously approaching and completing each day, as well as conscious voice positioning—sacred thought and speech—and conscious breath positioning—tonglen—are just a few of the simple techniques for practicing compassion and loving-kindness.

Pema Chodron offers simple exercises for prayerful meditation and tonglen—exercises we can begin to practice *during* our day-to-day activities and interactions. Flexibility and creativity are great assets in our quest to practice compassion and loving-kindness and to integrate spiritual fitness into our ordinary lives. The simplicity of her instruction and guidance supports and encourages us to be flexible and creative in our implementation of these practices.

Expanding Our Vision of Approach

For those of us who are earnest and sincere in our quest toward true zendurance, I strongly recommend reading books that address spiritual fitness beyond our practice of zendurance athletics. Reading of this kind can greatly expand our vision and open up our awareness to the sacred opportunities of our daily lives, assisting us with the essential process of *integration*. On the other hand, if we limit our reading diet to books and magazines that focus only on our endurance athletic activity, our vision and awareness will remain narrow and our ability to develop, practice and integrate spiritual fitness will be weak and limited.

HEARTCORE INTEGRATION: SUMMARY

The Essential Event

Integration—event 4 of our Zen pentathlon—is the most essential *and the most difficult* element of zendurance. In the "Tri Zen" section, we began to orient and transform our endurance athletic training into *zendurance*—a viable practice for developing spiritual fitness and for cultivating an experience of our effortless power, our sacredness, and our true spirit nature. However, if we cannot integrate and apply this experience within our daily lives, then our practice of zendurance is an isolated monastic activity that can only carry over into our mundane daily lives in very limited, narrow, and specific ways. Our zendurance training may then become simply an addictive spiritual escape from the rest of our not-so-spiritual day-to-day experiences. (I speak from experience here.)

We concluded the "Tri-Zen" section by briefly studying the nature of our three energetic intelligences. In "HeartCore Zendurance," we have looked at the six branches of traditional spiritual practice and how those six branches provide the leg strength that assembles and stabilizes our three energetic intelligences into a powerful triangle of intelligence. We have also considered some of the ways that we—as zendurance athletes—can develop the leg strength of our energetic intelligence triangle.

We can see now that overall spiritual fitness is contingent upon *integrating* all three of our intelligences together to create that stable and powerful triangle through balanced and equal leg strength. To truly integrate our zendurance practice into our lives as ordinary human beings, we must become just as fluent and articulate in the medium of interaction and relationship and in the medium of compassion and tolerance as we are in the medium of breath and movement. We can develop an intimate feeling and articulation for all three mediums—just as we can develop an intimate feeling and articulation for swimming, biking, and running.

Every Ordinary Moment

Our intention in this "HeartCore Zendurance" section is to strengthen the other two legs of our energetic intelligence triangle without piling on more formal practice—without adding more daily activities to an already full schedule. We *have* added the practice of creating and maintaining a shrine as well as one or two periods of quiet, contemplative, and devotional time each day. This simple meditation, prayer, and devotional practice helps us to develop and strengthen our conscious and diligent *approach* to our daily lives—*including* our athletic training. The benefits that we experience *and the benefits that others experience* from these simple and brief practices of compassionate and tolerant approach are immense compared to the small amount of time and energy we invest. As I suggested earlier, we can substitute this contemplative, prayerful, and devotional practice in place of that other devotional practice with the initials "TV."

Integration is *not* contingent upon devoting extensive amounts of time to conducting formal spiritual practices on all three legs of our energetic intelligence triangle. Integration *is* contingent upon *approaching every moment* of our ordinary lives as a sacred opportunity to practice and to strengthen our spiritual fitness through loving-kindness, tolerance, and compassion—for others and for ourselves.

We first learn how to consciously navigate through each sacred moment by deliberately approaching our endurance athletics as a zendurance practice—staying present and mindful in each breath, each stride or stroke, and each moment of our training session. As we become more familiar with and skilled at navigating through the metaphysical landscape of approach, we begin to transform each moment or our ordinary lives into a sacred opportunity to practice spiritual fitness.

Voilà!

Voilà! That's integration! That's the main event of the Zen pentathlon! And do you know what's really great about all this? Well, as we honor and approach each sacred moment of our lives, we plant the imprint seeds that will transmit that sacredness into our future. Gradually our own lives and the universe we live in become healthier, more harmonious and sacred. We are able to effortlessly integrate and dance with the sacred imprints that flower for us, that play back to us. Through this approach and practice of sacredness and true integration, we experience the mastery of our destiny.

ZEN PENTATHLON
CONTRIBUTION—THE FINAL EVENT

Introduction

This Zen pentathlon is quite a bit different from a conventional athletic triathlon or pentathlon. Here is a brief review so far—in notated form:

Event 1, Contemplation: Returning to our true essence—to the calm, still, silent, open, and empty Zen center of our energetic intelligence triangle.

Event 2, Approach: Consciously recognizing, honoring, and moving into each moment as a sacred opportunity to practice spiritual fitness—to practice Zen centered presence and brilliance.

Event 3, Practice: Consciously and diligently choosing to be Zen centered and present in this very moment—the *only* moment there is. Through practice, we actualize the sacred opportunity of now.

Event 4, Integration: Consciously and diligently practicing spiritual fitness fluidly and continuously in *every* moment of our lives—not just in our training sessions. Through integration, we practice spiritual fitness in *all* conditions and circumstances. With flexibility and creativity, we are able to effortlessly and seamlessly transition from one moment and activity to the next.

A Little Fuzzy

In a conventional athletic triathlon, the swimming, biking, and running events are separate, well-defined, and distinct entities—with clear transitions from one to the next. In our Zen pentathlon however, the events are not so separate, well defined, or distinct. Meditation for instance, is a *practice* (event 3) of *contemplation* (event 1). We regard prayer and devotion as *practices* (event 3) of *approach* (event 2).

We are also beginning to see how a specific practice that links two of our intelligences together along one of the practice legs of the triangle can also strengthen the other legs of our energetic intelligence triangle. For example, prayer and devotion are practices that link our pu'uwai and mana'o intelligences through the medium of compassion and tolerance. However, they can also enhance our skill and articulation in the medium of interaction and relationship. As a result, prayer and devotion also strengthen the service-diet leg that links our pu'uwai and na'au intelligences. Likewise our diet can enhance our athletic training—the meditation-yoga leg of the triangle, which connects our mana'o and na'au.

All of our ordinary daily activities can be transformed into spiritual practices that are a little of this and a little of that—practices that occur in more than a single medium to link and integrate all three of our energetic intelligences. We will consider this in the entry, "Practical Navigation."

Contribution

The fifth event of our Zen pentathlon is *contribution*. As ordinary human beings who happen to engage in the formal zendurance practice of athletic training, how can we actually *contribute* to our world and our universe? In order to successfully complete the Zen pentathlon, what is it that we must contribute? Do we need to gain formal recognition as great civic leaders and community members? Should we generously donate large amounts of money to charitable and altruistic endeavors? Can we fulfill our contribution by winning world-class endurance races and by inspiring others toward physical fitness?

Typically—through our mana'o intelligence—we want to identify and to distinguish our contributions as well-defined and specific activities and accomplishments. *Contribution*—as the event of completion in our Zen pentathlon—may very well include such charitable and altruistic activities and accomplishments. This is not, however, the true essence of contribution.

Zen Pentathlon Flower

For a clearer understanding of the nature of contribution, let's imagine the first four events of the Zen pentathlon as the petals of a flower. Let's envision a *lotus flower,* since it is a significant image in traditional Eastern spiritual paths. The very first petals of our Zen pentathlon lotus flower that open up are the *petals of contemplation.* As these petals fully open, the next inner petals of the lotus begin to unfold—and these are the *petals of approach.* They unfold outward from the center of our lotus flower, surrounded by the petals of contemplation. Then from the center of these lotus petals of approach are born the unfolding *petals of practice.* The lotus flower of our Zen pentathlon continues to unfold and open from its *Zen center.* The *petals of integration* are the next to open up from this lotus Zen center. They are embraced and encircled by the petals of practice, which are embraced and surrounded by the petals of approach, all of which are held and embraced by the petals of contemplation.

Again, from the very center of our Zen pentathlon lotus flower, the *petals of contribution* unfold and open—born out of our integration. All the petals of our lotus flower and all the events of our Zen pentathlon unfold and begin in our *Zen center*.

Contribution—The Mastery of Integration

As we gain mastery at *integrating* our Zen centeredness and presence into each moment of our daily lives as ordinary human beings, we are continuously planting and cultivating beneficial and harmonious imprint seeds in the garden of our universe. Through the progressive mastery of integration, we diligently plant and cultivate these imprint seeds and lovingly tend the garden of our universe with every thought, word, feeling, and action. The effects of our Zen gardening are infinitely far reaching—rippling outward throughout our universe.

This is our *real contribution*. Each and every moment of our ordinary lives, we are tending the garden of our universe with *loving-kindness, tolerance,* and *compassion*—through every thought, word, feeling, and action. True contribution does not require heroic deeds, brilliant schemes to save the world, fame and fortune, world-class racing performances, or any other elaborate and large-scale endeavors. True contribution unfolds naturally and simply from the Zen center of our flowering lives—surrounded and embraced by the lotus petals of contemplation, approach, practice and integration.

It Happens Now

We do not have to worry, struggle, plan or exert any great effort in order to contribute. We can only contribute in this present moment. We can only integrate with this present moment. We can only practice in this present moment. We can only approach this present moment. We can only contemplate *being present* in this present moment. We simply allow our sacred lotus flower of loving-kindness, tolerance, and compassion to unfold through contemplation, approach, practice and integration. At the very heart center of our loving-kindness, tolerance, and compassion, our precious lotus flower of contribution is unfolding each moment.

This is *HeartCore* Zendurance.

PRACTICAL NAVIGATION

INTRODUCTION

The Map

We have now drafted quite an elaborate metaphysical map. It includes the energetic intelligence triangle, with its three practice legs. Each practice leg is comprised of two forms of spiritual practice that connect two of the energetic intelligences. Our map also includes the Zen pentathlon lotus flower, with the five steps—or events—unfolding from its very heart center. Just like a conventional road map, our metaphysical map can be a very valuable guide—once we gain some practical navigational experience.

Using the Map

So, before moving on to "Zendurance Racing and Performance" —where we put the icing on the cake—let's get a little navigational exercise with our new map. Let's consider how we can use this metaphysical map—specifically our energetic intelligence triangle—to navigate through a few ordinary nonathletic activities in our daily lives. This exercise will enable us to better recognize and approach these activities as opportunities for spiritual fitness. As a selection of activities let's look at domestic chores, communication, social and play time and . . . well, how about sex?

DOMESTIC CHORES

Intelligence of Activity—All Day

The word *activity* already indicates that each of these selections engages our na'au intelligence of activity. Yet how na'au conscious are we of housekeeping, yard work, food preparation or shopping? How consciously present are we in our bodies during our domestic chores? Are we well aligned with gravity? Are we physically grounded and moving from our na'au center? How intimate and articulate is our *feel*?

From the moment we arise in the morning until we retire at night, we are engaged in *activity*—we are occupying and engaging our bodies—even if that activity is stillness. Being continuously and completely present in our bodies and intimately aware of our breath and our movement is a powerful practice of presence. If we keep our attention in our bodies seamlessly and continuously, then we are *anchored* in the now. When we lose touch, we are losing ourselves to the external world and to the ego dialogue of our mana'o.

All of our daily activities can be transformed into Zen practices that engage and link up *all three* of our energetic intelligences. Each activity is a unique blend. It is worth repeating: True integration and spiritual fitness occur as we engage and coordinate all three of our energetic intelligences in each present moment.

Even Cleaning and Yard Work?

Cleaning and yard work—as examples of domestic chores—clearly engage our na'au intelligence of activity. There is just as much opportunity for efficiency, economy of movement, alignment, grace, and fluidity in these activities as in our zendurance training. It's just that domestic chores are not endowed with the same potential for glory and prestige. The skillful means and keen, attentive perception of our mana'o intelligence is also essential during our domestic chores, so that we are competent, efficient, safe, and thorough in our activity. When we are truly present and attentive in our housekeeping, we are also *connecting* with the energetic quality—the mana—of the objects in our houses and their arrangement. The same is true in our yard work—we connect with the mana of our yards, the energy and consciousness of our plants. This connectivity and attentiveness comes from our pu'uwai intelligence.

Our Whole World Is a Shrine

Our homes and our workplaces, our yards, our whole planet Earth—all of these are our *shrines*. They all reflect the harmony, loving-kindness, tolerance, and compassion we embrace as we tend the garden of our universe. When we *approach* domestic chores as a sacred opportunity to practice spiritual fitness, we plant harmonious and beneficial imprint seeds in that garden. I mentioned earlier just how powerful this can be—with the example of our daughter Erin's high school graduation party. Each young person who came into our temple-home was clearly in touch with his or her sacredness.

We can regard housekeeping as an opportunity to attend to our inner shrine, while yard work and exterior maintenance serve as opportunities to attend to our outer shrine. We can consciously engage in cleaning windows as a practice to bring clarity and resolution to our vision and clear the vital link between our inner and outer sense of self. Each domestic chore can be a sacred activity— it's all in our approach and our creativity.

As we engage in such seemingly mundane or domestic activities, we can observe—from our Zen center—just how we are engaging and coordinating our three energetic intelligences, and how we are navigating the approach to each task.

COMMUNICATION

The Activity of Communication

For most of us, the activity of communication—with our family and friends, as well as in our workplace—may be the most frequent and common daily activity of all. Again, as an *activity,* we *do* engage our na'au intelligence. The practice of staying grounded in our bodies—intimately conscious of our breath and our energetic feeling— keeps us present here and now. This physical energetic presence enhances our ability to accurately and honestly listen to others and to ourselves. It also enhances our ability to articulate and speak intelligently.

Voice Positioning

Earlier we considered the practice of voice positioning—consciously centering our voice equally between our heart and our brain. Our speech accurately indicates the quality of our mana'o and pu'uwai connection. We can observe and practice the same kind of positioning with our listening. We can train our listening observation to occur equally between mana'o and pu'uwai.

As with all activities, we begin to transform our communication into spiritual practice and integration by first returning to the Zen center of our intelligence triangle. From the calm, still, silent, open, and empty Zen center, our voice positioning and our ear positioning are balanced and centered. We no longer wander off into autopilot reactive speech—speech that perpetuates the patterns of negative imprints in our relationships. Just as important as deliberately choosing our words and communications is our discernment of when not to communicate—when not to respond to or engage in speech that will give energy to negativity.

Listening

Paramount to the activity of communication is our ability to *listen*. As an example of the importance of listening, consider that our ability to safely navigate a car is first and foremost contingent on accurately observing—seeing—where we are driving. Likewise, in order to navigate in our communications, we must accurately see or listen to others. We must accurately hear what others are saying without dressing it up in our own ego-derived reactions, fears and desires. Listening begins with *contemplation*—moving away from the ego-generated noise of our mana'o intelligence and returning to our silent Zen center.

Connecting and Compassion

Regardless of how technical—mana'o oriented—our communication may be, it is always an activity that *connects* us to one another, an activity that *circulates* information. Our connective, integrative and circulatory brilliance is sourced from our pu'uwai intelligence—for both listening and speaking. When we are Zen centered and present in this connective intelligence, our intuition sharpens and we begin to tap into our natural sixth sense—our psychic abilities.

Many times we have made mention of the *tangibility of compassion*. Part of this tangibility is our ability to exchange places with someone else—to feel what she or he feels. This ability develops as we gain spiritual fitness and strengthen the harmony and integration of our mana'o and pu'uwai. *Compassion* becomes an essential element in all our communications—even the most technical. Compassion gives us the ability to accurately perceive others *and to perceive how it is that they perceive us*. With keen and accurate perception, we can communicate clearly and accurately—not just from our own perspective, but from the listener's perspective as well. After all, how many times have we communicated something in a way that we thought was crystal clear, only to have it misconstrued? This occurs as a result of imprints we plant by misconstruing our perceptions with our own ego-derived desires, fears, attachments, and aversions.

In *The Diamond Cutter*, Geshe Michael Roach refers to this compassionate and connective ability as "exchanging yourself" and clearly indicates how empowering this process is in our interactions and relationships—even beyond verbal communication. In this activity, we thoroughly blend the mediums of relationship and compassion. Since *most* of our daily interactions include communication—both listening and speaking—as the primary component of connection and exchange, then our communications are rich opportunities to develop and practice the tangibility of compassion. This opportunity exists in *every* relationship—with those who are intimately familiar and those who are apparently unknown to us.

Communication starts with compassionate listening—with exchanging yourself. Since communication is our principal way of connecting and integrating, we begin to see how the most ordinary and common daily activities are transformed into the practice of spiritual fitness through compassion—the harmonious integration of our mana'o and pu'uwai intelligences.

SOCIAL AND PLAY TIME

Are We Having Fun Yet?

We usually associate social time with getting together with friends and family for recreation and fun. How do we know when we are having fun? One of the most significant signs of fun—and one of the most beneficial activities—is humor and laughter. We can distinguish between the healthy humor and laughter of our heart and the sardonic humor and laughter of our brain. Mana'o humor usually involves diminishing others in order that we look good—a dysfunction of the isolating, distinguishing and separating process of the mana'o intelligence. *Hearty* laughter, on the other hand, is an activity of connecting with others, an activity of compassionate exchange in which we share and celebrate our humanness.

The healthful benefits of heartfelt laughter are scientifically documented—see Paul Pearsall's *Heart's Code.* These benefits include stimulating the thymus gland—located very close to the heart—which serves a key role in developing certain immune cells called T lymphocytes.

Recreation—Re-Creation

Social, party, and recreational time is our opportunity to creatively celebrate and acknowledge our sacredness—our spiritual essence. These recreational times can include music, singing, dancing, sharing food, expressive conversation, and body language, as well as creative and spontaneous activity. Recreational activities are literally just that—an opportunity for "re-creation," for regaining and renewing our creative spiritual essence.

This *play* time is our opportunity to innovatively and creatively engage all three of our energetic intelligences with genuine *spontaneity*. We can regard the term *spontaneity* as a combination of the words *respond* and *naïveté*. When we are spontaneous, we are engaged and interacting in the present moment without fears, desires, agendas, or judgments.

Painting Our Experiences

Let's imagine that our three energetic intelligences are the three primary colors—red, yellow, and blue. Combining the three primary colors in various proportions will yield the entire spectrum of colors. With just three energetic intelligences, our pallette of experience can be *infinite*. We can color our lives with exquisite beauty by creatively mixing and combining our three energetic intelligences. Social and play times offer us the greatest opportunities to creatively paint with our three energetic intelligences—to reveal the infinite magic and mystery of our spirit essence. Truly, every moment of our lives is an opportunity to creatively paint with our three intelligences—to paint the experiences of our lives.

Intoxication

So what about intoxication—isn't that also associated with party time? The truth is that humans—and some animals—have sought out and used intoxicants for millennia. Our endeavors for intoxication have been guided by a presence or absence of wisdom and judgment that ranges from divine and brilliant discernment to blind ignorance. In an unhealthy and dysfunctional context, we use intoxicants as an escape from our fears, pain, anguish, remorse, and resentment. In a healthier context, we use them to creatively mix the paints of our intelligences and to access our energetic intelligences along paths and through connections that are not otherwise evident to us.

With intoxicants, we can open and discover new access and new links among our three intelligences *or* we can weaken and deteriorate the existing access and links—sometimes temporarily and sometimes permanently. It is a very fine line of distinction between the creative and the destructive. Ironically alcohol—the most popular of all intoxicants—can cloud our discernment the most.

Even our endurance training and racing can be a form of intoxication—one that we shall discuss in "Zendurance Racing and Performance." It takes very wise discernment and self-honesty to determine what our individual limits and capacities are and what our true intent—our *approach*—is. Of all the intoxicants, laughter is probably the healthiest and safest.

Quality Play Time

Even when we are in peak training—*especially* when we are in peak training—it is a wise and healthy practice to engage in social and play time. It is essential to break away from the serious mana'o-based self-reflection and isolation to get a bigger picture.

In a social context, it is best for us to seek out creative, spontaneous, humorous, and compassionate people—those who are present here and now. Ask yourself: *Is my play time serious or humorous? Is it structured, patterned, and predictable or creative, spontaneous and imaginative? Is it light or heavy? When I'm socializing, do I end up talking mostly about work and training or am I present here and now?* We can consciously orient our social recreation and our creative playtime so that it genuinely supports and enhances our health, creativity, and well-being.

Solitude

Our creative activities do not always have to be social and outward. We may also include creative activities that we engage in alone—like painting or writing. Even gardening can be creative. We are best to listen to the wisdom of our hearts in choosing our recreational activities.

Yes, our social and recreational activities are essential to our health and balance. These activities are another rich opportunity to practice our spiritual fitness—our Zen center and presence.

WELL, HOW ABOUT SEX?

A Perfect Combination

It is appropriate that we should follow up the activities of communication as well as social and playtime with the activity of sex. Sex is, after all, a form of communication and a form of recreation. We regard sex as perhaps the most intimate form of interaction and communication, a form that includes the physical contact of touch—the language of *feel*.

With sex, the compassionate ability of exchanging yourself—as discussed in "Communication"—has a whole new relevance. It is often just as exciting and gratifying to perceive our partner's feelings and sensations as it is to experience our own. This ability to accurately perceive and respond to our partner's feelings is a significant skill in the *art* of lovemaking—a skill derived from the connective brilliance of our pu'uwai intelligence. As the intelligence of transmitting and receiving, it is through our heart that we gain fluency in lovemaking. Perhaps the greatest quest of lovemaking is to dissolve the boundaries of separation and distinction and to *feel* a complete union with our partner. In this experience of true intimacy, our individual electrical fields merge and blend to become one unified field.

Sex is one of the most powerful practices for integrating our pu'uwai and na'au intelligences. It is therefore a practice of service and diet—of giving and receiving. In the union of sexual ecstasy, there is no distinction between giving and receiving.

Equanimity

It is easy to experience this kind of ecstatic union in those first encounters with a new lover, while the excitement of polar attraction is fresh and strong. The true test is to sustain this level of sexual intimacy even when the inevitable opposite of attraction finally surfaces in our intimate relationships—*aversion.*

Ultimately, the true test of *all* relationships is to develop and cultivate *equanimity.* Equanimity enables us to transcend those temporary oscillations between strong attraction (or attachment) and aversion. For many of us, when the pendulum inevitably swings from attachment to aversion, we seek out some justifiable excuse to toss our lover out of bed and into the laundry basket as we head out to search for another. Eventually the laundry basket begins to overflow and—through the imprint seeds we plant repeatedly that focus on sustaining attraction and avoiding aversion—we end up experiencing the same pattern over and over again.

At some point we must face up to the truth—"after the ecstasy, the laundry." When we can truly abide in equanimity, then our union in *all* relationships—from intimate sexual union to brief and casual conversation with apparent strangers—transcends the criteria of aversion and attraction. Equanimity enables us to navigate and develop much stronger and deeper connections with all other beings.

How do we go beyond attraction and aversion in our most intimate relationships? This is one of the truest tests of compassion *and commitment.* As endurance athletes, we are quite familiar with the commitment and discipline—clear vision—that it takes to move beyond our mental and physical barriers to athletic training. When we encounter difficulty and obstacles, we do not permanently abandon our endurance activities to take up something else, like golf or motorcycle racing. Of course the same is true for successful golfers and motorcycle racers. It may be beneficial however to pause, retreat, and take a break when we encounter difficult obstacles that we are not able to readily dissolve. A brief "vacation" may shift our perspective—that is, our creative approach to engaging our three energetic intelligences—so that we may gracefully and effortlessly navigate through the difficult experience.

Intimacy and the Mirror

As mentioned earlier, our most intimate relationships serve as our most accurate mirrors. If we don't like what we see in the mirror, getting another mirror is not likely to improve things. With clear communication and intention, it might be wise to gently set the mirror down for a short while and then return with a renewed sense of *compassion*—of peace and harmony between our mana'o and pu'uwai. If we continue to simply exchange one mirror for the next, we will continue to see the same reflection—just a little older and a little more worn out, from our own resistance and aversion.

Around the Triangle

To summarize so far, sex—as a practice of spiritual fitness— occurs primarily in the medium of interaction and relationship. In this medium, sex connects our na'au and pu'uwai intelligences along the service/diet or giving/receiving practice leg of our triangle. As an expression of love, sexual union also functions through the medium of compassion and can serve as a powerful format for prayer and devotion—when we approach it as a sacred opportunity. And, for sure, lovemaking includes breath and movement. It can be transformed into a high form of yoga and meditation. With sex, we can wrap ourselves intimately around the entire energetic intelligence triangle, through all three mediums.

Mutual Creativity

Sex is a great opportunity for creativity, for mixing the paints—the three primary colors of our three energetic intelligences—into the full rainbow spectrum of colors. Our sexual practice can provide a fantastic creative playground for exploring the vast wilderness of feelings and our electrical energetic essence. As the process of procreation—of creating new beings—sex is an incomparable creative activity. It is a powerful interaction and exchange of creative energies and a great opportunity to practice centeredness and presence. *Trust* is an absolutely essential ingredient in this mutual practice of spiritual fitness. We develop trust through honor and commitment.

Sex in Traditional Spiritual Practice

In the Eastern religions and traditional spiritual paths, sex has a long history in the context of spiritual practice. The Hindu culture of India developed the traditional practice of Tantric sex more than a thousand years ago. Likewise, the Taoist culture of China—where tai chi originated—also developed specific sexual practices and techniques. These ancient traditions recognize sex as an opportunity to enhance and strengthen our mana. After all, the root chakra—which is the source of creative fire and our sexual energy—is situated just below our second chakra na'au intelligence center. This sexual fire can be used to heat and to strengthen our mana.

Mantak and Maneewan Chia—husband and wife—have written some excellent books, including: *Taoist Secrets of Love: Cultivating Male Sexual Energy* and *Cultivating Female Sexual Energy*. In Western culture, we typically regard sex as a necessity to release the buildup of fiery sexual energy. Through the Taoist and Tantric practices, we can begin to circulate and strengthen our sexual energy by developing our neurological intelligence and by transforming our approach. We begin to experience sexual union with our partner at greater expanded levels.

In a durable, trusting, and intimate relationship—based on equanimity that transcends attraction and aversion—we can develop spiritual fitness that brings us to greater and more gratifying levels of union between our masculine and feminine energies.

And remember—with an approach of loving-kindness and compassion—*have fun!*

T-2: TRANSITION TWO

Looking Back

Wow! We really have covered a lot of ground now. We have progressed from the physical endurance activities of swimming, biking and running all the way to the spiritual fitness practices of loving-kindness, tolerance and compassion. Is there a thread of continuity throughout this vast expanse? After all, that's quite a transition. On the surface, there is a big difference between lacing up our shoes to go for a run and lighting up candles on our shrine for the meditative practice of approaching our day.

We have now reached T-2 in *Zendurance.* Let's go back to Hawaii Ironman for some perspective on this transition. Imagine that we are just arriving at T-2 at the Old Airport Park, just north of Kailua. Way back at 7 A.M., we began our day with the 2.4-mile swim in the cool, crystalline turquoise waters of the Pacific. Now we have completed that 112-mile bike ride through the windswept and sun-scorched lava desert of the north Kona coast. It's almost impossible to find even a thread of continuity throughout this long journey, either. The sensation of that cool blue water evaporated long, long ago.

We *do* have at least one thread of continuity throughout this vast wilderness of endurance experience—our breath and our move-ment. Along with our continuous *feeling*-presence in our bodies, our breath and movement have given us a very lucid and conscious thread of continuity throughout this ocean-to-desert odyssey. They have anchored us continuously in *this present moment* for a total of 114.4 miles so far.

What a Challenge So Far!

One hundred and twelve miles of biking is *not* an easy endeav-or. Likewise, "HeartCore Zendurance" is *not* an easy read. It is, however, the most crucial material of this book. Like that 112-mile bike ride, we cover the most ground in "HeartCore." There are times we may wish to quit reading (or re-reading) this section. Of course there are also those times on the 112-mile bike ride when we may want to quit riding: *Just get me off this bike!* Even a marathon in the searing midafternoon sun can look pretty attrac-tive after about ninety miles of wind, desert, and bike.

Handling the Whole Map

Through "HeartCore Zendurance" our metaphysical map has expanded considerably since T-1 at the end of "Tri-Zen." Back then it was just three energetic intelligences, along with the zendurance practices of yielding, blending, and aligning. Now our feeble little heads are spinning with practice legs, Zen pentathlon lotus flowers, the mediums of breath, compassion and relationship, as well as shrines, a healthy diet and planting imprint seeds in the garden of our universe. We are starting to feel like master jugglers in the circus, frantically trying to keep all this metaphysical stuff up in the air without letting it all crash to the ground.

Relax! All this metaphysical stuff stays in the air all by itself. It doesn't rely on any of us. It's all completely available and accessible to us at any moment. The three energetic intelligences of mana'o, pu'uwai and na'au exist and resonate throughout our universe independent of any of us. We do not have to maintain these intelligences—only our access to them. Our infinite access to them is available right now, in each and every present moment. The practice legs that link them together and help us strengthen our access to them are infinitely available for us right now. If we approach each moment as a sacred opportunity for practice and if we are *creative* in our approach, then our navigational skills will come naturally.

The metaphysical nature of all of this makes it impossible to hold or to grasp any of it. This is especially disconcerting to our mana'o intelligence, in its endless effort to view and to hold things as distinct, isolated, and well-defined elements.

Keep in Touch

Let's go back to "What Is Feel?" for a moment. Our tactile sense of *feeling* is just as energetic as any element of our metaphysical map. *Feel* cannot be held as a distinct, isolated, or well-defined "thing." We ourselves are energetic electrical entities who are constantly changing, metamorphosing, evolving and transitioning. There just ain't nothin' to hold on to. The best we can do is to simply practice loving-kindness, tolerance, and compassion.

The purpose for reading "HeartCore Zendurance" is not to rationally comprehend or memorize the material. Rather, we begin to recognize our infinite opportunity *and* our natural and creative ability to access and engage our three energetic intelligences—to mix the paints—in each moment of our lives. We begin to awaken to our lucid consciousness and spiritual fitness through breath and movement, as well as our infinite capacity for tolerance and compassion and the interactivity of relationship.

Reading material like "HeartCore," the books mentioned therein, or similar material that speaks especially to our hearts will provide us with a steady diet of healthy spiritual food. Every time we eat some of this spiritual food, we assimilate some of it, while the rest passes on through. If our diet is sensible and consistent, if we do not starve ourselves of this spiritual food, then—with training and exercise—we will effectively develop our spiritual fitness.

Icing the Cake

In the next section, "Zendurance Racing and Performance," we are going to see just how our "Tri-Zen" and "HeartCore Zendurance" practices have prepared us for one of the greatest passions in our lives—our racing performance. It's time to demonstrate and celebrate our spiritual fitness in one of our favorite arenas. It's time to *race!*

When it comes to our goal races, many of us know from experience that when we arrive at the starting line, we have already done the really hard work. We have already baked the cake. Now it's time for the icing and decorations!

WHEN WE REACH THE STARTING LINE,
95 PERCENT OF THE WORK IS COMPLETE.
THE RACE IS THE ICING ON THE CAKE.

3

ZENDURANCE RACING AND PERFORMANCE

WHY RACE?

THE HEART OF RACING

RACING AND EGO

CENTERING AND PEAKING

GIVEAWAY RACING

ZENDURANCE PERFORMANCE

PERFORMANCE AND STRESS

CHEMISTRY AND ZENDURANCE PERFORMANCE

THE NATURE OF OUR RACE ENTITY

EMBRACING ATTACHMENT: WHY NOT RACE?

COMPETITION: A PETITION FOR COMPANIONSHIP

WHY RACE?

Solitude and Communion

In our explorations of Zendurance as a healthy, functional spiritual path, we have focused primarily on our endurance *training* activities and how we can transform these daily activities into a meditative zendurance practice. This is the principle aim of "Tri-Zen." We have also considered how we can integrate this zendurance practice into our day-to-day lives as ordinary, healthy human beings in "HeartCore Zendurance." These two processes comprise the essence of zendurance as a complete and healthy way of living, loving, and growing.

Our zendurance training includes the essential element of *solitude*. Solitude enables us to begin the five-step Zen pentathlon through contemplation. As the historian Gibbon once said, "Solitude is the school of genius." Through the meditative contemplation of solitude, we access our true creative nature—the pure potentiality and infinite possibility of our calm, still, silent, open, and empty Zen center. Most traditional spiritual practices place some degree of emphasis on solitude. We recognize that in some extreme cases—the hermetic monks in the caves of the Himalayas, for example—solitude is a total way of living.

Other traditional spiritual paths place a great deal of emphasis on communion and companionship. In "HeartCore Zendurance," we considered how our interactions with others are a fundamental and essential part of our spiritual path—especially as we learn to integrate our zendurance practice into our lives as healthy, ordinary human beings. Siddhartha, the first human to attain Buddhahood, discovered his enlightenment—after many years of extreme asceticism—by following the *middle path*. This middle path includes a balance of solitude *and* companionship.

Is Racing Required?

If zendurance *training* is our solitary activity of contemplation, approach, and practice, then zendurance *racing* must naturally be our communal athletic practice of integration and contribution. Does this mean that we are *required* to participate in races so that we can complete the spiritual pentathlon process? *No.* There are many, myriad activities we can engage in that enable us to com-

232   SHANE ALTON EVERSFIELD

plete those two remaining steps of integration and contribution without racing.

In truth, it is *essential* that we *do* engage in communal activities other than racing to complete the Zen pentathlon. After all, the essence of zendurance is to live our lives *completely*—moment to moment—as spiritual beings. As human spiritual beings, we are more than athletes—99.99 percent of us also have families, friends, jobs and/or community activities. These are the arenas where our opportunities for integration and contribution are most promising, as we considered in "HeartCore." In this section, we will examine how these practices *outside* of athletics actually empower us as racers and can enhance our race performances.

So Why Race?

So, racing is *not* necessary in our realization of zendurance as a complete spiritual path in life. Well then, *why race*? If racing is not necessary, what are the opportunities inherent in racing that can empower and enrich our practice of Zendurance?

The most obvious aspect of racing is the motivation it gives us to train diligently and consistently. Many of us have experienced this same motivation in the form of deadlines in other areas of our lives. These deadlines offer us a clear time frame in which we must accomplish a well-defined task. Racing is quite similar. Once we have sent in the entry form and fee, we have created a real, tangible commitment with ourselves to arrive at the starting line well prepared to cross the finish line.

Early on, in "Starting Line," we considered the nature of discipline. We considered how our *clarity of vision* provides us with a healthy sense of motivation and discipline. Submitting that race application provides us with just such a clear vision. It is, however, important to distinguish between a *goal*—a clearly defined objective or milestone along our path—and our *direction*—where it is that our path is ultimately leading us. Our commitment to a race provides us with a *goal*—a clear vision—whether that goal is simply to finish the race gracefully or to finish within a specific time frame. Our commitment to zendurance—as an approach to our training and our lives—provides us with our *direction* and assists us in navigating our chosen path. Our *direction* is the big picture, so to speak. Our *goals*—just like mile markers on the race course—provide us with clear indicators of our progress along the chosen path.

Goals, in the form of races, are not necessary for all zendurance practitioners. Some of us progress along our zendurance paths, setting and realizing goals in our lives without ever racing. Even without racing, the clear vision that motivates our zendurance training practice is already part of the bigger picture of our lives and adequately supports and empowers us through the steps of integration and contribution.

Then there are those of us who *thrive* on races. For some of us, racing can even be addicting. (We will consider this as well.) The practice of racing can provide us with something even more valuable than goal-oriented motivation. Zendurance racing can also challenge and enhance our overall spiritual fitness in ways that zendurance training alone cannot. This is the subject of our next entry, "The Heart of Racing."

THE HEART OF RACING

True Meaning of Competition

Racing is often synonymous with *competition*. What is competition? If we examine the parts of this word, we can interpret the meaning to be "a petition for *companionship* or company." There is nothing in this interpretation to suggest or encourage aggressiveness, conflict or the notion of beating others. In its pure essence, a competition is simply a gathering of individuals.

In the context of a race, this petition for companionship—this gathering—is usually comprised of volunteers and spectators, as well as athletes. All three groups of individuals contribute vitally to the quality of our race. Consider the Hawaii Ironman: Over fifteen hundred athletes compete in this event, supported by more than five thousand volunteers—with estimates running as high as eight thousand. The support of the volunteers and race staff is essential to any endurance athletic competition and is often one of the most memorable aspects of the race experience for many athletes. Spectators are also a significant element in many endurance events, including our loved ones, who line up along the course—especially at the finish line.

Pu'uwai Intelligence and Racing

In relationship to our intelligence triangle, we have considered how the solitude of our daily zendurance training primarily engages and coordinates our mana'o and na'au intelligences and most clearly resembles the traditional spiritual practices of yoga and meditation. The companionship and support of racing engages our pu'uwai intelligence. Our heart center intelligence is clearly expressed through the charitable intentions of many of our races and by organizations like Team in Training, Joints in Motion and Challenged Athletes Foundation.

Giving and Receiving

Pu'uwai intelligence is also essential in the relationship between volunteers and athletes. In this relationship, we discover the traditional spiritual practices of service and diet—blending our pu'uwai and na'au intelligences. What do volunteers do for us as athletes? They serve us and support us. Among other services, volunteers give us liquids and food. This is the literal giving and receiving of service and diet.

The traditional practices of prayer and devotion integrate our mana'o and pu'uwai intelligences. Both spectators and volunteers attend races out of a devotion to the athletes and to the health and fitness that athletes emulate. Volunteers may also choose to participate out of a sense of devotion to the charitable causes that many races benefit. Volunteers and spectators—through their cheers, their gestures, and their words of encouragement—are essentially praying for us as athletes. These are sincere prayers for our graceful passage and successful completion.

As athletes, we are obviously at the receiving end of this devotion, prayer, service, and diet. Yet racing is an opportunity for us to give as well. Certainly we are contributing a lot of energy as we race and we have also given and invested a lot of time and energy in the training that has brought us to this moment. Our race performance provides inspiration to both volunteers and spectators. Our daily devotion to and discipline in training inspires our families and friends—especially if this activity is in a healthy balance with the rest of our lives. We may even be a great source of inspiration to those in our community—even those we have never met—when they see us training while passing by in their cars. Our pu'uwai intelligence of circulation—giving and receiving—is functioning on many levels and weaves a complex tapestry through our training and, even more so, our racing. This circulatory intelligence extends far beyond the boundaries of our logical mana'o intellect and our five senses.

The Heart of Racing

Pu'uwai intelligence is the source of the synergy, the magic, and the mystery we experience in racing. As the intelligence of circulation and integration, our heart's intelligence functions to links us all together, to assemble all of us into a single living and breathing entity that we label our "race." At an endurance event as grand as a marathon or a triathlon, all of us—athletes, volunteers and spectators alike—clearly experience the synergy and collective intelligence of something far greater than our individual identities. It is the spirit of the *race itself.* The empowerment, insight, and inspiration that we experience as a part of this greater organism demonstrate clearly the expansive wisdom and powerful capacity of our pu'uwai intelligence. Our race entity can provide us with vivid and

undeniable experiences of our true nature beyond individual ego—
our collective spirit of pure potentiality and infinite possibility.

Our Athletic Family

In many fields of endurance activities, there are athletic clubs
that organize weekly training activities—such as masters swim
sessions, evening runs, or Saturday long rides. Many such clubs
also put on races. Club-sponsored races are often filled with
"aloha" and a strong embracing sense of family—truly a petition for
companionship. Participating in athletic club activities can help us
disarm our fears, engage our pu'uwai intelligence, and experience
a genuine and loving connection with our fellow athletes—even as
we put in a high-intensity race performance. Since we feel the
embrace of trust and friendship through athletic clubs, it can be
easier to open our hearts. Competing with friends through club
affiliation allows us to relax and to be present with others beyond
our fears. Local athletic clubs offer us the opportunity to practice
family in a purely athletic context.

The Human Race

For those of us familiar with the history of Hawaii Ironman,
there was one particular moment in the televised coverage of the
February 1982 race that reached deeply into the soul of each viewer and revealed the essential nature of endurance racing. It was not
the start of fifteen hundred swimmers thrashing in Kamakahonu
Bay, at the start of the 140.6-mile race. It was not a long duel
between two leaders or even the victorious breaking of the finish
line tape by the winner. It was Julie Moss collapsing three times in
the final three tenths of a mile and being passed by Kathleen
McCarthy as Julie *crawled* the last thirty feet to the finish line. (An
ironic side note: The finish line was eventually moved sixty feet
back down the road.)

This event somehow conveyed to the passive and removed TV
audience the true nature of endurance racing. Julie vividly portrayed the endearing capacity in each of us to courageously and
compassionately embrace our human limitations—without self-
pity. The empathy it evoked in each viewer was tangible and undeniable. The media of our culture is born almost completely out of
mana'o intelligence and typically ignores and excludes our
pu'uwai—yet there was no denying or hiding this heart-rendering
experience. To this day, the most riveting aspect of the televised

coverage of Hawaii Ironman, the most powerful element of witnessing *any* endurance race—as an athlete, volunteer, or spectator—is our tangible *connection* with one another, through our collective pu'uwai intelligence.

The award-winning television coverage of Hawaii Ironman has not earned acclaim simply by covering the contest for first place. Rather, we are moved to tears by real human beings gathering every ounce of their compassion, courage, faith, and commitment to complete this rite of passage (or to support those who are) with dignity, grace, patience, humility, and integrity. In this context, endurance racing becomes a metaphor for life. It is a pilgrimage with clear parameters—a start, a finish, a defined course or path, as well as rules and conditions designed to make us "equal" for fair competition and mutual communion.

Assets for Racing—Individual and Collective

In this metaphor, as in life, we are endowed with *two valuable assets*. First, each of us *individually* is endowed with an infinite experience-ability and unlimited access to our three energetic intelligences. It is our diligence and commitment to zendurance training that largely determines how much of this infinite potential each of us realizes with regard to endurance athletic capacities.

The second essential asset that we are each endowed with—in both racing and in life—is the company and *companionship* of each other. Through this communion, the synergy of our *collective* energy and intelligence is far greater than our individual and isolated energies and intelligence. In racing, as in life, it is by sharing our pain and ecstasy, our fears and brilliance, our vulnerability and invincibility that we inspire, empower, and enable each other to continue on with grace, humility, dignity, and integrity. Great performances—in racing and in life—come from this collective, synergetic empowerment, mixed with our infinite individual experience-ability. During our greatest performances, these two assets—individual "experience-ability" and collective integrity—blend seamlessly together, becoming indistinguishable.

Summary

Zendurance racing is a conscious practice of accessing and channeling our pu'uwai intelligence. Through our heart's intelligence, we can link up and blend with the collective intelligence and energy of our living, breathing race entity. Only through this pu'uwai link-up to our race entity do we have the opportunity to channel this collective energy and intelligence.

As individuals, racing provides us with an opportunity to test and evaluate our zendurance capacity as well as the effectiveness of our technical and creative approach to training. More importantly, racing provides us with an opportunity to see just how effectively we can transcend our individual, ego-based fears, desires, greed, and limitations so that we can truly access the greater empowering energy and intelligence of our race entity. Herein lies the true source of great race performances—of remarkable accomplishments and genuine satisfaction, as well as profound and illuminating life experiences.

RACING AND EGO

"If you magnify the pure spark of spirit through the puffy lens of ego, you risk burning a hole through your soul."
—Tom Robbins, *Fierce Invalids Home From Hot Climates*

Fear and Anxiety

Virtually all of us have experienced the pre-race jitters brought on by our fears, anxiety, and uncertainty. Where do these nerve-fraying jitters come from? What causes our fears and anxieties? What can we do to alleviate this nervousness?

For some of us, the fear and anxiety we experience before a race can be more energy consuming and exhausting than the race itself. This jittery condition can significantly hamper our performance potential and can be detrimental to our physical health as well as our mental and emotional health. Some of us who get completely overwhelmed by pre-race anxiety may avoid racing altogether.

Our fear and anxiety are usually strongest before a goal race—an endurance race that will push us beyond our strongly held conceptions of who we are and what we are capable of. Perhaps we are attempting to finish a race that is longer than any previous race or training session we have ever completed. Or maybe we are attempting to finish a race faster than we have ever covered that same distance. In either case, we are challenging our perceived limitations and capacities. Our true essential spirit nature is infinite and boundless—and this is what we intend to express and to manifest by going beyond our previous achievements.

If our true nature is infinite and boundless, then why do we experience the jitters? Those fears, doubts and anxieties come from our ego-based addiction and attachment to security and certainty. We examined the nature of ego as a function of *mistaken identity* in "Intelligence of Tri Zen." In this scenario, we incorrectly identify our isolating and distinguishing mana'o intelligence as being our true, essential nature. In this mistaken identity, we shift our center of being away from the infinite, boundless, creative, and pure potentiality of our true sacred nature—the Zen center of our intelligence triangle—where anything is possible. We get stuck in the isolating and distinguishing mana'o intelligence, where we view competition as *me against them.*

Racing as a Challenge of Centering

From this ego identity, it is only natural that we experience fear, anxiety, and nervous jitters. Racing is an excellent and challenging opportunity to practice centeredness—our ability to remain steadfast in the Zen center of our intelligence triangle. When we slip into ego, we can no longer access our na'au and pu'uwai intelligences. Without our na'au intelligence of activity and movement, we are paralyzed with fear. Without our pu'uwai intelligence of circulation, we are disconnected and shrouded in doubt and isolation.

Racing mastery begins with Zen centeredness. Effective, intelligent racing originates in our ability to orchestrate and blend *all three* intelligences—without slipping into the mire of ego. This is the true challenge of racing. Can we embrace the *wisdom of uncertainty* without grabbing for the attachment of security and certainty? In his book *The Seven Laws of Spiritual Success*, Deepak Chopra eloquently expresses the empowering possibilities of *uncertainty* in the Sixth Law, the "Law of Detachment."

We have already considered detachment as the process of disengaging from our ego-driven attachment and our mistaken identity with mana'o intelligence. This detachment transforms our mana'o from the indiscriminate and flailing ego-driven chainsaw into the swift and silent sword of skillful means. In this process of disengaging and returning to the Zen center, we give up our attachment to the *security* and *certainty* that our ego so desperately clings to. This process of detachment does not require that we become *apathetic*—we simply *disengage* from our mistaken identity—ego.

When we are truly Zen centered, we are calm and completely present with uncertainty—with *not knowing*. We can patiently and calmly contemplate *questions* and remain *open* to possibilities—without attachment to the immediate gratification of answers or the security of closure. Odd as it may seem, our calm, still, silent, open, and empty Zen center is the *source* of uncertainty. Out of this fertile ground of uncertainty springs our infinite creativity and our true, open, and genuine presence in this moment.

The *wisdom* of uncertainty empowers us with the ability to respond *brilliantly* in this moment. Through this wisdom, we find the courage and the willingness to venture into unfamiliar territory, knowing full well that in this unfamiliar territory, we are gifted and endowed with infinite compassion, creativity, and freedom. We willingly relinquish our attachment to everything familiar—both in our surroundings and in *our own character*. This attachment to the familiar is a desperate clinging to our past patterns playing out over and over again. Our attachment and past patterns imprison and cripple us in the present moment. By moving into the unknown, we move into the infinite field of possibilities and cultivate an attitude of openness where our responses in this moment are fresh, creative, and brilliant.

An Exotic Vacation

As an illustration of this, imagine traveling to an exotic place with unfamiliar geography and a strange culture. At first we feel unsettled, strange, and out of place—*uncertain*. As we begin to relax and open up to our *wisdom* of uncertainty, we begin to experience the mystery, adventure, and excitement of this fresh and unfamiliar place. We start to trust our spiritual fitness *and intelligence*. We begin to masterfully mix the paints of our three energetic intelligences into fresh new colors. These new colors reflect back to us our own magic and mystery. The wisdom of uncertainty endows us with the ability to navigate through the unknown, finding the excitement and exhilaration of each new moment.

Exhilaration

Is this not the *true spirit* of racing? Honestly, if we knew exactly how our race was going to turn out well ahead of time, how much motivation would we have to train? How attentive would we be to the quality of our training sessions? Spectators are attracted to a race by uncertainty and the potential for surprising, unpredictable and remarkable performances. They are drawn by excitement, magic, and mystery.

When we are Zen centered in our intelligence triangle, then uncertainty—the infinite field of possibilities and potentiality—is like a pristine, breathtaking wilderness. From the mistaken identity of ego, the same wilderness is threatening and terrifying. It is not the wilderness or the uncertainty of racing that can be scary, it is our perception of it. When we are Zen centered, we embrace the *wisdom* of uncertainty and find exhilaration, inspiration, and excitement in the days leading up to our big race.

CENTERING AND PEAKING

Introduction

For most of us, the fear, anxiety, and nervousness we experience before a race vanishes just as soon as the race begins. Immediately we find ourselves in a calm and centered place. Why is this?

In "What Is Feel?" we examined the phenomenon of muscle memory along with the process of clearing past traumatic experiences and fears through our zendurance approach to training. As we activate our neurological and muscular systems during our zendurance training—from our calm, still, silent, open, and empty Zen center—those traumatic cellular memories are cleared and replaced with a calm, abiding serenity. Consequently, as soon as our race starts, we begin to activate those nerve and muscle cells through familiar movements. The calm, clear, and abiding serenity replaces or mana'o-based, ego-centered fears. In this kinetic state, it is much easier for us to stay Zen centered in our intelligence triangle. After all, this is the essence of our zendurance training.

The Recovery Dilemma

Finding this Zen centeredness can be particularly challenging in the final weeks and days before our race for two reasons. First, the uncertainty of our race is looming ever closer each day. Second, we are decreasing our training as we taper in order to recover for our significant goal race. This reduction in training means we are spending less time in our zendurance meditation, where we so frequently experience the familiar serenity held in our muscle memory. This is the dilemma of recovery that we often experience before racing.

Those of us who rely solely on our endurance training as a way of staying centered and calm may choose to train with little reduction in duration or intensity right up to race day—just to maintain some semblance of sanity, even if it is at the expense of our recovery and race performance. There *are*, however, other ways of practicing Zen centeredness without our usual quota of endurance training so that we can allow our bodies to recover and to peak for a great race performance and still avoid the fatigue of pre-race jitters. Let's consider some of these alternatives.

Centering Through Diversity

The very essence of zendurance as a way of life is to integrate the spiritual fitness that we have developed through our zendurance training into each and every moment of our lives. The preceding section, "HeartCore Zendurance," is a guide to initiating this *most essential* integration. As we gain experience in the practical art of HeartCore Zendurance, we empower ourselves with this most precious and valuable ability—seamless, graceful, and continuous Zen centeredness and effortless power—regardless of the quantity, intensity, or proficiency of our endurance training. True mastery of HeartCore Zendurance liberates us completely from the necessity of having to practice or train in order to experience Zen centeredness. Attaining this level of mastery is the essence of all spiritual paths. It is an exceedingly difficult and arduous path, yet the rewards and benefits for all are immeasurable.

In the practice of HeartCore Zendurance, we begin to approach this mastery of continuous and seamless Zen centeredness and effortless power by integrating and equally balancing *all three* of our energetic intelligences. We know already that our individually oriented zendurance training focuses primarily on the integration of mana'o and na'au intelligences. Zendurance *racing*, however, requires a well-developed pu'uwai intelligence. This indicates the value of expanding beyond our athletic training to the practice of HeartCore Zendurance in our daily lives to develop and articulate our pu'uwai intelligence—even for the sake of racing performance alone.

The Gift of Family

Those weeks and days before a goal race leave us with more time away from training. In addition to rest and recovery, this free time provides a great opportunity to diversify our zendurance practice to the HeartCore level. We can spend more quality time *practicing* family—one of the best pu'uwai practices. Increased quality time with our family and loved ones can do wonders for our happiness, health, and well-being—as we rest and recover before the big one. What a great time to express and share our gratitude and appreciation—for our health and for the love, support, and nurturing we receive from our family and friends. If our race entails traveling, the companionship of our family or friends transforms the trip into a vacation. As we travel and prepare to race, let's remember to embrace the *wisdom of uncertainty*. Children are masters at that.

244   SHANE ALTON EVERSFIELD

Activities of service, such as volunteering—perhaps volunteering for a race that we do not compete in—can be very gratifying and appropriate during our rest and recovery just before or after our big race.

Emphasize Meditation

If our zendurance practice includes meditation, yoga, or tai chi, we may increase the duration, frequency, and quality of these practices as we decrease our training volume and intensity. Even our reduced endurance training sessions provide great opportunities to sharpen our focus on movement meditation.

Our training activity immediately preceding a goal race is usually comprised of easy, low-intensity sessions that include a few very short, high-intensity bursts. During the low intensity base of these sessions, we can practice our tai chi approach—very slow, effortless, and seamless movements executed with deliberate and perfect form. We can diligently practice total yielding in our swimming, complete blending with our bikes, and perfect alignment in our running. During this easy, low-intensity base, we can really strive to *breathe our movements*—to breathe slowly and deeply and to completely coordinate our movements with our breath. During each of the very short, high-intensity bursts, we can strive to maintain the same tai-chi-like quality. Our form and effort in these bursts should appear and feel as easy and as calm as the low-intensity base. Our meditative zendurance approach is the thread of continuity between these two extremes during these final training sessions.

Be Connected Here and Now

In the last few days just before the race, our wisdom of uncertainty begins to peak. Our presence in *this* moment—the *now*—becomes absolute. From the time we awaken in the morning, each and every movement is slow, fluid, effortless, and centered. Every word we speak is soft and calm. Every breath is conscious, deliberate, slow, and deep. We are kind, patient, tolerant, and compassionate in each and every interaction with others.

This is especially true with our fellow competitors—let's call them companions—and the volunteers we interact with during the check-in, registration, and pre-race meetings. We are attentive to any and all opportunities to support and facilitate our fellow athletes. We are generous with our knowledge of the race course and registration procedures, of good restaurants, activities and so forth. During our final training sessions, as we get oriented and familiar with the racecourse, we share that knowledge and familiarity with others. This is especially true if we are locals, or have participated in this race before. We share our knowledge of what to expect during the race—wind and water conditions and other possible weather factors.

Our final training sessions are a great time to join up and train with other athletes, even complete strangers. These connections can be quite spontaneous and need not last for the whole training session. We constantly remind ourselves that we are here for *competition*—a petition for *companionship*. When race day arrives, our pu'uwai intelligence is peaked so that we link up easily to the incredibly powerful, energetic, and conscious entity of our race. How we embrace and support our fellow athletes and volunteers in the days before the race largely determines how the race entity will embrace and support us.

Lighten Up!

Another valuable asset as we prepare for our big race—and an extremely valuable asset throughout our lives—is the lightness of *heartfelt* humor. Such genuine humor is not derisive or degrading to others. It is humor that comes from a wise and compassionate recognition of our commonly shared human condition or predicament. What exactly is that human condition? It is simply our tendency to fall into the *mire*, the mistaken identity of ego—our isolating, distinguishing mana'o-based survival mode.

When we *really* take ourselves seriously—like the days before a big race—we easily slip into that fear-based survival mode, *me against them*. The seriousness of survival mode is perhaps the most difficult time to find humor in *any* situation. Yet humor of the heart gracefully releases us from the stronghold of ego and moves us back to Zen center. Humor touches our hearts and reconnects us with the wisdom of uncertainty. It is most difficult to find humor when we are experiencing frustration and aggravation, when we feel powerless and things are not going as expected. It takes tremendous courage and humility to step back and laugh at ourselves during these trials and tribulations. Humor is a most effective tool for moving from resistance and frustration into choice and effortless power. (Yeah, this is definitely one of my weakest sports—how about you?)

It is no coincidence that the words *human* and *humor* are so similar, so close. *Human* can refer to our tendency to slip unknowingly into our mistaken ego identity. *Hey, I'm only human. Humor* identifies our ability to catch ourselves as we slip into ego, to laugh at ourselves and to return to our Zen center of the intelligence triangle by *lightening up.* In this process of lightening up, we release our burden of expectation, and our desire and attachment to certainty—the oppressive weight of our ego. We return to the light, to the brilliance of our spirit essence.

Hearty laughter is a prominent character trait of many of the world's most respected and accomplished spiritual masters—indeed many of the world's *happiest people.*

Living Examples

As athletes, let's consider a few examples of how valuable humor can be. The first example comes from Kara Douglass Thom's book *Becoming an Ironman.* Bob Babbitt—recently inducted into the Ironman Hall of Fame—recalls the experience of his first Ironman in 1980. It's one of the funniest stories I've ever read. In those pioneering days (1980 was the third running of Ironman), just finishing the race was virtually unexplored territory, filled with uncertainty. Back then each athlete arranged his or her own support crew. Very little information was available on how to train, how to prepare, how to fuel, how to race, or even what the racecourse was like.

Bob arrived on Oahu with saddlebags, a tent, and sleeping bag, figuring that—given the distance of each leg of the race—this must be a two-day event. He did not realize this was a nonstop, one-shot deal until the day before the race—that's when he reluctantly removed the saddlebags from his bike. Because he did not know how to change a tire, his bike was equipped with solid rubber tires. Since the event was being held in Hawaii, Bob figured that twenty loaves of Hawaiian sweet bread would be appropriate nutrition for the race. Bob Babbitt actually *gained weight* during his pilgrimage.

What strikes me about his recollection is how he responded to his ignorance and the uncertainty of this ordeal with humor and naïveté. His lack of knowledge and training made him a prime candidate for misery, yet his humor and positive outlook transformed this ordeal into a somewhat graceful and smooth accomplishment.

Many of us have met or at least heard of the legendary Cowman. Another hard-core pioneer in the world of organized ultra-endurance athletics, Cowman helps us to remember the "bovine" in each of us. Built like a Viking and now more than fifty-five years old, Cowman is not likely to be out there burning up the race course. Typically you will see him sauntering along, wearing his heavy cow horns and carrying a camera. He's more eager to stop and talk and to capture a photo opportunity than to get to the finish line.

While this casual attitude may seem to oppose the whole spirit of racing, it's actually quite healthy if we consider our race as a metaphor for life. Do we really want to streak to the finish line of our lives as quickly and urgently as possible—without ever pausing to savor the moment and enjoy the companionship of others? Cowman's approach strongly engages pu'uwai intelligence in his eagerness to celebrate companionship as the true essence of competition. His performance is not about speed and grace. It is about the joy of being alive and in the company of others. "Ah-moo-ha!" According to Cowman, that's how cows in Hawaii say "Aloha!"

Cowman is a rare and unique character. On the other hand, most of us are far more goal oriented and performance conscious. We enjoy the high intensity—mentally, physically, and emotionally—of training and racing to expand our boundaries, conceptions, and limitations. In the exhilaration of this drive and intensity, I constantly remember one particular expression or slogan that helps me keep it light. I humorously share the expression with others when they tell me how inspiring my discipline and devotion are or compliment me on a race performance. I graciously accept their encouragement and praise. Then I laugh and remind them—as well as myself—that, *Hey, I'm just a legend in my own mind.*

GIVEAWAY RACING

Introduction

In the true essence of competition, it is congregation and celebration that really engage our pu'uwai intelligence and inspire and nurture our true spirit nature. With sincere gratitude for the companionship—like Cowman—we can deliberately choose to race without the consuming, glory-seeking motivation of our me-against-them ego and simply enjoy the camaraderie of our athletic clan. This provides us with an unsurpassed opportunity to *open up* and to join with the greater entity of the race itself—without the preoccupation or attachment to some desired outcome. We can deliberately choose to kick back and relax through a casual approach to some of our less-than-significant and nongoal races.

Let's call these giveaway races. We choose to participate in these races *without concern for our placement results.* Instead we earnestly focus on being calm and serene, concentrating on our zendurance meditative approach toward effortless power. With clear and deliberate intent we simply *cruise* the race. We allow others to pass us by unchallenged as we abide in our Zen center—that calm, still, silent, open, and empty space of deep inner listening and contemplation.

Imagine that! Racing from a place of calmness, stillness, silence, openness, and emptiness—from a place of absolute relaxation. Our form is beautiful and graceful—as though we were *dancing* rather than racing. We observe quietly how our ego flares up as we watch athletes who are usually much slower than us go sailing by. We simply *relax* and let it be. We just keep on dancing effortlessly and gracefully and we find *peace* with all of it. We are relaxed and genuinely present with everyone before, during, and after the race. We look to our companionship with others as our inspiration and satisfaction, rather than our individual performance. This is how we learn to embrace the true meaning of competition—a petition for companionship.

The Rewards of Our Giveaway

What can we expect to receive in exchange for our giveaway race? We have the precious opportunity to clear our cellular nerve and muscle memories of exertion, pain, and tension, along with the emotions and attitudes of anxiety, fear, aggression, and nervousness that we usually associate with performance racing. This clearing is the most effective remedy for the jitters and will facilitate us in being calm and relaxed before and during our performance and goal-oriented races.

We also develop a stronger ability to access and draw upon our pu'uwai intelligence and to tap into the collective power and intelligence of our race entity. We gain the experience and capacity to remain Zen centered without being sucked into the drama and attachment of our ego. We are able to thoroughly enjoy and to be completely present in the powerful wisdom of uncertainty. In the long term—the big picture—these benefits far outweigh the recognition and reward of placing high and performing at peak in every single race. Go ahead, *share* the glory!

Racing Like a Drunken Sailor

I had the opportunity a few years ago to study briefly with Peter Ralston, a truly progressive and pioneering artist in the field of martial arts and author of *Cheng Hsin: Principles of Effortless Power*. Peter has been a great inspiration for the vision and development of zendurance. Earlier in his life—long before I met him—Peter had become a very accomplished fighter in many martial art forms. At this time, he began to explore and to study in earnest the more subtle and profound principles of effortless power. This was a deep internal investigation into areas of experience that few, if any, martial artists have ventured into in modern times.

When he began this investigation, he radically changed his approach to competition. He completely gave up trying to accomplish anything in the fighting ring. Peter's focus was complete and total relaxation during competition. His attention was fixed solely on blending and integrating with his opponent and on accurately and instantly perceiving the opponent's intentions and agendas. This accurate perception was only possible for Peter by being completely present in the moment—without any intentions or agendas of his own. As he expressed it, he "fought like a drunken sailor." A soft and yielding approach to his fighting, as well as complete presence and awareness in the moment, were essential conditions for him to discover and *allow* the principles of effortless power to arise within his experience and in his interactions with his opponents.

As a result of his complete surrender and integration, he began to *clearly perceive* his opponent's intentions and actions *even before*

these actions were initiated. Through his total relaxation and surrender, he was completely present in the moment, without any agendas or desires. Appropriate, effective, and brilliant responses would
arise through Peter without any reasoning or constructing on his
part. In this complete state of presence, his opponent's actions and
techniques were useless—no matter how innovative, unique or
sophisticated. Peter made *no effort* to accomplish anything except to
be completely present and to blend thoroughly and seamlessly.

We may recall our image of water, from the entry on swimming.
Water is able to flow and shape-shift instantly. From experience, I
can say that sparring with Peter is like *sparring with water.* For
every move I make, Peter is responding, shifting and reshaping
instantly. I had the very clear visceral experience—the *feeling*—that
any action I took simply rebounded from Peter back at me.

Peter simply became transparent, invisible. I could not *feel* any
solidity in him. I felt only myself through him. He was a mirror and
I was my own undoing, my own demise—*every time.* In his completely open state—in his absolute presence here and now—Peter
simply *allows* the principles of effortless power to arise each
moment. This requires absolute softness, suppleness and surrender. His approach is so powerful and so effective that he won the
World Championship Full Contact Martial Arts Tournament. Peter
is the only non-Asian ever to do so. His relaxed, playful and creative approach is absolutely effective even in a potentially deadly
fighting competition. (Yes, people have been killed in this tournament. There is no protective gear, no weapons, and no rules.)

This is the very same approach we can explore in our giveaway
races. From the moment we arise in the morning, we can focus on
being completely present here and now, on being Zen centered so
that we can instantly and effortlessly access and channel all three
of our energetic intelligences. As we travel to the starting area and
prepare for our giveaway race, we keep the *clear* intent to stay present and centered—we notice immediately when we begin to slip
into the me-against-them survival mode of ego. *We give it up!* This
is absolutely our complete focus as we gather for the start—*connecting* with our athletic companions through pu'uwai intelligence.
We strive to *disarm* ourselves by being light, humorous, relaxed,
kind, generous, humble, and supportive of others.

We begin the giveaway race thoroughly relaxed—drunk on the
intoxication of moving and dancing gracefully and effortlessly with
our companions. (While we are on the subject of intoxication, the

giveaway race is a good opportunity to abstain from adrenaline-tweaking caffeine. We are more apt to relax without it.) The relaxation and intoxication grow as we flow easily and effortlessly through the race. Each stride or stroke expresses and emanates our serenity and effortless well-being so that our companions can absorb and enjoy this serenity as well—similar to a practice of tonglen, as mentioned in "HeartCore." At the finish line, we thoroughly enjoy the afterglow as we celebrate the grace and serenity of our race and the breakthrough accomplishments of our companions. Go ahead, *share* the glory! When we celebrate the accomplishments of others, we can enjoy their glory. Everyone is willing to share the experience of glory. After all, there is no glory if it is not shared and celebrated in the presence of others.

The Dress Rehearsal

For those of us who are type A's, the giveaway race is a very *daring* endeavor. After all, what will others think of us if we finish out of the running? Will we lose respect? Will we ever be able to show our faces in this town again? Will we simply become legends in our own minds? For us, the giveaway race holds the greatest potential for insight and wisdom. It is like a *dress rehearsal.*

In the days leading up to our next significant goal race, we will be glad that we made the giveaway—that we experienced the dress rehearsal. It is a small price to pay for the *freedom* we will gain—the freedom from anxiety, fear, and stress, the freedom from our ego's attachment. The giveaway race can renew our joy in racing and performing. It is invaluable in building a bridge that allows us to approach performance racing with the same zendurance meditation we experience in our training. This bridge we build is constructed with relaxation and detachment so that we can embrace and appreciate the wisdom of uncertainty.

Remember, the dress rehearsal of the giveaway race has nothing to do with fast race performances. It has *everything* to do with the quality of our *presence* in the here-and-now—before, during, and after the race. It is a dress rehearsal for the orchestration of all three intelligences so that we may respond brilliantly to the uncertainty of the moment. If we really relax and enjoy the giveaway races, we will begin to relax and enjoy all our races with the same grace and effortless ease—even the big one.

ZENDURANCE PERFORMANCE

Introduction To Performance

The term *performance* applies to both athletics *and* to the performing arts—the live arts of theater, music, and dance. As a term common to both areas, *performance* indicates that certain similarities exist between the performing arts and athletic performance. In both areas, the performance can involve a group of people—such as a symphony orchestra or a basketball team—or the performance may be solo, such as a violinist or a marathoner.

In both athletics and the arts, performances are live—they embrace the exhilaration and wisdom of uncertainty. There is no retake or second chance as there is in filmmaking or music recording. A live performance is a unique event that can never be repeated in exactly the same way. In both art and athletics, performance is an act of creativity here and now. The totally committed and invested performer—artist or athlete—draws upon every resource of intelligence and presence, every means of perception and expression to be fully present and brilliant in *this very moment*—here and now.

In both art and athletics, there is often thorough and detailed preparation—referred to as *rehearsal* in the arts, and *training* in athletics. In the arts, this process of preparation often culminates with a dress rehearsal. We just considered the athletic cousin to the dress rehearsal—the giveaway race.

A significant element in the actual dress rehearsal/giveaway race, and even more so in the actual live performance or goal race, is our audience. In endurance athletics, our audience includes spectators, volunteers, *and* other athletes. The audience is a great source of motivation and inspiration for artists and athletes alike. The presence and support of others can evoke and elicit from the performers some profound accomplishments and realizations—whether it is the graceful, efficient, and spirited movement that produces a fast race or the sensitive and intimate expression that yields a flawless and sterling music recital.

Defining Performance

Even with all these common elements, what makes an *athletic* performance and an *artistic* performance so closely similar that

they share the word *performance*? What does performance mean?
One interpretation of *performance* is "the *perfection* of *form*." After
all, isn't that the essence of all those countless hours spent in
either rehearsals or athletic training sessions—to *perfect our form*?

Early in this book, we considered the nature of form in the context of endurance athletics by using the compass metaphor.
Perfecting our form is like skillfully using a compass to accurately determine a precise direction in which to travel. Maintaining
that perfect form is like gracefully and efficiently moving forward
in that very specific direction. The grace and efficiency of our form
enable us to accomplish more—to go faster and/or farther—with
less energy.

Our ability to develop, recall, and maintain perfect form is
based on our *feel*—our feeling intelligence. Our athletic form—be
it swimming, running, or cross-country skiing—is based on the
coordination and integration of our neurological and muscular
memories—what's known as engrams. Through diligent and consistent training, we develop a strong, intelligent, and articulate
neurological system so that we can accurately recall and repro-
duce our efficient swimming, biking, or running form and—with
flexibility and adaptability—respond appropriately to the unique
conditions of the present moment. Our appropriate response to
the now—which includes yielding, blending, and aligning—produces efficiency, grace, *and speed.*

The Process of Perfecting Our Form

Great endurance athletic performances are based upon the efficiency, grace, and speed we develop as we perfect our form through
training. This includes both our high-intensity breakthrough sessions and our low-intensity *feel* sessions. While agony, pain, and
even injury may sometimes accompany great athletic performances, they are not the fundamental basis of perfecting form. Typically
in our training programs, we emphasize and focus our attention on
high-intensity and long-duration training sessions. We can identify
these as our significant breakthrough workouts. During these sessions, we are stressing—literally damaging—our muscular, metabolic and neurological systems. Generally the muscular system
incurs the most stress, the neurological system the least.

Recovery is just as essential as these stressful breakthrough
workouts for the process of strengthening our muscular and metabolic systems. This recovery process includes both rest and low-

intensity, short-duration recovery workouts. After stressing our muscular and metabolic systems, an adequate period of recovery will allow these systems to *adapt*—to heal and rebuild *with added strength and capacity*. When the recovery process is not adequate, then adaptation does not occur—we don't experience any improvement. Rather than enhancing and perfecting the efficiency, grace, and speed of our form, we *diminish* it.

Neurological Intelligence and Form

As mentioned in "What is Feel?" it is our neurological system that is most easily educated and is most responsive to training— more so than either our metabolic or muscular systems. Neurological strength may be defined as our capacity to *conduct* electricity and to *articulate* that electrical field or matrix into patterns or *engrams* that produce efficient and graceful movements. It has nothing to do with big, bulging muscles. Our neurological system has the greatest ability to morph—to learn, adapt, and develop. While we usually focus most of our training efforts on developing muscular strength and focus least on neurological strength, we need to develop all three systems to truly perfect our endurance athletic form.

In our zendurance approach to athletic training, we are cultivating and developing efficient, graceful movement and Zen centeredness so that we may navigate the path toward effortless power. Our neurological system is *essential* in this navigation. In the zendurance approach, *both* our breakthrough *and* our recovery workouts offer us the valuable potential to strengthen and to educate our neurological system in order to perfect our form. A recovery session can be the most valuable opportunity to intimately focus on the feeling intelligence of our form—without the distraction and concern for either high-intensity output or sustained long duration.

Our recovery sessions are no longer for unconscious junk miles. These intimate *feel* sessions are for perfecting our form by focusing solely on our neurological intelligence, unhindered by stress. With a strong foundation of neurological intelligence, our zendurance approach to breakthrough sessions—both high intensity and long duration—is to maintain the same clear, conscious, serene, and intimate quality of feeling intelligence that we experience in our low-intensity sessions. During our breakthrough workouts, we maintain the same *tangible* qualities of yielding, blending, and aligning—even as we stress our muscular, metabolic, and neurological systems.

Imprints and Performance

Let's reconsider the phenomenon of imprinting that we first examined in "HeartCore," so that we can see just how *vital* an intelligent neurological foundation is for producing brilliant race performances. To review, we know that our thoughts and speech, along with our actions—including our athletic training activities—constitute our response to events and circumstances. They determine what seeds or imprints we plant in our subconscious that will flower or surface in our future. Remember?

This is how we literally—either consciously or unconsciously—design our own future. *That future includes our goal races.* How we respond now determines what we will be responding to in the future. In this context of setting up our future performances by the *quality* of our actions *now*—every swim stroke, every pedal stroke, every run stride—determines our athletic performance in the future. Our dress rehearsals or giveaway races are valuable opportunities for us to *clear* our relationship to racing. What are we clearing? Essentially we are clearing out our ego. We are moving into the clear and empty Zen center of our intelligence triangle.

If the essence of a great performance is the perfection of form, this must include planting in our subconscious the seeds or imprints that will flower with grace, efficiency, and effortless speed on race day. We can virtually assure this through a sincere and diligent zendurance approach to every athletic training session—breakthrough and recovery alike—*and* a sincere and diligent zendurance approach to every thought, word and action in our daily lives.

Attitude and Approach

If our attitude and approach to training, racing, and living life are those of *resistance*—of battling the elements, of competing *against* others and staking *our* claim—then our endeavor for a great performance will manifest as a harsh and brutal battleground and an experience of agony. Likewise, if our attitude and approach to training, racing, and living life are those of *humility* and *grace* by yielding, blending, and aligning with the elements and with each other, then our endeavor for a great performance will manifest as a poetry of effortless power. The elements, the circumstances of the race, and our fellow athletes will actually support and enhance our performance.

Performing Every Moment

All we have is *this present moment* to make the choice and determine our future. With this insight and wisdom, we can perfect our form in each and every thought word and action. This is *true* zendurance—easy to define yet incredibly challenging and difficult to enact and to master.

Our notion of training for a great performance has now expanded infinitely. Training to perfect our form now includes every moment of our lives. With this insight, our preparation for the big race and for a great performance includes *two* essential elements. First and foremost, true zendurance training and racing requires a perfect orchestration and coordination of all three of our energetic intelligences. This happens naturally and effortlessly when we are in the Zen center of our intelligence triangle—when we are effectively practicing HeartCore Zendurance not only in our training but also in each moment of our lives. The second essential element arises naturally from our condition of Zen centeredness—wise and effective athletic training. The *quality* of our training is a clear and direct reflection of our Zen centeredness. We train most effectively and intelligently when we engage and coordinate all three of our intelligences equally.

Through the *art* of effective and intelligent athletic training, we creatively balance both stress and recovery to produce optimal adaptation and capacity.

PERFORMANCE AND STRESS

The Nature of Stress

Let's look a little closer at the nature of stress and its functional mechanics in our lives. Phil Maffetone has written some very insightful material on managing stress and maintaining health. Maffetone identifies three sources of stress—physical, chemical and mental/emotional. Simply identifying and categorizing the sources of stress in our lives can facilitate us in managing our stress and balancing our health. Maffetone offers valuable guidance in understanding the nature of stress and how we can address each type.

Typically we view stress as bad, as negative and health threatening. However, when we train athletically—especially in our breakthrough sessions—we are deliberately and intentionally inflicting stress on our bodies. The truth is, without this athletic stress, we would not adapt and improve. The same thing can be said about our lives overall. If we experienced no lessons in life—no difficult and challenging situations—how would we learn and grow? Another illustration of this dichotomy of both benefit and detriment is one we considered in the entry "Swimming—Yielding," concerning the density of water. That density of water resists our forward progress. It slows us down and absorbs much of the energy we expend in swimming. Yet without the very same density and resistance, we would have no buoyancy and we would have nothing to catch in our hand and to pull on in order to propel ourselves forward.

Stress as a Choice

Both athletically and spiritually, stress is a catalyst for growth. Through our zendurance approach to performance training, we begin to realize a level of mastery at *using stress as a tool*. In this athletic context, we clearly experience our *choice* in creating, enduring, and embracing stress. When we *deliberately choose* the stress, we can develop a competence in using stress as a tool toward our growth and improvement.

In turn, through our experience in this athletic context, we can begin to create the same mastery with the stress in our everyday lives. Rather than blaming the world for inflicting stress upon us, we begin to clearly experience our *choice* and our capacity to embrace and orchestrate the stress in our daily lives. In our daily lives, we can gain the ability to balance both stress and recovery for the sake of our spiritual adaptation and strengthening—our spiritual fitness.

While we may eagerly embrace the athletic stress of our training, it can be much more challenging to see our *choice* and to accept our responsibility in creating the everyday stress of our lives. It is much easier and more compelling to convince ourselves that we are the victims. This disempowers us and leaves us with no choice in the matter. Culturally it does not appear that we are the source or the orchestrators of stress in our lives. The stress seems so overwhelming and beyond our control. We feel so powerless in the presence of life's everyday stress.

It is a valuable exercise for us to contemplate this challenge as we welcome and engage in the stress of our breakthrough workouts—where we consciously design and construct these stressful situations to improve our performance. There is a tremendous potential for empowerment if we can begin to see that we also design and construct the stressful situations in our everyday lives. These situations strengthen our spiritual fitness and improve our spiritual performance.

CHEMISTRY AND
ZENDURANCE PERFORMANCE

Law of Inertia

The Law of Inertia states: "A body in motion tends to remain in motion. A body at rest tends to remain at rest." So what can the Law of Inertia reveal to us about effectively orchestrating and mastering the balance of stress and recovery for performance gain in our lives?

Let's look at our zendurance *performance* training as an example. We will first examine the distinction between mastering our stress/recovery balance versus being a slave to it. Examining the chemical context of this balance can help us see this distinction and gain some insight that will help us in those final two to three weeks preceding our big race, when it is most crucial to thoroughly recover from the cumulative stress of our training.

The Endocrine System

In order for us to adapt and to grow—to strengthen and temper ourselves either athletically or spiritually—we must alternate between intervals of stress and recovery. We must gain equal fluency in both processes. One of the primary systems of the body that responds to this alternating process of stress and recovery—that enables us to adapt, strengthen, and grow—is the *endocrine* system, a part of our larger metabolic system. This complex chemical system responds to all forms of stress and recovery—physical, chemical, mental, and emotional. The endocrine system can profoundly change our physical, chemical, mental, and emotional state of being.

Under extreme conditions of chronic and unrelenting stress, the endocrine system can respond by breaking down and destroying our bones, muscle tissue, and even our vital organs. In this scenario, our endocrine system can effectively diminish our state of health, accelerate decomposition and aging, and bring us to an early death. Yes, the endocrine system *is* that powerful.

On the other hand, with clear vision, wisdom, and discernment—through a brilliant and well-balanced orchestration of stress and recovery—at a peak moment our endocrine system can make us superhuman. We are then capable of feats that, under normal conditions, would be impossible to attain—*like a spectacular race performance*. In this moment, we feel physically, mentally and emotionally immortal and invincible.

Human Being and Athlete

It is important to remember that our physical condition and our mental and emotional states contribute profoundly to the activity and response of our endocrine system. As an example, we may meticulously train our bodies athletically through an artful balance of stress and recovery, building toward a brilliant athletic performance—however, if we are experiencing chronic and severe mental or emotional stress without recovery, then our athletic performance potential *will* diminish. Like it or not, we cannot separate our athletic activities and performances from the activities and performances of our human lives.

Let's review the scenario I experienced pertaining to over training—our athletic version of too much stress and not enough recovery. The section "Starting Line" began with my experience of over-training for my first iron-distance triathlon, which prompted my commitment to write this book. A little later, in the "Zendurance" entry, we considered why we might be compelled to continue over training even when we clearly see the warning signs and our performance potential is diminishing. It all boils down to one thing: *addiction!*

Chemistry and the Law of Inertia

This addiction is very similar to the Law of Inertia. If we are in motion, we desire to remain in motion. If we are at rest, we desire to remain at rest. The chemical state of stress—let's call it motion—is very different from the chemical state of recovery—let's call it rest. If we are accustomed to the chemical state of stress and motion, we are physically, mentally and emotionally *familiar* with this state and we are predisposed to remain in this state. If we are accustomed to the chemical state of recovery and relaxation, we are likewise physically, mentally, and emotionally *familiar* with and predisposed to remain in this state.

We know from the Law of Inertia that it takes energy and focused intention to transform a body at rest into a body in motion. Likewise, it takes energy and focused intention to reverse this process—to transform a body in motion into a body at rest. If we are going to wisely balance between stress and recovery—both athletically *and* in our everyday lives—we must do so with conscious, focused intention.

When we first begin to train as endurance athletes, it can take quite a bit of discipline—in the form of clear vision and conscious, focused intention—to get up off that couch and exercise. As seasoned *Ironheads*, after a decade of obsessive swimming, biking and running, it can take just as much discipline—also in the form of clear vision and conscious, focused intention—to dismount from the bike, get back on the couch, and rest.

Orchestrating Our Chemistry

The chemical states that our endocrine system generates are *very powerful and pervasive*—physically, mentally and emotionally—so our clear vision and conscious, focused intention must be sourced from *outside* this powerful sphere of influence. There is only *one* source outside this powerful sphere of physical, chemical, mental and emotional influence—the Zen center of our energetic intelligence triangle. *All three* of our energetic intelligences—mana'o, pu'uwai, and na'au—are within the endocrine system's chemical sphere of influence. Only from our Zen center can we *stand at the podium, take up the conductor's baton, and masterfully conduct the massive and grandiose Endocrine Philharmonic Symphony Orchestra.*

Addressing the Recovery Dilemma

Through our performance-oriented athletic training programs *and* throughout our human lives, we must orchestrate the dynamics of stress and recovery from the calm, still, silent, open, and empty space of our Zen center. As athletes, this can be most difficult at the time when it is most crucial—in the last weeks and days before the big race performance. The goal race is a great indicator of just how skillful and strong we are at being Zen centered. Can we remain steadfast outside the powerful and pervasive chemical sphere of influence of the endocrine system and the *Almighty Ego*?

During these last few weeks and days, we are tapering our athletic activity. Since we are doing less training, we are no longer activating the serenity and calmness that we have instilled in our nerve and muscle cell memories during the zendurance meditation of our athletic training. Chemically we are not producing the high levels of dopamine and endorphin that we usually enjoy—that give us that runner's high. Just when we need that calmness and serenity most of all, we are scaling back and withdrawing from the very activities we rely on for the chemistry that helps us cultivate and develop our inner peace—our zendurance training. What a dilemma!

To top it all off, as our endocrine system shifts into deep recovery mode, the chemical state of our bodies, minds, and emotions changes profoundly. In those final weeks and days, our bodies and personalities are morphing into creatures that we hardly recognize. As we go into deep recovery mode, we begin to feel physically lazy and sluggish. We feel *heavy!* This can be very disconcerting, very unsettling, and very scary. After investing so much time and energy into honing the edge of our performance knife it suddenly feels so *dull!*

HeartCore

It requires great skill and spiritual fitness to stay Zen centered as our body, mind, and emotions change—as our na'au, mana'o, and pu'uwai intelligences take on new personalities. First and foremost, our diligent practice of HeartCore Zendurance in every moment of our daily lives provides us with the spiritual fitness—the centering strength—to remain in the center of the intelligence triangle. Without this HeartCore practice in our daily lives, our virtual withdrawal from endurance activity and from the chemical endocrinal state of stress that is so familiar to us can be overwhelming.

Athletic Training Techniques

In addition to the HeartCore practice of our everyday lives, there are some training techniques that can help us remain at ease and gracefully progress through our final and crucial recovery and preparation for the big one. The most important training technique is one that is part of many conventional training programs, like the one outlined in Joe Friel's *Triathlete's Training Bible.*

During the months of training that lead up to a significant goal race, we train progressively longer and/or harder each week for a two-to-four-week period and then ease up considerably and recover for a week or so, before resuming again. This cycle is not only invaluable for physical recovery and adaptation but also allows us to become familiar with the chemical landscape of recovery—physically, mentally, and emotionally. During these periodic recovery weeks, we become familiar with the profound chemical difference of our body, mind, and emotions during recovery.

These periodic recovery weeks are when we plant the seeds or imprints into our subconscious that will flower during our most crucial recovery stage just prior to our significant goal race. These recovery intervals are a great opportunity to invest more of our time and energy into real HeartCore Zendurance—diversifying our practice to other valuable areas of our lives, especially our families and relationships. These recovery weeks afford us the opportunity to diligently and gracefully practice yielding, blending, and aligning in *all* areas of our lives.

Another training technique, also included in many training programs, concerns the actual training we do in those final weeks and days. Generally our sessions during this recovery period are short and, for the most part, conducted at low intensity levels. During these easy sessions, we include very short, high-intensity blasts or bursts—say, thirty seconds each in duration—with adequate, very easy recovery intervals of at least two or three minutes between them. (If you are performance oriented, I strongly suggest you study a well-designed and comprehensive training program or work with a coach.) These short blasts briefly afford us the opportunity to remember our form at race intensity.

In our zendurance approach, we begin these sessions with easy, low-intensity activity and focus completely on the *feel* of our perfect form. We begin by dialing in our most graceful, efficient and effortless form, our most tangible sense of yielding, blending, and aligning. In our short high-intensity bursts, we stay with the same grace, serenity, efficiency, and effortlessness. Although the low-intensity base of these sessions is distinctly different from the high-intensity blasts, our focus is to establish a seamless continuity throughout by maintaining our meditative approach.

Endocrine Philharmonic Symphony Orchestra

Realizing a degree of mastery in conducting the Endocrine Philharmonic Symphony Orchestra from the podium of our Zen center empowers us with the opportunity to produce astonishing athletic performances. This same mastery can also lead us to profound revelations—peak enlightenment experiences—*satori*, as they are called in traditional spiritual practices. These moments of crystalline clarity can be unforgettable and life changing. They usually occur during or just after our peak performances, but can also occur unexpectedly during a particular training session.

The afterglow we often experience following the finish of a major race is a phenomenon of the altered chemical state of our body, mind and emotions produced by our very own Endocrine Symphony. We literally create our own body- and mind-altering drugs. Dopamine and endorphin—produced by our endocrine system during intense endurance activity—are quite similar to *morphine*. And yes, just like morphine they can be very addictive. Remember our version of the Law of Inertia: It takes conscious, focused intention to transform a body in motion—producing adrenaline, dopamine, and endorphin—into a body at rest. We can only source that conscious, focused intention from the Zen center of our intelligence triangle.

Finish-Line Afterglow

The postrace afterglow is a time of celebration and great clarity and revelation. The companionship we enjoy, the connections we make with our fellow competitors, volunteers, and race staff as well as our families and friends during and after our race, can be deep, significant heart-to-heart experiences that reveal and express our true spirit nature. If we are completely present in these precious moments, we can thoroughly absorb them, especially through our pu'uwai intelligence. These experiences can vividly reveal to us and clearly express to others our true spirit essence—our pure potentiality and infinite possibility.

The postrace afterglow—courtesy of our Endocrine Symphony— is a precious opportunity to generously share our spirit nature and to clearly perceive and acknowledge this same spirit nature in others. In athletics, we often identify the spiritual presence that seems to transcend our normal human capabilities—like a great race performance—as *glory*. That glory is *tangible*—we can feel it, regardless of whether we are the performing athlete or the perceiving spectator, the supporting volunteer or the loving family member or friend. When glory is present, it is abundant. Glory must be generously and graciously shared. In our essence, *we are all* that same spiritual presence that transcends normal human capabilities.

THE NATURE OF OUR RACE ENTITY

Pu'uwai Intelligence

We have considered briefly the notion of each race coming to life as a *conscious entity*—an entity that we merge with, that evokes in us an experience of being much more than an individual competitor. We have identified pu'uwai intelligence as a key element in this merging, especially in connecting with the human companions—athletes, volunteers and spectators—who comprise so much of our race entity.

Another example of this kind of collective organism, this phenomenon of an entity greater than our individual selves, is our families. As we considered in "HeartCore Zendurance," our pu'uwai intelligence is essential here, too—in cultivating and strengthening our collective *family entity*. Our experience in the practice of family applies directly to how we engage and integrate with our race entity.

Na'au Intelligence

Our na'au intelligence also contributes to our race entity. In "What Is Feel?" we looked at the phenomenon of extending feel. I recounted my experience as a dancer of creating a collective field of *intelligent* energy that filled and permeated the space as we danced in and through it. As dancers, each of us could extend our individual sense of feeling into this intelligent energetic field. Through this extension, we could accurately and intimately feel each other's presence and movements as well as our own—even without visual contact. Simultaneously we would experience both our individual identities as well as our collective field intelligence.

As athletes, many of us have felt this collective field of energy just before the start of a big race—a highly amped energetic entity. It takes skill and experience to stay calm and centered as part of such an intense, high frequency field of energy.

Movement Quality

The *quality of our movements*—whether aggressive and forceful or graceful and calm—significantly contributes to and determines the character of our collective race entity. As performing athletes, each of us contributes to the overall experience of the race. The quality of our movements during our race performance reflects the approach we have used in preparing for the race. Again, we must remember that *all* our thoughts, words, and actions in the past have planted the seeds and imprints we contribute to the race entity today. Months in advance, as we are laying the foundation for our race, we must ask ourselves, *Do I wish to create a brutal war or a graceful pilgrimage?*

Mana'o Intelligence

Our mana'o intelligence contributes to our race entity in two obvious ways. First, the *rules* and *regulations* that define the operating parameters of our race are an essential application of mana'o intelligence. Second, the *skillful means* we employ in our training and racing strategies are a vital part of our race performance.

Both the race staff and the sanctioning body that governs our race—by setting and enforcing the rules and regulations—provide very clear parameters and definitions that are essential to our race entity. These include the course layout, accurate distant measurements as well as rules for our behavior—such as rules for no-draft zones and subsequent penalties. There are also clear definitions of illegal doping and performance-enhancing drugs, as well as permissible forms of support and aid. All these regulations figure prominently in the character of our collective race entity and ensure our equality as the individual components of this entity by clearly defining the *agreements* we are all committed to honor. Clear and concise agreements are a vital and binding function of *any* collective entity—a competition, a family, or a business partnership.

Our training and racing strategies contribute to our race entity in much the same way that the quality of our movements and actions does. Together, our strategies and the quality of our form—smooth and graceful or aggressive and forceful—substantially determine our *approach* to the race. As the second step of the Zen pentathlon, our approach to *any* activity has a significant bearing on the outcome. Our *approach* predisposes us to—either consciously or unconsciously, either deliberately or recklessly—plant the seeds and imprints that will flower in our future. The skillful means of mana'o intelligence is a very key player in our approach.

Additional Elements

There are other elements that contribute to our race as a living, breathing, conscious entity. So far we have looked at how our three energetic intelligences contribute in the context of our collective *human* element. The character and intelligence of our race entity also includes significant elements outside the human realm.

The most obvious nonhuman element is the physical location of the race. The topography, flora and fauna as well as the climate and weather conditions on race day are all profound characteristics of our race entity. Most obviously, factors like temperature, topography, and humidity directly affect our performance.

Planet Earth

We must also recognize and honor the dynamic *conscious* and *intelligent* nature of these geographical elements. Our planetary entity is a living, breathing and intelligent organism—not an inanimate object. As individual human entities, we are each an integral and inseparable part of this greater entity and intelligence—whether we choose to be conscious of it or not.

Those vanishing cultures that we so naively call indigenous are completely conscious of and attentive to their inseparable connection with our planetary entity and intelligence. These people thrive on an articulate relationship with our planetary entity. They are as articulate in their *dialogue* with our planetary entity as they are with each other. The people of these cultures live in a humble, graceful, and patient manner, honoring the greater collective Self over the lesser individual self.

"I believe that as Native people, we are the land and the land is us."—Tom D. K. Goldtooth, Dine and Mdewakanton Dakota Indian

Even in our aseptic modern cultural ways, this truth still stands *undeniably*. While we may acquire packaged and processed food from the supermarket—never bending down once to touch the actual Earth that it comes from, or reaching out to touch the plants and animals that bore it—*all* of this food comes from our greater planetary organism and ultimately from our sole source of physical energy—the sun. Our bodies are composed of this Earth and sun. In "HeartCore Zendurance," we looked at diet as a branch of spiritual practice that connects and blends our pu'uwai and na'au intelligences. It is our most fundamental practice of receiving. Every time we eat—and as endurance athletes, that can be frequently—we are blending with our greater living Earth entity.

Just one solo swim out into the deep and wild blue yonder of the great Pacific Ocean is enough to humble even the most arrogant of us to this living entity. There is nothing like stepping down from the top of the food chain.

Myth of Kona

There is a phenomenon here on the Big Island of Hawaii that— through Hawaii Ironman—is known as the Myth of Kona. This myth has nothing to do with the fame and prestige or the media hype that surrounds the World Championship Triathlon. This myth was alive and well long before triathlon was ever conceived and long before Captain Cook blundered upon the Hawaiian Islands. Hawaii Ironman is just one personification, just one expression of this powerful, articulate, intelligent island entity. Hawaiians have long respected and honored this intelligent and powerful entity in the form of Pele for more than a millennium. Pele is recognized and honored as the Goddess of Creation. Her home is currently the active volcano Kilauea, the birthing source of new land. Even in this present moment, when so many of the world's myths have died, Pele lives on.

Tourists and natives alike have vividly seen her in the form of a woman of varying age and stature. Some have seen her materialize or disappear right in front of them. The circumstances of her appearance or manifestation are inexplicable. For instance, a couple ventured out onto the new lava flow along the shoreline at the base of Pu'u O'o, the active vent of Kilauea. It was there that he proposed marriage to her. After she accepted, a woman appeared in a long black gown with high-heeled red shoes, smoking a long cigarette. It would have been impossible for her to walk miles on the rough and undulating surface of the lava flows in those unscuffed, red high heels. She slowly gaited around a tall buckle in the lava and was gone. The couple could find no trace.

Less fantastical—yet no less powerful an indication of the intelligent consciousness of this land—are the literally hundreds of accounts of tourists who have been foolish enough, through either naïveté or belligerence, to take lava rocks from this island as possessions and return home with them. Usually within a matter of days, they send them back to one of the parks or to acquaintances with a woeful letter of the ill-fated experiences they have endured. It is a well-known and respected fact that this land is *not* an appropriate souvenir.

Superstition?

Does all this still sound like superstition, like foolishness to our mana'o intelligence? Of course! Mana'o functions by distinguishing, by separating—it refuses to recognize intelligence beyond the duality of separate and distinct *you and me,* beyond what normally reaches our five senses. As a Big Island resident, I can tell you from years of swimming, biking, and running here, that the Myth of Kona is *real!* The essence of this myth is the mana—the conscious energy—of this land. I feel it most powerfully in those areas of Kona where the land is in its natural state and where the ancestral burial sites and cultural states are respected, are honored and remain intact. This energetic *feeling* of mana is not quite the same as a typical physical feeling.

While Pele has yet to make a literal appearance in the form of a woman during the race, without fail many athletes *feel* her presence. The pure and raw elements—including the great blue waters of Pacifica, the howling Ho'omumuku winds of Kohala, the sweltering heat and the endless and infinitely undulating lava fields— all touch us and etch Pele's presence deeply within our bodies, hearts, and minds.

Brutal Warrior or Open Channel?

Some athletes arrive in Kona—or at any race, for that matter— resolved to do battle *against* the elements, *against* Pele. This is a resolve of the ego—the *mistaken identity*—that foolishly operates under the premise of mind *over* manner. This kind of resolve seals off any access and connection to the integrity of pu'uwai intelligence, to the greater intelligence of our race entity, to the mana and ultimately to our true spiritual nature. While the ego may regard itself as infallible, no matter how strong the will of the ego may be, it does inevitably expire.

A great deal of our zendurance path is founded on that principle Buddhist tenet that we create our universe from the inside out— both individually and collectively—through the imprint seeds we plant in our subconscious. Through this tenet, we clearly determine for ourselves just how the elements will treat us on race day. Environmental conditions that we perceive as being *brutal* may very well be an accurate mirror of our own egocentric interpretation of competition as *me against the world.*

Our zendurance approach is to connect and integrate with our greater race entity—to *offer* ourselves as channels or conduits through the humbleness, grace, and emptiness of our Zen center. We surrender the little self into the pool of the greater Self—our collective race entity.

This is the true essence of zendurance racing. It is the true essence of spiritual life, regardless of religious affiliation. In this true essence, our zendurance racing is simply a way of practicing, mastering, and perfecting our ability to be clear and open channels in *all* areas, in *every* moment of our lives. With this zendurance approach to racing and to our lives, we can realize strength, capacity, and intelligence beyond our individual identity. Performance at this level is the perfection of our true spirit form as an expression of our pure potential and infinite possibility.

EMBRACING ATTACHMENT: WHY *NOT* RACE?

The Next Piece of Candy

For some of us, racing is a way of life. It is something we have done for many years. Racing is so ingrained that we can't even imagine our lives or our day-to-day training without it. After finishing a significant goal race, we immediately set our sights on the next big one and resume training to carefully build toward it. We are eager and willing to register for significant goal races well in advance. In the case of the most popular Ironman races, like Canada, the registration fills up in eight hours—a year in advance!

This advanced registration gives us the anticipation of the next "piece of candy." Granted, this *is* an effective and healthy form of motivation so that we continue to progress and grow as athletes— to refine and perfect our zendurance training. It also helps offset any postrace depression. However, our avid pursuit of race performances may have pitfalls as well. Placating ourselves with the anticipation of the next significant goal race can become a way of future tripping—of living in and clinging to our fantasies and dreams of the future, sometimes at the cost of being present here and now—both in our training and in our daily lives as ordinary human beings. The cost can also include the quality of our families and relationships, as well as our jobs. Our attachment to racing can become an addiction when we begin to compromise other areas of our human lives.

Racing for Life

When racing does become a way of life, we have progressed well beyond the initial phase of cultivating the discipline to train and then to finish a race. Many of us skillfully embrace the challenge of balancing our lives as healthy human beings with our passions and endeavors as athletes. We learn to embrace and temper the hungry need to perpetually set new goals and constantly forge ahead into new territory. That new territory may be a race of longer duration or a faster performance at the same distance—the challenge of improving our finish times. As we ripen with age, even the most successful pursuit of increased speed will eventually level off—although the pursuit of grace and effortless power may continue to develop and improve indefinitely.

For each of us, the ultimate challenge becomes gracefully relinquishing the hunger and attachment we may have toward always climbing the ladder of goals and personal accomplishments, or even our fixation with maintaining some level of status. It may be beneficial for us—and our friends and families as well—if we gracefully resolve this attachment before we are forced to do so by serious injury or other extreme circumstances. Relinquishing our attachments *now* can greatly empower us with a new level of mastery in our training and racing as well as our overall lives.

Just to Maintain Status?

I was acutely aware of this attachment after my first Ironman. As a rite of passage, that first Ironman is a powerful and transforming experience. As an achievement, as an accomplishment, the title of "Ironman" and the "M-dot" that symbolizes that accomplishment can be very powerful, attractive, and seductive elements that feed the ego.

John Collins, one of the originators and first finishers of Ironman back in 1978 said, "You have bragging rights for the rest of your life." *Well*, says the ego, *that's just fine and dandy, but how long before the expiration date? When does it change from "I am an Ironman" to "I was an Ironman?" How often do I need to finish an iron-distance race in order to keep my status current?* My ego had settled on a minimum of one per year to maintain my status. Seven months after my first finish, I bagged my second in Brazil—despite suffering from chronic adrenal fatigue syndrome. Whew! I kept my status current through 2000!

Breaking Open the Heart of Racing

In 2001 I knew in my heart—my pu'uwai intelligence—that I had to address this attachment. As a resident of Hawaii Island—known as the Big Island—I am eligible for one of the thirty resident slots for Hawaii Ironman, offered each year at the Keauhou-Kona Half-Iron. While I have yet to qualify by international standards, I enjoy big-fish-in-a-small-pond status locally. I train and compete at Keauhou with relative certainty that I will have the honor and privilege to represent Kona at the starting line each October for the World Championship—where my status becomes "little guppy in the Big Pacific."

In May 2001 I earned a local slot again at Keauhou. As I enjoyed the afterglow of the finish-line party, I made the most difficult decision in my athletic career—to *decline* the slot I earned and let it roll down to someone else. It was time to let go of my status and my identity as an Ironman. My attachment to that identity was stifling other areas of my life. For instance, parked just outside the finish area, my unregistered, uninspected, and uninsured truck was sporting bald front tires—although I had just purchased a new training tire for my bike. I had barely enough fuel to get back home. Could I really justify a $375 charge on my credit card for the entry fee?

By this time I had begun to formulate and to write this book. Now, just like training for and starting a race, I was going to finish the book. As I informed my friends and fellow athletes of my decision there at the finish-line party, many responded with bewilderment. I was clearly committed to continue training and participate in other less significant races. Having given up caffeine, I was no longer suffering from chronic fatigue or overtraining. I could easily have accepted my slot and trained intelligently enough to finesse my way to another Ironman finish. However, through my pu'uwai intelligence, I was clear that I had to make the big giveaway—to give up my cherished ego-centered attachment to the identity and status as a current Ironman.

In the tender first few hours after the finish of a long race—when our hearts are open and our pu'uwai intelligence is piqued—our discoveries, experiences, and sharing of deep inner truth can be quite revelatory. I shared my decision and the basis for it with one of our Kona legends—Papa Pea, Peaman's father, who has finished at least eight Ironman races. Like the others, he was bewildered by my choice to decline—until I explained the basis for that decision.

I shared with him how powerfully seductive and addictive the M-dot Ironman identity was to my ego—how easily it could become the sole basis of my self-esteem. Papa Pea shared with me his experience of failing to complete the swim leg of the 2000 Hawaii Ironman by the official cutoff time—at age sixty-six. I was on swim patrol that year and witnessed this. He exited the water with tears of shame and disappointment at not being allowed to complete the event. So dedicated is Papa Pea to making this annual rite of passage that—in the few years he has not qualified, with the help of friends and family—he has done the whole course in one day, a week or so in advance of race day.

As we sat on the grass there at the finish-line party, tears welled up in his eyes. He told me of the fear he had experienced after missing the swim cutoff time—fear of losing all respect from his family and friends. What he discovered instead, during the ensuing weeks after that Ironman, was that many people—both close associates and complete strangers—approached him and embraced him with love and appreciation for being the warm and wonderful human being that he is. His heart connection, his humor, his love and compassion, his grace and humility, and his health meant more to us than whether he had another Ironman notch in his belt of athletic achievements.

Shortly after my heart-to-heart connection with Papa Pea, I sat down on the lawn with another middle-age local Kona multi-Ironman finisher, Bill Hall. "How was your race?" I asked. "Oh," Bill replied casually, "I didn't race." Bill elected that very morning not to race. Seven weeks earlier, still feeling the effects of a flu, he raced Lavaman, an Olympic-distance tri and DNF'd. After a short rest, he resumed training. By the time Keauhou came knocking on his door at four o'clock that morning, he knew his health was not stable enough to respond. He had come to the finishers' party anyway, just to make peace with himself. I congratulated him for his honest perception and his wise discernment. His health and well-being were more precious to him—as well as to his family and friends—than whether he could have, would have or should have raced.

Fasting for Clarity

Once we attain a level of proficiency and mastery at setting and attaining admirable goals through our zendurance approach to training and racing, there is the difficult challenge of giving up—at least temporarily—the need to climb the ladder of achievement. If we truly want to see how our zendurance training functions as a daily *practice* toward inner and spiritual growth and fitness, we may consider, for a period of time, giving up or "fasting" from significant goal races.

During this fast, we still practice our zendurance training for the sake of its functional value as a spiritual practice—without the ego-driven need for achievement, recognition, and glory. We want to be especially attentive to our motivation and purpose for training as a form of yoga and meditation. Our experience of discipline may change. We are familiar with discipline and the correlation with clear vision. While we are fasting from significant races, our clear vision must extend beyond goals and achievements. We must clearly envision the *direction*—the big picture—of our zendurance training as a spiritual practice that enhances our health, our calm presence here and now, and our happiness. Without the distractions and attractions of an upcoming goal race, we can really focus on the *quality* of our awareness and our mindfulness as we train. We can begin to observe how we integrate our zendurance training into others areas of our lives, how it enhances our lives *and* the lives of those around us.

Investigate and ask questions. *What is my motivation? Where is this process leading me? Do I train out of a genuine love for the craft? Is my training playful? How do I experience quality in my training beyond the race performance element? How does my zendurance practice as an athlete enhance my spirit presence—rather than my ego presence—when I am around others? How do I share this presence and contribute my experience valuably with others? Do I enjoy the same satisfaction when I am training without a goal race on the horizon? Can I enjoy and accept lesser challenges in my zendurance practice with the same love and enthusiasm? As a multisport athlete, how do I approach and regard each unique activity (swimming, biking, running) as a zendurance practice?*

Without our ego-driven mana'o scheming and planning out our training for the next goal race, we have the opportunity to center our awareness on the *feel* and the *playfulness* of our training. This abstention can offer us a great opportunity to transform our training into a true Zen practice, with progressively less and less ego attachment. We can renew and refine our meditative zendurance approach to training as a way to develop spiritual fitness and inner clarity in all areas of our lives.

During this reprieve from goal racing, we may still choose to participate in less ego-significant races—even at high levels of performance. Congregating and celebrating are healthy activities. Without the ego supplication of a significant goal achievement, we are free to *enjoy* the companionship of our fellow athletes—our endurance family. We can rediscover just how empowering we are for each other.

When we resume the pursuit of goal-race performances, we will return with a stronger capacity for spiritual fitness—for genuine Zen centered presence in the moment. We will discover a *new* sense of intelligence and mastery in our performance-oriented training and racing. This is a result of balancing our three energetic intelligences and abiding in our true home—the Zen center of our intelligence triangle. We will return with a renewed sense of gratitude and appreciation for the opportunities that goal-oriented training and race performances offer us.

With clarity and discernment, we are more apt to choose and train for races that *appropriately* enhance our spiritual fitness and intelligence. As we choose races of progressively longer duration, we can naturally expect to invest more of our time and energy into training. The patience, discipline, grace, and efficiency that we develop through progressively longer training sessions and races can be an effective way for us to temper and build our spiritual fitness and intelligence.

Eventually we may realize that increasing the duration of our races and training sessions no longer serves our spiritual fitness and intelligence. We may discover that there is more for us to gain spiritually if we *decrease* the duration of our races and training sessions and invest our time and energy in *other* areas of our lives. This can be a difficult concession to make if we are passionate about our zendurance practice—both training and racing.

We are more apt to enjoy the health of our zendurance practice and to integrate it into our daily human lives if we can honestly identify and embrace our attachments to training and racing. Making the choice to temporarily *abstain* from something we savor—such as performance training and racing—can help us to disengage from our attachments. Through this abstention, we discover a higher level of mastery and spiritual fitness. We develop the discernment to balance the dreams and aspirations of the glorious athlete with the health and well-being of the ordinary human.

4

FINAL MILES

KNOW FEAR

BEYOND ZENDURANCE

Introduction

John Collins once said—back in the early days of Ironman— that just finishing the 140.6-mile race gives you bragging rights for the rest of your life. In the context of other long distance endurance races, finishing an iron-distance triathlon is *not* really all that extraordinary. Events like the Tour de France, the bicycle Race Across America, the Western States 100-Mile trail run, the Run Across America, the Manhattan Island Swim Marathon, and the English Channel Swim pose challenges even greater than iron-distance triathlon.

Still not convinced? Recently we have seen the rise of Ultraman, double and triple iron-distance tri's and even tris that are *ten and twenty times iron distance*! At twenty times iron-distance, that's a 48-mile swim, a 2,240-mile bike, and a 524-mile run. Most of these "ultra-ultra" events are conducted on closed-circuit courses that allow the athletes to eat, sleep, shower, and receive massage and medical treatment on site. We are also witnessing a rise in popularity of the twenty-four-hour and several-day adventure races.

Is there a limit to human endurance? Here is a better way to phrase the question: Is there a limit to our human potential for spiritual fitness and intelligence through the practice of zendurance? This question has intrigued and inspired humans for more than a thousand years in many cultures on every continent. Our modern-day endurance pursuits—in the context of athletic competition—are actually quite mundane in comparison to the purely spiritual pursuits of endurance that many of our sacred indigenous cultures have engaged in. In myriad forms, endurance has long been recognized as a path toward spiritual fitness, intelligence and enlightenment.

Beyond the context of athletic competition, the spiritual path of endurance has led to feats and accomplishments that even the most seasoned ultra-endurance athletes might have difficulty accepting. Some of these feats involve endurance forms that are familiar to us, such as running.

Marathon Monks

In his book *The Marathon Monks of Mount Hiei*, John Stevens describes a group of monks in Japan who run daily as a part of their traditional spiritual practice. They commit to a rigorous seven-year training program. During a particular hundred-day stretch, they run 52.5 miles each day. They maintain a vegetarian diet throughout their seven years and even do "death defying" fasts. They also wear handmade straw running shoes. The monks are part of the Tendai sect of Buddhism.

Lung-gom-pa Runners

Alexandra David-Neel was a French orientalist. As a practicing Buddhist, religious historian, and linguist, she lived in Tibet for fourteen years during the early 1900s. Tibet has long been regarded as the last home of mystery and, until recently, remained hidden, remote and sealed off. In her second book, *Magic and Mystery in Tibet*, published in 1932, she includes the chapter "Psychic Sports."

The title alone introduces a whole new context to the world of sports. Just imagine if someone perfected the art of teleportation. Imagine that this person could travel energetically by dematerializing from one location and rematerializing in another—*without* the use of *Star Trek* gadgetry. Now suppose that person enters a marathon and is able to teleport to each given checkpoint along the course and then physically cross the finish line. Suppose the athlete accomplishes this *without* the use of any sophisticated equipment, but simply by psychic means. Would this be grounds for disqualification? Is teleportation addressed in *any* of the rulebooks? Okay, maybe we *are* stretching the imagination here. But let's entertain some of the phenomena that Alexandra David-Neel witnessed in the early twentieth century—in that last home of mystery.

She begins "Psychic Sports" with a few personal accounts of the *lung-gom-pa* runners. The individual runners she observed on three separate occasions high on the Tibetan plateau were "tramping at a rapid pace and without stopping during several successive days and nights." In her first observation, she and her traveling party of six were riding across a "wide tableland" when she noticed a moving black spot far in front of them. Through her binoculars, she could see that it was a man moving "with an extraordinary swiftness." This man continued to advance rapidly toward them.

She expressed to the Tibetans in her party an interest in meeting and questioning this man, whom they identified as a lung-gom-pa runner. They explained to her that a lung-gom-pa must enter a state of trance to run in this way, and that if she were to break that trance it would be injurious and possibly fatal for him. When this runner reached the traveling party, David-Neel could see his trancelike expression. His eyes were wide open and gazed fixedly up into the sky. His gait did not resemble a run so much as a leaping walk—as though he was running on the moon. "It looked as if he had been endowed with the elasticity of a ball and rebounded each time his feet touched the ground. His steps had the regularity of a pendulum." He wore robes that identified him as a Tibetan Buddhist monk. He seemed completely unaware of his observers.

They turned around and followed him for about two miles, until he left the path, ascended a steep slope, and disappeared into the mountains. The terrain was too rough for them to follow on their horses and mules. They turned around again to resume their journey. Four days after their encounter, Alexandra and her party arrived at the encampment of some herdsmen. They, too, had seen this lung-gom-pa, the day before Alexandra observed him. She calculated that he must have been running—or "leap-walking"—in that fashion for the entire twenty-four-hour period between the herders' camp and their encounter. *Psychic* endurance?

Even more remarkable perhaps is the formal training that these monks undertake to gain this capacity. The training techniques do not develop muscular strength and aerobic endurance at all—they develop the athlete's psychic abilities. The initial training consists of three years and three months of strict meditative seclusion in total darkness. During this solitary retreat, the psychic athlete practices specific breathing exercises.

One of the exercises that the monk practices is to slowly inhale for a long time—as if completely filling his or her body with air. Then, while holding this breath, the monk jumps or rises into the air while remaining in a motionless, cross-legged meditative posture. Essentially the purpose of this intensive training is to develop the skill of levitation. The proficiency test for this athlete is to sit in a pit that has a domelike covering over top with a hole in the center. The distance from the floor of the pit to the hole is twice the standing height of the person. The initiate must levitate up through the hole while remaining in the meditative posture. (Folks, don't try this at home in your living room.)

Alexandra David-Neel offers a brief description of the trancelike technique used by the lung-gom-pa, after passing the proficiency test. The initiate is given a mystic formula—a kind of mantra. The silent recitation of this mystic formula must be coordinated with the breath and the cadence of the steps. The lung-gom-pa must not speak and must keep his or her attention focused, while the eyes are fixed on a single distant object. In this state of trance, there is just enough normal consciousness that the runner is aware of obstacles, the direction of travel, and the destination. There are specific times of the day and terrain conditions that are most favorable for the beginner—although masters can maintain the trance for several consecutive days on almost any terrain.

The prospect of levitation is difficult for our mana'o intelligence to fathom. Alexandra David-Neel also describes briefly seeing a naked man in a forest in Tibet with iron chains wrapped around his body. Deep in meditation, he did not at first take notice as she and her companions approached. When he was finally aware of their presence, he leaped up in his chains and disappeared into the woods "more quickly than a deer." One of her companions explained that—as a lung-gom-pa—his body had become so light from his practice that he wore the chains to stay on the ground.

Tumo

Also in "Psychic Sports," David-Neel describes a feat of endurance known as *tumo*. Unlike the lung-gom-pas—which were quite rare even eighty years ago—tumo practitioners are still common and are not limited to Tibet. In this practice, the yogi-athlete is able to sit in meditation and generate a tremendous amount of warmth.

There are numerous accounts in the Orient of hermits who sit outside naked or clad only in thin cotton garments. Through a specific and elaborate process of breathing, meditation, and visualization, these individuals can generate enough body heat to melt the snow around them. One of the requirements for the practice of tumo is that they do not eat or drink anything beforehand.

Spiritual Endurance

Many native cultures have developed practices for enduring extreme climatic conditions. A common element throughout these endurance practices is that the skills and abilities are developed not through direct physical training, but through breathing, meditation, prayer and visualizations. In his book *Bone Games: Extreme Sports, Shamanism, Zen and the Search for Transcendence*, Rob Schultheis investigates the heightened and extraordinary states of consciousness and the elements of shamanism that can lead to such remarkable feats of endurance. He cites numerous examples from many cultures and many contexts—religious and shamanic as well as athletic.

Truly remarkable feats of endurance are not based on sheer physical strength—they are based in spiritual fitness and intelligence. In India there are accomplished yogis who can defy our modern scientific explanation of human possibility. These masters can voluntarily stop both their breath and heartbeat for a length of time that would normally be fatal or cause irreversible damage. Such feats can only be accomplished through *spiritual* fitness. *Yoga* means "union"—the union of our three energetic intelligences at the Zen center of our intelligence triangle. We will consider just one more example of endurance as a sacred practice toward spiritual fitness.

Native American Sun Dance Ceremony

For half a century the U.S. government legally prohibited the practice of Sun Dance. In the past thirty to forty years, the Sioux Nation has revived this annual ceremony of prayer and sacrifice— usually held in early-to-mid-summer. Those who participate do so as a result of a vision or a dream. Sun Dance is not regarded as a mere test of manhood or a feat of endurance. There are no finisher's shirts or medals for Sun Dance. Preparation for a Sun Dance is based on a diligent and *sacred* approach—with sincere prayer as well as very specific and deliberate ceremonies.

Traditionally a Sun Dance lasts for twelve days. The first four days are for preparing the campsite and the dance circle as a living shrine to honor the Great Spirit. During the next four days, the dancers prepare and receive instructions from the medicine men. The final four days are for the dance itself. For the first three days of the actual dance, the participants dance from dawn until dusk in the sun's intense heat and light without food or water. As they dance, they gaze at the sun and blow on whistles made from eagle bones.

Throughout these days of dance, the elders, medicine men, and family supporters continue to pray for the dancers. On the fourth day—following prayers and offerings to the rising sun by the medicine men—the dancers go to the sweat lodge for purification. Afterward, they are painted and adorned, and then are led by the medicine men back to the Sun Dance circle for the final day. Many singers and drummers surround the dancers to perform the seven

Sun Dance songs. It is here that the dancers are *pierced*.

Traditionally, there were four different ways of piercing. Today most Sun Dancers use Gazing at the Sun Leaning—the one most often used traditionally. The flesh of the dancer's breasts is pierced about a handwidth above the nipples. A wooden stick or an eagle's claw is stuck through each piercing. These sticks or claws are attached to leather thongs that hang from the *can-wankan*—the sacred pole that was erected in the center of the circle during the ceremonies of the first four days of preparation. The dancers lean back, allowing the thongs to pull at their pierced flesh and muscle. They raise their arms in prayer as they blow on their eagle-bone whistles. Now the dancers stay in one place—leaning back, always turning to gaze steadily into the light of the sun.

The commitment to dance is usually for at least four consecutive years. The four days of actual dancing each year are regarded as an expression of prayer and sacrifice for a much deeper spiritual commitment that includes every aspect of the dancer's daily life throughout the rest of the year. Those who commit to Sun Dance for several years actually commit deeply to a daily life of service and spiritual fitness. Sincere service and generosity of oneself is the real training for the Sun Dance. Dancers who break free easily from their piercings during the final day of Sun Dance demonstrate their ability to break free of the ego in their daily lives. They demonstrate true spiritual fitness.

These brief examples demonstrate the infinite potential of zendurance as a practice for developing spiritual fitness. They help to sober our feelings of superiority and elitism as endurance athletes—a healthy measure if we are truly earnest about endurance training as a spiritual path. They emphasize for us the value of *sacredness* in our approach and practice.

Conclusion

To conclude "Beyond Zendurance," let's consider one more example of our infinite potential and capacity outside the endurance arena—as demonstrated through the traditional practice of tai chi. In the not-so-distant past, there were great masters who had developed extraordinary skills of yielding, blending, and aligning. These masters could absorb the energy of tremendous impact and could repel others with great force simply by touching them.

I have seen film footage of one of these great masters from Thailand, from the 1980s. He was sparring with one of his students, using a form called Push Hands. In this form, while remaining stationary, the opponents try to uproot one another. The master's opponent began to strike him in the torso. As he dropped his arms, his entire body became soft—like Jell-o. Each blow created jiggling waves through his body, as he remained relaxed and stationary. He raised one arm, unfolding and extending the fingers of his hand. The back of his fingers gently brushed his opponent's upper chest as he extended them. The master sent his opponent flying backward about five feet before he fell to the ground on his back.

This same master then sat blindfolded in a chair at one end of the large studio. One of his students ran at him with a large wooden ram, about eight feet long, striking him in the stomach. The master absorbed the impact of the blow and then repelled the ram, sending his assailant and the ram back across the room. His chair never moved. Impossible?

I have also read several accounts of the great Chinese masters, some of whom lived into the mid-to-late twentieth century. These masters demonstrated similar abilities. One account in particular stands out: A small and elderly master, weighing no more than 90 pounds, easily held off six black belts of karate who were armed with wooden swords. When any of them got within two yards of him, he raised his hand and repelled them—*without ever touching them!*

Accounts of these remarkable feats are too numerous to be fairy tales. Of course they are difficult for us to conceive. We usually experience power as being limited to physical, external forces that require muscle. How are these feats possible? These traditional masters demonstrate for us the infinite potential of yielding, blending, and aligning. When we have the awareness and intelligence to align literally every cell, every molecule of our body with gravity, then we can activate, translate, and articulate that energy.

In the "Running—Aligning" entry, we used the image of a gravity laser. Through perfect alignment and complete energetic grounding, these masters have literally turned their bodies into gravity lasers. They demonstrate the incredible potential inherent in the intelligent skills of yielding, blending, and aligning.

Our potential for spiritual fitness and intelligence and for effortless power is infinite—provided we honor and abide by the laws of harmony and integrity that govern our universe. If we violate these laws, we have nothing but ego left.

GENUINE FITNESS, INTELLIGENCE AND POWER

Spiritual Fitness

One of the distinctions between traditional spiritual forms of endurance and our modern athletic endurance races has to do with the methods of training, preparation, and approach. Our conventional athletic methods focus on *physical* training—first building our aerobic base fitness and then carefully peaking for a goal-race performance. The training and preparation in traditional spiritual forms of endurance focus on overall *spiritual* fitness and intelligence—often including very specific ceremonies of prayer, devotion, and meditation. Traditional "spiritual athletes" approach their endeavors in a very diligent and sacred way. Many of these traditional forms include little if any formal physical training—as we have considered with the Tibetan runners and the Sun Dancers. Spiritual fitness is the ability to remain steadfast and seated in the Zen center of our intelligence triangle.

The Zen Center Question

What exactly *is* our Zen center? Throughout this book we have described our Zen center of the intelligence triangle as the "calm, still, silent, open, and empty space of deep inner listening and contemplation." But can we actually see, hear, taste, smell, or touch this calmness, stillness, silence, openness, or emptiness? These adjectives seem to *defy* our senses—yet we know undeniably when we are sourcing our awareness, our experiences and our lives from this place of *witnessing*. How do we know? Energetically we can *feel* that calm and abiding place of witnessing. *This* sense of feeling is not the same as our physical sense of touch. We cannot physically locate or touch the calm, still, silent, open, and empty Zen center—nor can we touch any of the energetic intelligences—yet they are all somehow tangible and accessible to us.

As athletes, we have developed this energetic tangibility by transforming our aerobic training into the moving meditation of zendurance. This ability to *feel* energy is like a *sixth sense* for us. Our sixth sense seems to have one foot in the physical realm and one foot in the metaphysical—the realm that cannot be measured or quantified. Even beyond our athletic training as a zendurance practice, our sacred approach to the everyday experiences of our daily lives also requires this very same energetic sixth sense.

Power—Beyond Five Senses

While we have not yet clearly defined our Zen center, we acknowledge that we *are* developing and strengthening a sixth sense that enables us to locate and to *feel* that place within us. Gary Zukav begins his book *The Seat of the Soul* by introducing a distinction between what he calls the "five-sensory human" and the "multi-sensory human." As he explains it, one is not superior or inferior to the other. There is, however, a distinction between the potential of our five physical senses and the potential when we expand into our multisensory capacity. Our "sixth sense" of energetic feeling is an example of this expanded multisensory capacity. It has opened us up to a vast metaphysical landscape that includes the energetic intelligence triangle and our Zen center.

Based on this distinction between our five-sensory and multi-sensory capacities, Zukav goes on to explore our notions of *power*. Within our limited five-sensory physical capacity for experience, we navigate through our lives using *fear* as our primary guidance system. Where does this powerful conditioning of fear come from?

As five-sensory humans, each of us is separate from one another and alone in the universe. Beyond the phenomena of pregnancy, birth, and identical twins, our five physical senses alone provide absolutely no proof or indication that we have any tangible connection with one another. This solitary confinement is *certainly* a cause for fear. Acting out of this primary experience of fear, each of us strives to maintain the power to control our environment and those within it.

An athletic example of this fear-based need to control and dominate is the way we skew our experience of competition. Instead of embracing competition as a petition for companionship, support, and inspiration—when we are trapped within our lonely fear-based physical reality—competition becomes *me against them*. From this fear-based experience of power as an external force, we approach endurance athletics as a pursuit of physical strength—focusing our training programs just on physical conditioning. If we limit ourselves solely to this pursuit of physical power, we have no chance of developing or experiencing the effortless power of zendurance or the joy of true competition.

Authentic effortless power *does not* give us the capacity to physically control our environment, the circumstances of our lives, or those around us. Before we look further into effortless power, though, let's return to our earlier question: What exactly *is* our Zen center of the intelligence triangle?

Back to the Zen Center Question

We cannot define our Zen center in a way that is tangible to our five senses. Yet we do detect a tangible quality to our Zen center through our sixth sense. We begin to develop this sixth sense through *contemplation*—as we disengage from and simply witness our thoughts, emotions, and bodily sensations, without identifying with them. What is left beyond these basic elements of our experience? What *is* our true nature, our true essence? It is *love*. It is *spirit* and *consciousness*. We are love. We are spirit and consciousness.

Our divine essence—conscious spirit love—is boundless and infinite. That is why we cannot directly perceive "it" with our five physical senses. Buckminster Fuller defined *gravity* as "the physical manifestation of love." Gravity is not something that we can actually see, hear, touch, taste, or smell, either—but we *can feel* it and we can see its effects. Just like love, gravity is also boundless and infinite. Just as gravity permeates all things physical—without exception and without pause—our conscious spirit love permeates everything—without exception and without pause.

Love is our universal common denominator—our oneness. As individual entities of our conscious loving spirit, we are each shaped into unique souls—fractals of our God essence. This individuality or separateness allows our God essence—our conscious spirit love—to hold up the mirror of relationship in order to experience itself as ourself. We are love's longing for itself. There can be no experience without the mirror of relationship.

The Zen center of our intelligence triangle is—for each of us—*the clear and open window to our soul.* That calm, still, silent, open, and empty space of deep inner listening and contemplation is the accessible and tangible surface of our soul's brilliant God consciousness. Our Zen center is that place where our soul and our human existence can *touch* one another. It is our mana source.

Painting the Experiences of Our Lives

Our infinite spectrum of experience requires three primary elements—just as painting requires three primary colors. Pu'uwai, mana'o and na'au—our three energetic intelligences—are the three primary colors of our experiential palette. These three primary colors endow us with the unlimited potential to paint infinitely diverse and unique experiences of ourself—of our loving conscious spirit essence. *All three* of our primary colors—our energetic intelligences—are vital in order for us to experience the infinite spectrum of our loving God essence.

Our pu'uwai intelligence endows us with the intelligent capacity to connect and integrate with our divine loving essence. Pu'uwai is the *source* of our multisensory capacity—the intelligence that enables us to expand beyond our five physical senses. Without pu'uwai intelligence, we are alone and separate.

Our mana'o intelligence endows us with the skillful capacity for distinction and isolation. This is absolutely essential in the arena of experience. Mana'o is the intelligent source of *duality*—of *me* and *you*—that allows for perception and expression. Duality creates the mirror of relationship so that our God essence can experience itself as ourself.

Our na'au intelligence endows us with the intelligent capacity to be present here and now—in *this* moment and in *this* place. Na'au is our intelligent source of activity, of manifestation. It is the vehicle of grounding—the stage where our experience occurs.

Painting with Fitness and Intelligence

Each of these three intelligences is an infinitely powerful universal force—like a mighty river. As human beings, when we slip away from the Zen center—from the clear and open window to our God essence, the seat of our soul—we are engulfed and swept away by the powerful current of one or more of these unlimited and infinite forces. We are no longer conscious and awake as multisensory beings. Until we make the conscious choice to return to the refuge of our Zen center, we will be at the mercy of these forces: We will blindly and recklessly flail the chainsaw of reason. We will be helplessly swept away in the current of our emotions and feelings. We will be thoroughly consumed by the sensations and instincts of our bodies.

Spiritual *fitness* begins with the capacity to wake up at any moment and to return immediately to the refuge of our Zen center. The true essence of spiritual fitness is the grounding and stamina—*as well as the loving-kindness*—to remain seated and awake at that clear and open window to our soul.

Spiritual *intelligence* is our capacity to pick up the palette of our three energetic intelligences and to brilliantly and creatively paint the experiences of our lives—without falling back into the paints—as we gaze through the clear and open window to our individual souls and our collective God essence.

What's Possible?

Sri Chinmoy is one of the greatest living examples of our human capacity for spiritual fitness and intelligence. Born in Bangladesh in 1931, he entered the Sri Aurobindo Ashram at the age of twelve, after both of his parents had died. He spent the next twenty years at the ashram building a spiritual practice that included meditation, athletics, musical composition, and writing. In 1964 he left the ashram for New York City to share his inspiration and intelligence and to continue his path of service.

Quoting from the Sri Chinmoy Website, "Sri Chinmoy's life is an expression of boundless creativity. His vast output spans the domains of music, poetry, painting, literature and sports. His contributions in each of these fields is striking and far-reaching." Sri Chinmoy has produced more than fourteen hundred books of poetry, essays, plays and short stories. He has also produced over 150,000 meditative artworks and thirteen *million* soul-bird drawings. Sri Chinmoy plays twelve musical instruments and has composed countless musical compositions.

As an athlete, he was a 100-meter sprint and decathlon champion in his youth. (And we think three sports is challenging—how about ten?) He has completed twenty-two marathons, five ultramarathons, and has set many world records in weight lifting. At least one of these weight lifting records he set using just *one* arm. This remarkable feat defies modern scientific analysis—which calculates that the weight he lifted should have crushed the bones in his arm. Now in his early seventies, he remains physically active and healthy.

Sri Chinmoy has inspired many endurance athletes, as evidenced by the ultra-endurance events that bear his name. This includes the Sri Chinmoy 5000K—the world's longest certified foot race. (That's a 3,100-mile race, folks.) In Australia, the Self Transcendence Triathlon Festival is put on annually by an athletic organization that bears his name. One of the races in this festival is a three-day triathlon—with a 15-kilometer swim that laps a 500-meter course, a 400-kilometer bike on a 2.2-kilometer, loop and a 100-kilometer run on a 1.4-kilometer loop.

Sri Chinmoy firmly believes that physical fitness is a vital component of spiritual practice and spiritual strength. If we truly intend to reach our greatest potential as athletes and as human spiritual beings, we must combine physical and spiritual fitness.

He recognizes *aspiration* as "the heart's ceaseless yearning for higher and deeper realities." It is "the spiritual force behind all great advances in religion, culture, sports, and science. By living in the heart and aspiring for continual self-transcendence, men and women can bring forward the best in themselves and find their path to true satisfaction." As someone who demonstrates such a remarkable capacity for spiritual fitness and intelligence, Sri Chinmoy's emphasis on the intelligence and guidance of the heart is noteworthy.

"When the power of love replaces the love of power, Man will have a new name: God."   —Sri Chinmoy

Effortless Power

I was first introduced to the expression "effortless power" through the title of Peter Ralston's book *Cheng Hsin: The Principles of Effortless Power.* The pursuit of effortless power is the true path of all the purest internal martial arts forms. What distinguishes these martial art forms as pure and internal? They train and develop much more than sheer physical strength and force. These forms recognize the functional value *and the power* of contemplation and approach, along with the discipline of practice. They recognize that genuine power is based not on control and manipulation, but rather on subtle and profound skills like yielding, blending, and aligning.

As zendurance athletes, we have direct training and racing experience with these subtle and profound skills. Through yielding, blending, and aligning we are honing our efficiency—our ability to do less and accomplish more. Efficiency—the "path of least resistance"—is essential to any quest of endurance. With this efficiency, we experience better performances, less injury, and more satisfaction as athletes.

Through the practices of HeartCore Zendurance, we are diversifying and applying these skills beyond athletics into our daily lives.

We are *creatively* integrating the subtle and profound skills of yielding, blending, and aligning into our relationships and families, our occupations, and our ordinary day-to-day activities. We are experiencing more harmony and grace, less resistance and frustration and more satisfaction as human spiritual beings. We are planting positive and beneficial "imprint seeds" in our own future and the future of those around us. We are blending together our lives as both aspiring athletes and ordinary human beings. These are all sure signs along our path toward effortless power.

Three Practices for Effortless Power

In "Zendurance Racing and Performance," we considered the wisdom of uncertainty—based on Deepak Chopra's sixth spiritual law of success, The Law of Detachment. From this same book, *The Seven Spiritual Laws of Success*, we look to the fourth law, called The Law of Least Effort, for more insight on effortless power.

Acceptance

Chopra outlines three conscious practices that we can implement in our commitment to effortless power. The first practice is *acceptance*, which begins with contemplation. From our Zen center, we can open up and accept the present moment as it unfolds. We can embrace all current circumstances, situations, and relationships as they are, without resisting. If we struggle against the present moment, then we are actually struggling against the *entire universe*. Acceptance is a lot like our practice of *yielding*.

Acceptance does not mean that we must like or agree with the present moment. We must recognize that these likes and dislikes are *our own* feelings, *our own* approval or resistance. We do not blame or credit them to someone else or something outside ourselves. This recognition enables us to take *responsibility* for how we feel.

Responsibility

The second practice in our commitment to effortless power is *responsibility*. Responsibility endows us with the ability to respond creatively and intelligently to the circumstances, situations, and relationships *as they are now*—without wasting energy and expending effort to resist them or judge them. Our experiences with *blending* enhance our ability to accept and to respond to this present moment.

It is through our ability to respond creatively and intelligently to this present moment that we can plant the imprint seeds of harmony in our future. A functional understanding of the principle of karma—of planting imprint seeds—is essential in our quest for effortless power, particularly in the practice of responsibility. Responsibility begins with our *approach* to each moment and each experience. In our quest for effortless power, we diligently choose to approach, honor, and respond to each experience as a sacred opportunity for growth, fitness, and intelligence.

Defenselessness

The third practice in our quest for effortless power is *defenselessness*. The practice of defenselessness is similar to our athletic efficiency practices of hydrodynamic swimming, aerodynamic cycling, and gravi-dynamic running—all practices of making ourselves small. In our pursuit of athletic efficiency, we know that minimizing our impact and our resistance by streamlining our body's position reduces considerably the effort we expend in our endurance activity.

The practice of defenselessness *also* involves streamlining our position. In this practice, the position we are streamlining is our *point of view*. We can conserve an immense amount of energy when we give up defending our point of view, blaming and judging others and seeking approval. Our point of view is generated by our *ego*. In the practice of defenselessness, we abstain from defending our ego. This helps us considerably to remain steadfast in the Zen center of our intelligence triangle. Our practice of *aligning* with gravity—minimizing our impact and our friction—is very similar to the practice of defenselessness.

Summary

When we consider the practices of acceptance, responsibility and defenselessness, as well as the wisdom of uncertainty and the operational principles of karma—of planting imprint seeds—then our long-held notions of *power* begin to transform. This is particularly true in our expanded capacity as multisensory beings. Genuine effortless power requires that we yield to, blend, and align with the circumstances, situations, and relationships of *this present moment*. It requires steadfast centering and our willingness to relinquish our attachments.

We are still endowed with our desires and our intention—but without attachment to the outcome. Genuine effortless power requires absolute faith and trust in the divine balance and love of the universe. It also requires that we remain open, alert and connected to this divine balance and love. If we abide by these requirements, then our desires—through focused intention—will come to fruition effortlessly.

As we progress through the final miles and approach the finish line, let's investigate one more triad—one last triangle. Let's call this one the *challenge triangle* because it identifies the three challenging conditions of human existence. These conditions provide us with truly challenging tests throughout our lives to develop spiritual fitness, spiritual intelligence, and effortless power.

FINAL MILES

The Challenge Triangle

The *triangle* has been a key element throughout this book. We began with the three athletic activities of conventional triathlon—swimming, biking, and running. Through these three endurance forms, we have identified and explored the intelligent skills of yielding, blending, and aligning—the next triangle or triad. It is important to note that *every* form of endurance activity—even those we did not consider in this book—provide us with the opportunity to examine *all three skills*. All that is required is a diligent and creative approach.

Next, we introduced the trinity of our sources of intelligence—pu'uwai, mana'o, and na'au. These are the apexes of our intelligence triangle. The three legs that connect these apexes to one another comprise the trinity of practice legs—meditation/yoga, service/diet and prayer/devotion. Now let's look at one more triangle—the challenge triangle.

Those Final Miles

In the final miles of a long endurance race—especially a goal race—we must often dig deep. We must reach deep into the core of our being for the energy, focus, and courage to push on to the finish line. In these final miles, we get up close and personal with our pain and suffering, our doubts and uncertainty, our fatigue and our fear. We realize that our mental willpower—courtesy of the ego—is absolutely powerless in this moment of truth. We are fighting the battle of the inner warrior. Our most effective weapons in this inner battle are spiritual attributes like grace, humility, patience, and compassion. These are the tools that can help us to remain steadfast in our Zen center. In these final miles, we must embrace the toughest of challenges.

In our everyday lives as human beings, we must also face some difficult challenges and conditions. Unlike our experiences with endurance racing, however, we can choose to embrace these challenges at *any* moment—without waiting until the final miles of our lives. If we choose to avoid them throughout our lives, they will always lurk close by—in the shadows of our subconscious. Then we *will* be compelled to face them in those final miles.

Daily Choice

As endurance athletes, we make a conscious choice daily to embrace the challenging opportunities of aerobic training in order to cultivate and develop aerobic fitness and intelligence. As human beings, we can also make the conscious choice in our daily lives to embrace and transform the challenging conditions of human existence as opportunities to cultivate and develop spiritual fitness and intelligence.

Three and Three

In triathlon we have three athletic activities—*three challenges*—to work with in cultivating and developing our aerobic fitness and intelligence—swimming, biking, and running. Our very existence as human beings also provides us with *three challenges* to work with in cultivating and developing spiritual fitness and intelligence. In Buddhism, these challenges are known as the *three characteristics* (or *conditions*) *of human existence*. These are three conditions that *each* of us experiences—whether we are rich or poor, good or bad, gifted or cursed, saints or sinners.

The Moment of Truth

These three challenges are *impermanence, selflessness,* and *suffering.* What is your first reaction to these conditions? Resistance? *No way! This sucks! These definitely do not apply to me. Screw this finish line! It's time to close this book for good and turn on the TV!* These conditions are not very attractive are they? They are downright *terrifying* for me. Before we run away, though, let's try a different approach.

Responding to the Challenge

As endurance athletes, through diligent and consistent training, we have learned to embrace and to respond to the challenges provided by our athletic activity. When we first begin, our athletic training may not be much fun—but the gains we experience by responding to these endurance challenges obviously outweigh the sacrifices that we make and the discomfort and monotony that we encounter. We choose to maintain a daily relationship with the challenge of aerobic fitness through our practice of zendurance because we would be miserable if we avoided it and chose instead the life of a couch potato.

The three characteristics of human existence provide us with even greater potential for fitness and intelligence—if and when we choose to *accept* and *embrace* them. (Remember the practice of acceptance in our quest for effortless power.) Unlike swimming, biking, and running, we *cannot* avoid *any* of these three conditions—no matter how smart, how rich, or how charming we may be. Since we cannot avoid them anyway, let's at least take a cautious little peek at each one, shall we? After all, these three challenging characteristics provide the powerful and enduring framework for our human existence.

FINAL MILES: IMPERMANENCE

"Whether the reality of change is a source of freedom for us or a
source of horrific anxiety makes a significant difference."
—Pema Chodron, *The Places That Scare You*

Everything Changes

If there is a single popular expression among the widely diverse
sects of Buddhism, it is this: "Everything changes." Impermanence
—or *change*—is a basic and *essential* element of each and every
experience in our lives. Why is impermanence essential to our
human experience? Each sensation, feeling, and thought that
comprises our experience has a beginning, middle, and an ending.
Each one arises and then passes away. Each one is *temporary*.
After all, if these sensations, feelings and thoughts were *perma-
nent*—without a beginning or ending—then how could we possibly
detect them? How could we *experience* them? Without this tempo-
ral, dynamic quality in our lives, we would have no experiences.
There would be no growth, no progress in our lives.

Fear of Change

Our typical way of responding to impermanence is to *resist*
change. We go to great effort and great expense throughout our
lives to stabilize and to *secure* our environment and our lives. We
make every attempt to *stop* the flow of time. Why do we so strongly resist impermanence and change? What do we *fear* about impermanence?

When we open up and investigate the nature of impermanence,
we discover that it delivers each and every one of us to the same
place. Impermanence leads to the inevitable conclusion of human
life—something we call death—and that's one finish line that most
of us are not exactly racing toward. Yet a race without a finish line
or an adventurous journey without a destination can feel like aim-
less wandering.

Our reaction to these inevitable changes in our lives—*including
our deaths*—is that we made a mistake somewhere. We didn't man-
age to keep things in order. Yet no matter how good or bad we are,
all of us—saints and sinners alike—arrive at life's finish line. Is
there any consolation, any comfort or refuge for us, or do we just

wallow away hopelessly in this condition of impermanence? How can we gracefully embrace the condition of impermanence and transform it into an opportunity to develop our spiritual fitness and intelligence?

Responding to Impermanence

The *first step* in transforming the condition of impermanence from bad news to good news is the first step of the Zen pentathlon—*contemplation*. Only from the Zen center of our intelligence triangle are we able to embrace and to be completely present with the condition of impermanence—the ocean of change in our lives. From our Zen center, we can disengage from all the fears, anxiety, and resistance that have been sucking up our vital energy and distracting us from true intelligence. Through contemplation, we can really begin to *investigate* the true nature of impermanence with curiosity, patience, and keen, open perception.

We know already from our athletic training just how valuable this open-minded and Zen centered approach can be—when we transform the hardship and drudgery of our endurance training into zendurance meditation. Through the same steadfast centering and contemplation, and the same open-minded approach, we are able to examine the fears and resistance that we have to the inevitable changes and impermanence in our daily lives.

Kind and Gentle

As we begin to discover and to examine our own fears and resistance, it is best if we refrain from self-criticism, judgment or evaluation. These only serve to add more resistance and anxiety. Our intention—through Zen-centered contemplation—is to *gently embrace* our fears and resistance without being swept away by them. This embrace enables us to disarm them so that they gradually dissolve. Responding with judgment, self-criticism, or the like only serves to strengthen and entrench them.

Swimming Through Impermanence

Let's draw a little more on our experience as endurance athletes, so that we can determine how to effectively use the condition of impermanence as an opportunity for spiritual fitness and intelligence. If the condition of impermanence is like a vast ocean of change, then our zendurance approach to *swimming* can provide us with some valuable and applicable skills.

As beginners, we start out swimming without any awareness for the fluid medium of water—it is completely alien and threatening to us. We experience only resistance and the immensity of its volume. We have no knowledge of swimming technique—no *feel* for swimming or for the water. Similarly, until we begin to accept and to embrace the condition of impermanence, we have no awareness for the graceful and fluid nature of change—it is completely alien and threatening to us. We experience only difficulty and resistance—resistance that we ourselves create. We feel overwhelmed by the immensity of that vast ocean of change. In both our swimming technique and our approach to impermanence, we are so unconscious that we cannot *feel* the disturbance we are causing and the resistance we are creating as we flail away.

This comparison of the medium of water to the condition of impermanence is a very accurate one. Both water and *time* are in constant motion. Our fear of water and our fear of impermanence are quite similar—a fear of being fluid, of giving up our stability and solidity.

As zendurance swimmers, we know from the experiences of our training and racing just how essential it is to develop keen and subtle sensitivity to the medium of water. This intimate *feel* for the fluidity of water is built upon the intelligent and sensitive discernment to distinguish between a smooth, graceful flow over our body's surface and a turbulent, resistant flow. With this intelligence and discernment, we begin to *embody* the fluid nature of water.

Our swimming technique improves (that is to say it *changes*— thanks to the condition of impermanence) as we learn to minimize our disturbance, as we learn to be receptive and yielding to the fluid nature of water. Our technique also improves as we learn to maximize the *benefits* of water's dense and resistant qualities. Remember, it is the density and resistance of water that enables us to move forward with each stroke, with each handful of water. Water's density is what keeps us buoyant. Our yielding and receptive zendurance approach to swimming includes a dynamic give-and-take relationship with the water.

We can include this same give-and-take dynamic in our response to impermanence—as we swim gracefully and efficiently through the ocean of change. The fluid and ever-changing dynamics of impermanence can be an overwhelming source of turbulence and difficulty in our lives. Yet it is this very same fluidity and change that we grasp hold of as a way of propelling ourselves through growth—the way we grasp hold of each handful of water in our swimming.

Streamlining

All of the sensitivities and techniques that we are developing in our swim technique are just as vital in our zendurance approach to the challenge of impermanence. We can develop the same subtle sensitivity to the flow of time and change in our lives that we have developed toward the flow of water over our bodies. We can strive to become sensitive enough to this flow of change to feel it in every area of our lives, just as we strive to become sensitive to the flow of water over every part of our body's surface. This enables us to streamline—to minimize our turbulent resistance and our effort. Our zendurance approach to swim training can take on a whole new role in our lives. It becomes a conscious way of refining our approach to impermanence—as we learn to swim efficiently and gracefully through the ocean of change that engulfs us.

Aging Gracefully

This open, receptive and yielding approach to the condition of impermanence enables us to *age gracefully* as athletes. (*Youth is a gift of nature. Age is a work of art.* Remember?) We cannot stop or prevent our athletic bodies or our aerobic capacity from gradually dwindling with age. However, rather than kicking and screaming, we may develop the intelligent sensitivity that enables us to move through the aging process gracefully and fluidly.

The Wisdom of Uncertainty

Another valuable asset we have already begun to develop and strengthen—especially in our zendurance approach to racing—is the *wisdom of uncertainty.* The condition of impermanence generates uncertainty in *all* areas of our lives. If we choose to respond with attachment—struggling to stabilize and secure our lives—we end up imprisoned by our own fears of impermanence.

In "Zendurance Racing and Performance," we looked at just how exhilarating and refreshing the condition of impermanence and uncertainty can be. When we respond to the condition of impermanence with the wisdom of uncertainty, we step through the door of fear, out on to the vast and fertile ground of freedom and creativity. Freedom and creativity are only available to us in this present moment. They are not available to us if we constantly dwell in the past or project into the future. The pervasive and persistent condition of impermanence in our lives *provides our only guarantee* that this infinite potential of freedom and creativity is available to us each and every moment.

Without impermanence and uncertainty, our lives would be stale and repetitious—devoid of any mystery, any challenging opportunity to cultivate and develop spiritual fitness and intelligence. We would become lazy and listless, with no aspiration. Responding with alertness and open receptivity, with the flexible wisdom of uncertainty to the condition of impermanence and change helps to ventilate our lives, to bring oxygen to our spirits.

FINAL MILES: SELFLESSNESS

Is Anybody Home?

The second condition of human existence is *selflessness*. Yikes! Now that really sounds like a *terrifying* prospect! That's like saying we are empty and lifeless—as if there isn't anybody home—even while we are still alive. This seems even more threatening than impermanence. The condition of selflessness can make us feel utterly hopeless. Surely Buddha Sakaymuni must have been *mistaken* when he identified this as a condition of human existence. Or . . . perhaps *we* are mistaken in our *interpretation* of the condition of selflessness.

The Buddha was not implying that we must disappear or that we must annihilate our ego if we choose to follow a spiritual path. Selflessness does not forbid us from experiencing and enjoying our lives. We are not required to resign immediately, bow our heads and go directly to the finish line of life.

Extension of Impermanence

We can approach the condition of selflessness as an extension of impermanence. We have already considered that impermanence is an essential element of each and every experience of our lives. We know that if nothing ever changed, then the phenomena of experience and growth would not be possible.

As humans, we are just as impermanent as everything else is. For example, every cell in the human body lives for only *seven years*! So every seven years, the body we inhabit is a new and different body. While our body is on a seven-year cycle, our thoughts, feelings, and emotions arise and dissolve one after another in just seconds or minutes. *None* of these elements of our experience constitutes who we *really* are. But what about our memories of the past—they remain constant, don't they? They may remain somewhat constant, but our *present* relationship to them is always changing. We are not alive in the *past*; we are alive *here* and *now*.

Nothing about us is fixed or definite—*not even our precious personality*. It is our personality that we are most prone to identify as our true self—and *this is our primary delusion.* Now we are beginning to see just why the condition of selflessness is so *threatening* to us—it threatens our personality. But what is our personality really?

Personality and Athletic Gear

To consider this question, let's use an analogy: Let's compare our personality to our *collection of athletic equipment*. As athletes, we carefully select and acquire specific pieces of equipment that are essential to our endurance training and racing. For triathletes, this collection of gear can be quite extensive. We find out just how extensive and how cumbersome that collection is when we travel a long distance for a race—particularly if we travel by air. Often we must take along both our training gear and our racing gear. We require a bike case, a big gear bag, and perhaps a wheel case—and, once we arrive we have to rent a van just to haul it all around. Not only do we incur the expense of acquiring all that gear *and* the proper containers and vehicle to transport it—we must maintain it as well. Whew! It takes a lot of commitment and dedication not just to train, but also to stay equipped in this sport. Despite this equipment burden, it is well worth it!

Our Collection of Identities

So, how is our personality similar to our collection of athletic gear Our personality is a collection too. Rather than swimming goggles, bicycles and running shoes, our personality is a collection of *identities*. These identities include concepts: *I am a triathlete; I am a producer; I am a mother.* They include likes and dislikes: *I like reggae music; I don't like aggressive people.* Our identities include opinions: *I think every road should have a bike lane.* Our activities and habits: *I train fifteen to twenty hours a week; I always shower and drink coffee in the morning.* Our ambitions: *I'm training for the Boston Marathon; I'm going to retire when I'm fifty.* Our accomplishments and experience: *I've done ten marathons in the past five years—all under 3:50; I have a Master's in Business Administration.* Our identities even include our possessions: *I've got a Calfee Tetra Tri bike; I drive a Honda hybrid car.*

Just like our collection of athletic gear, we carefully select and acquire each specific item of our personality. Either consciously or unconsciously, we *choose* the identities that we deem are essential to our overall personality. These collections can make us more diverse and more functional. As triathletes, our extensive collection of athletic equipment can provide us with the vital tools to become skilled and accomplished multisport athletes. In a similar way, our collection of identities can provide us with tools to be diverse and functional human spiritual beings.

Burden and Distraction

These collections—both our athletic gear *and* our identities—can also *burden* and *encumber* us—making it difficult to function and to participate. As athletes—if we are obsessed with having all the latest, greatest, innovative, high-tech, high-end gear—then we lose sight of endurance athletics as a challenging discipline for growth and fitness. We no longer experience the happiness and satisfaction of our zendurance practice. Instead we are *burdened* by the equipment we have, by the financial setback it brings and the compulsion to acquire each new breakthrough and innovation. We end up training less in order to work more so that we can afford more *stuff.* We spend more time and money maintaining what we have and more time researching and keeping up with the latest breakthroughs. Hey, are we in this for equipment or experience?

We can suffer the same burdening encumbrance if we are obsessed with our personality as a collection of identities. We become vain and self-absorbed—unable to be fully present in this moment. When we are *attached* to our collection of identities, we lose our flexibility and our skills of yielding, blending, and aligning. We resist change as we struggle to preserve and maintain our collection of personality traits. Hey, are we in this life for the image or for experience?

Two Extremes—Athletic Gear

There are actually *two* dysfunctional extremes to this equipment/personality scenario. One extreme is to accumulate an *arsenal* of equipment—a stable of bikes and wheels, closets full of clothes, shoes, and sunglasses. Then, of course, there is the treadmill, the stationary bike trainer, and the pool. Most of us would have to work ten or twelve hours a day, seven days a week to afford all this gear—as well as the means to transport it all and the facilities to house it. That leaves little, if any, time to actually train and race.

Then there is the other extreme: We have a minimum of worn out equipment, no job, car, or house—but unlimited hours to train. With these extreme conditions, we may be unencumbered, but we are also unequipped, hardly able to eat, and unable to afford the cost of maintenance or race fees.

In this scenario of extremes, we realize that somewhere in between these two, there exists a happy medium. This is also true with our *personality.*

Two Extremes—Personality

At one extreme, we can be very obsessed with building and maintaining a glamorous, highly polished identity—one that always appears stable, well composed and never ever vulnerable, at fault, or wrong. As a result of this obsession, we become heavily burdened and encumbered by the weight of our *self-importance*. This self-importance is a clear indicator that we are strongly attached to our personality. No matter how well known, how accomplished, or how saintly we may be, our self-importance limits our potential for spiritual fitness and intelligence. We end up living in a narrow world, governed by our likes and dislikes, imprisoned by our limited self-definitions. Self-importance leaves very little room for the wisdom and freedom of uncertainty.

The other extreme in the personality scenario is the complete *absence* of any identity—no concepts, thoughts, likes or dislikes, opinions, possessions, plans, ambitions, or visions. At this extreme, we simply sit in a dark cave and meditate for the rest of our lives, practicing pure selflessness. After a while, our friends and families forget about us. With years of disciplined practice, we can be absolutely present in each moment—free of thoughts and ambitions, of likes and dislikes, and so on—as we sit silently in our dark cave. To what end?

Here again, we realize that somewhere between these two extremes there exists a happy medium.

Assets

So what does this whole side trip about personality and athletic equipment have to do with selflessness—the second condition of human existence? Just as our athletic gear enables us to train and race, our personality is a carefully acquired collection of *assets* that we have to use as tools in our journey through life. Obviously our athletic gear is not who we are as athletes. Likewise, our personality is not who we are in life. Embracing the condition of selflessness and transforming it into a challenging opportunity for spiritual fitness and intelligence does not mean that we must destroy, discard, or deny the assets of our personality. That would be as ludicrous as triathlon training and racing without any equipment.

Responding to Selflessness

So if we are to transform the condition of selflessness, how do we deal with our personality—with our elaborate collection of identities? As with everything else, we begin with step 1—*contemplation*. We disengage from our personality and return to our Zen center—the clear and open window to our soul. In our practice of meditation, we have contemplated these powerful questions: *What is the true essence of these thoughts, emotional feelings and physical sensations? Who is perceiving these experiences? Who am I really?* These questions do not elicit answers—they simply bring us back to *selflessness*—to the infinite openness and potentiality of our awareness.

In truth, our personality, too, is essentially empty and selfless. The thoughts, concepts, and opinions that constitute our identities are empty and impermanent. Everything we regard as *me* or *belonging to me* is part of the impermanent flow of experience. Our experience *and our personality* unfold and evolve according to the operational laws of the universe—it is not under our "control." However, even in this condition of selflessness, we are each still endowed with a *choice*.

Our choice is in how we *approach* this ever-changing flow of experience—how we swim through it. If we choose to be Zen centered in our approach, we are transforming the condition of selflessness into an empowering opportunity. In the most basic terms, *selflessness is a flexible identity*. It is *not* the annihilation of identity. With a flexible personality, we are inquisitive, adaptable, humorous, creative, and brilliant in this present moment—unencumbered with self-importance. The flexibility of selflessness enables us to willfully engage and disengage the various identities of our personality that are appropriate in the present moment's experience.

The Art of Transition

In our athletic equipment analogy, this flexible identity compares with our ability to *transition* from one sport to the next. In a smooth and seamless transition, we are able to change equipment easily and quickly. The *art* of transition is one of the most empowering and exhilarating aspects of triathlon, because we are literally changing from one *personality* to another—from cyclist to runner, for example—in just seconds. We pride ourselves as multisport athletes in our flexibility and selflessness to instantly and seamlessly transition from swimmer to cyclist to runner.

It would be absurd for us to carry our bike over our shoulder during the run of a triathlon, yes? This illustrates how cumbersome our attachment to our identities can be as we go through life. We can become so certain and attached to who we *think* we are that we cannot transition and participate in our ever-changing experience.

Eventually, with faith and trust, we soften enough to embrace and accept our selfless, egoless nature. We abide steadfastly in our Zen center—at the window to our soul. This is the one empowering *choice* we can make. It is a gradual and profound process of freedom and liberation—of lightening our cumbersome load and becoming enlightened. Can we see now that the condition of selflessness is a cause for joy rather than a cause for fear?

Relationships and Selflessness

Perhaps the biggest arena in our lives for embracing the challenge of selflessness is in our relationships with one another. The *me-you* dualistic nature of relationship can really challenge us to examine the strong attachments we have to the identities of our personality as we hold up the mirror. Remember that the mirror of relationship is a *playback of the imprints* we planted and recorded in the past.

One of the principal sources for our undesirable and negative playbacks in relationships is the imprints that we have planted through *self-importance.* In a state of self-importance, we are inflexible and unwilling to disengage from our most cherished identities. Recalling our earlier illustration, self-importance is when we insist on carrying that bike over our shoulder as we set out on the run. The condition of selflessness invites us to exercise *flexibility* in our relationships—to compassionately and intelli-*gently* engage and disengage our identities so that we plant positive imprints and cultivate harmony and integrity.

Zendurance Training and Selflessness

As we examined the first condition of human existence—impermanence—we identified specific elements of our zendurance athletic training that provide us with a foundation of experience for transforming impermanence into an opportunity for spiritual fitness and intelligence. Let's consider now the specific elements of our athletic activity that provide a foundation for transforming the condition of selflessness.

Streamlining

In the entries on swimming, biking, and running, we considered the practice of making ourselves small as a way of minimizing our resistance in the water, in the wind and with gravity. This technique of streamlining our bodies as swimmers, cyclists and runners has provided us with proof that demonstrates the benefits of minimizing our resistant presence and impact—of diminishing our stable and solid form.

As we disengage from and dissolve our inflexible attachment to the identities and agendas of our personality, we are functional, graceful and fluid in our lives—without resistance and impact. By streamlining our point of view, our personality becomes a more functional *asset* in our lives. As we embrace the condition of selflessness, our personality becomes more versatile and efficient. Just as we become hydrodynamic swimmers, aerodynamic cyclists and gravi-dynamic runners, we learn to be lighter, more adaptable, flexible and brilliant with our personality. Our personality becomes more *spirit dynamic.*

Cycling Through Selflessness

There are specific elements in our zendurance approach to cycling that introduce us to the condition of selflessness as an opportunity for spiritual fitness and intelligence.

The most unique aspect of cycling is the bike itself—the emphasis on equipment and our ability to blend with it. There are two primary components to this process of blending with our bikes. First, we must have a well-fitting bike that is appropriate to the kind of riding that we do. Second, we need to develop the ability to make this bike a natural and graceful extension of our body.

Recalling again our analogy of athletic equipment with personality: We can select a bike based on image—simply because it is high tech and looks cool. Or we can select a bike that best serves as an extension of our body and our sense of feeling, one that allows us to blend gracefully, effortlessly, and efficiently. We can use the same criteria in selecting the identities of our personality—choosing identities that enable us to function gracefully, effortlessly, and brilliantly in each moment. We are able to do this easily when we are *flexible, open, and receptive.* If we are inflexible, stiff and closed, then we will probably be very constrained and unable to function gracefully—even if we have lots of identities.

Like the bike portion of a triathlon, life is a long journey. We need to develop our *blending* skills if we want to make this journey with ease and grace. Blending is a fundamental skill in the process of transforming the condition of selflessness into a catalyst for spiritual fitness and intelligence.

As Novices

When we first begin bicycling, we do not have the sensitivity or the blending skills that help to make our bicycle an integral extension of ourselves. Instead of riding *through* our bike, we start out riding *on* our bike. This separation between body and bike—between self and other—is a tremendous energy sink. At first, we may not be aware of the resistance that exists in that separation—how much we fight our bicycle, by pulling and straining against it.

Similarly, in our daily lives, if we are not flexible in our identity, then it is difficult to blend with the world around us. We resist and struggle, trying to protect our identity. (Remember our discussion of defenselessness as a practice toward effortless power?) We may not be aware of the resistance that we cause with this inflexibility and the difficulties we create for ourselves. Instead it may appear to us as if the universe is doing it to us—that we are the victims.

With Experience

As we develop our blending skills through cycling, a whole new dimension of feeling opens for us. As with a virtuoso violinist, our bike becomes an intimately familiar and natural extension of our body. The boundaries that separate our body from our bike begin to dissolve through a gentle and patient approach and through diligent and consistent practice.

In our daily lives, as we become flexible with our identities and develop blending skills, we begin to dissolve our notions of a solid sense of self—with its hard edges and definite boundaries. We become flexible in our identity so that we can easily blend with all the events, circumstances and relationships of our lives. Our flexible identity endows us with the same virtuosity and mastery as the accomplished violinist or cyclist. We blend with each moment and each relationship as it unfolds—without the burdening encumbrance of attachment to our judgments, opinions, fears, and desires that can cause separation and isolation.

Collective Intelligence

As we develop blending skills in our cycling, we can actually *feel* a sense of intelligent awareness that includes our bike. As we incorporate these skills into our daily lives, we begin to connect to an intelligent awareness that is as much outside of us as it is inside. This is where pu'uwai intelligence is vital.

In "Zendurance Racing and Performance," we explored the nature of our race entity as an intelligent and articulate organism that is much greater than any single athlete, volunteer, or spectator within it. With pu'uwai intelligence, we can link up with this race entity. We are then capable of extraordinary performance levels. We can experience states of awareness and discover insights that are unique to this greater entity—moments of profound enlightenment. We create these experiences by letting go of our fearful limitations and our sharp definitions.

In our daily lives, as we soften our boundaries and definitions so that we can embrace the opportunity of selflessness, we will experience this same sense of enlightenment—without pushing our bodies past our notions of endurance and performance limits. We will gradually dissolve our long-held notions of a solid and stable self as we become flexible and adaptable with our identities.

Cycling as Our Preparation

All the blending techniques we are practicing in our cycling have "prepared" us for this second condition of human existence. We began the "Cycling—Blending" entry by identifying the crankset—with diametrically positioned pedals—as a kind of dynamic yin-yang. The art of circular pedaling is an essential element in the zendurance approach to cycling. Rather than producing power during just one segment of each revolution, we are learning to balance that power more evenly around the full pedal circle—with our legs and feet diametrically opposed. Circular pedaling creates a neurologically ingrained pattern of transforming those opposites into a dynamic circular balance. This nerve and muscle memory helps us transform our notions of self and other into a circular embrace of selflessness.

In addition to circular pedaling, we are practicing bike tai chi. This technique requires that we relax *into* our bicycle—that we soften our grip on the bike—our sense of control through strength. We learn to navigate using our pelvic center of movement and by extending our sense of feeling *into* the bike through the contact triangle with the saddle. We have also developed sensitivity in our feet so that we transmit power efficiently and directly—without misalignment or deflection.

Softening

If there is a common element to our bicycle blending techniques, it is the practice of *softening* our boundaries and definitions so that we can extend our sense of feeling awareness beyond our physical body. Similarly, the second condition of human existence—selflessness—invites us to *soften* our physical, mental, and emotional boundaries and definitions. We must soften the grip of attachment to our identities. Much to our relief, this condition of selflessness does not mean that we must discard or destroy our personality or our ego. Selflessness simply challenges us to be flexible and versatile with our identities—to transition gracefully and efficiently. This flexibility enables us to connect and blend with our infinite universal intelligence that is so much greater than our individual ego-self.

Imagine playing our lives with the articulation, mastery, and passion of a virtuoso violinist. The condition of selflessness provides us with this very opportunity.

FINAL MILES: SUFFERING

"To accept that pain is inherent and to live our lives from this understanding is to create the causes and conditions for happiness."
—Pema Chodron, *The Places That Scare You*

Introduction

The third condition of human existence is suffering and dissatisfaction. As with the first two conditions, when we first confront the condition of suffering, we may experience hopelessness and despair. Do we simply give up any vision or pursuit of happiness as we embrace these three conditions of human existence? Must all of our lives be so cursed? Let's exercise our spiritual fitness to remain steadfast right here and take a cautious little peek at suffering. Perhaps we will find some redeeming qualities—just as we have with impermanence and selflessness.

Suffering includes our physical pain, our emotional distress and grief, our anxieties and fears, our losses and disappointments. When we really open our eyes to the world around us, we see the incredible magnitude of this condition in its various forms—hunger, injury, disease, poverty, violence and cruelty. It can be quite overwhelming. Our natural reaction is to run away and hide from suffering.

Do we have to suffer? Is this a requirement from God? Do we suffer because we are bad, and deserve to be punished? Are we somehow inadequate? Have we made crucial mistakes in our lives? How can we possibly transform the condition of human suffering into a challenging opportunity for spiritual fitness and intelligence?

Even those of us who live physically comfortable lives—with adequate food, clothing, shelter, and medical care—still experience suffering. (In fact, the United States, with the highest standard of living, has the highest per capita instance of mental disease and incarceration in the world.)

When we really start to look closely at our daily activities, we begin to observe just how much these ordinary activities are governed by our *fear* and our compulsion to avoid suffering: We face the daily drudgery of commuting and working so that we can sustain our even improve our state of physical comfort and avoid that most graphic and immediate form of suffering—physical pain. We often keep ourselves so busy and so absorbed that we do not have to look deep inside ourselves and experience our deepest pain and suffering. This cycle is called *samsara* in Buddhist terminology—it is the escalating spiral of pain and suffering. The ocean of samsara expresses the enormity of our collective human condition of suffering.

Responding To Suffering

Where do we start in this vast ocean of pain and grief? In what direction do we go? As always, we begin at the calm, still, silent, open, and empty Zen center of our intelligence triangle. Only through *contemplation* can we summon up the spiritual fitness to approach our suffering. Rather than going to great pains to avoid suffering, from our Zen center we have the steadfastness to embrace and to investigate this condition. As we learn to stay calm and present with our suffering, we gradually begin to discern *three basic misunderstandings* that generate pain and suffering in our lives.

Three Misunderstandings

Our first misunderstanding is that we hope and expect that our lives and the world around us will remain stable and unchanged. *We resist the condition of impermanence.* We invest so much thought, time, money, and energy just trying to stabilize our lives and our environment. Then we suffer from the disappointment and the loss of that investment—due to our inevitable failure to prevent the ocean of impermanence from washing over us.

Our second misunderstanding is that we continue to maintain our separateness and to function in our lives as isolated and *lonely* entities. *We resist the condition of selflessness.* We navigate through our lives as though we are separate, solid and stable objects—like our cars—with fixed identities. We ignore the connective intelligence of our hearts. Here again, we invest so much time and energy just trying to preserve the distinction of self-importance and again we suffer in our inevitable failure.

The third misunderstanding that brings on our suffering has to do with our *interpretation of happiness.* We regard happiness as security and the avoidance of fear. We believe that fear is bad and should be avoided at all costs. Yet we do not need to be scared of our fears. We can remain steadfast in our Zen center—even in the presence of fear. Fear is a universal experience—it is part of our challenge to spiritual fitness.

Know Fear

As crazy as this may seem, each time we are able to remain Zen centered and present with our fears, we are actually moving *closer* to the truth and to genuine happiness. *How can this possibly be true?* Each time we disengage from and begin to dissolve an old pattern in our lives, we must embrace and experience the fear that has held that pattern in place—the fear, darkness, and ignorance that have imprisoned that part of us.

As an example of this, anytime that we approach and examine the conditions of impermanence and selflessness in our lives, we are really looking at *our own patterns and the fears* that hold them in place. Once we choose to embrace these patterns and fears, we begin to transform impermanence and selflessness into opportunities rather than burdens. These conditions of impermanence, selflessness, and suffering can be transformed into opportunities for genuine happiness and liberation—once we choose to embrace our fears associated with them.

Maitri

How can we possibly embrace and *befriend* our fears? Through our practice of contemplation—in traditional sitting meditation and in our zendurance training—we begin to discover and strengthen our *maitri*. Maitri is our loving-kindness toward our own selves and toward our feelings of vulnerability. Maitri softens us and opens us so that we can approach and embrace our fears and darkness with gentleness and patience.

Cultivating maitri does not mean that we will become weak and spineless or helpless and passive. Maitri comes from the spiritual fitness to remain steadfast in our Zen center without resisting, fighting or lashing out at our own fears and doubts. It endows us with the strength of the inner warrior to really befriend and intimately know our own fears—*without falling into them.* Our old patterns and fears can only dissolve in the light of our true wisdom and love. There is no other way to slay them. When we dissolve them with our maitri, then we experience the authentic happiness of liberation and freedom.

Knowing Fear Through Training

As endurance athletes, we already have experience with the conscious practice of embracing our suffering. Our athletic discipline already includes the process of dissolving old patterns and limitations—as well as the fears that hold them in place. In our daily commitment to training, we experience our aches and pains, weariness and doubts, fear and uncertainty—all the elements of our suffering—without succumbing to them. In doing so, we experience a daily redemption and renewal—the liberation, exhilaration and happiness that arise as we dissolve our old beliefs, limitations, patterns, and fears. We already know from our athletic training that a regular practice of embracing and being genuinely present with our suffering and our fear is a true source of happiness.

This very same knowledge applies to the ordinary activities of our daily lives. If we try to avoid suffering by avoiding the situations, circumstances, and relationships that would cause us to confront and investigate our old patterns and behaviors—as well as the fears that hold them in place—then we will remain spiritual couch potatoes. Our athletic training alone—no matter how pure—will not suffice in challenging our overall spiritual fitness. Simply put, we will continue to be held captive by our own fears beyond athletic endurance.

We *can*, however, choose to diligently approach the situations, circumstances, and relationships of our daily lives with the same maitri and the same inquisitive aspiration that we engage in our zendurance approach to athletic training. We can effectively apply the spiritual fitness we have developed through our zendurance training to the daily activities of our lives. All that is required of us is a clear and willful choice to do so.

Each time that we set out to train, we experience our doubts, fears, uncertainty, and resistance. These obstacles may appear to us in the form of fatigue, boredom, distraction, anxiety or agitation. Yet as we lace up our shoes and start out for a run, as we put on our goggles and dive in for a swim, we approach these obstacles with maitri and they dissolve. These very same obstacles also arise in our daily lives—in each situation and relationship that causes us to confront and experience our fears. We experience doubt, uncertainty, anxiety, boredom, fatigue, distraction, and agitation. We can respond to these obstacles with the same discipline and clear vision, the same sacred approach of contemplative steadfastness and maitri that we muster up for each athletic training session.

With a sacred approach of loving-kindness, we deliberately honor and recognize that our fear and suffering are part of the divine path of our lives. Rather than running from our fears or lashing out at them, we choose to befriend them, to know them intimately through the illumination of our light and love. With this sacred approach, we begin to welcome our fear and suffering as encouraging signs that we are actually approaching happiness.

Knowing Fear Through Racing

As we gather together in the days before a big race, we experience not just our own fears and suffering, but the collective fear and suffering of our companions as well. The ecstasy and happiness we experience at the finish line is generated, in part, by the support and inspiration we have shared with one another in the face of our fear during the race. With this support and inspiration, each of us embraces our suffering and ventures deeply into the darkness of our fears and doubts, to dissolve them with our light and love. It is very comforting and empowering for us to discover that we are not alone in our suffering and to discover the power of companionship—the power of our *collective* light and love.

We experience our greatest satisfaction and finish-line *satori* when we courageously approach our race with gentleness, humility and grace—rather than brutality, domination and fear. Only with maitri and compassion are we really able to embrace, inspire and empower one another. This is the very *heart* of racing. It is also the *heart* of living. *Maitri*—loving-kindness toward oneself—and *compassion*—loving-kindness for others—are two essential qualities for gracefully transforming all three conditions of human existence into opportunities for spiritual fitness and intelligence.

Running Through Suffering

As athletes, our daily discipline and dedication to training provide us with a strong foundation of steadfastness and maitri to embrace and transform our suffering. Let's look now at some of the techniques of our zendurance training that provide us with specific skills in this quest. Our zendurance approach to swimming has helped us develop the skill of yielding—a valuable attribute as we embrace the condition of impermanence and swim through the vast ocean of change in our lives. Our zendurance approach to cycling has helped us develop the skill of blending—a valuable attribute as we embrace the condition of selflessness. Blending teaches us to be flexible in our identity and to soften our boundaries and extend our sensitivities.

In the swim-bike-run triad, it is running that can be most painful—that can bring us up close and personal with our physi-

cal suffering. That's because running provides us with the most
direct relationship with *gravity*—with the weight of human existence. In the "Running—Aligning" entry, we considered three ways
of responding to our unceasing, lifelong relationship with gravity.

One way to respond is with resignation—to surrender to gravity
and to avoid it as much as possible. If we choose to resign to gravity, we eventually realize that we cannot—even for one instant—
avoid it. This is also true of our relationship to fear and suffering.
No matter how much physical and emotional comfort we insulate
ourselves with, no matter how many mental distractions we occupy ourselves with, we cannot hide from our fear and suffering.

The second way to respond to gravity is with resistance—to fight
gravity with brute physical strength and sheer mental will. If we
choose to respond to gravity with resistance, we will eventually
realize—through injury and extreme fatigue—that gravity will out-
last us. Gravity is much greater than our physical strength or our
mental will. This is also true of our relationship to fear and suffering. If we choose to fight our fears, to wage war against our suffering, we will only strengthen them.

Our third response to gravity is to *align* with it. By aligning with
gravity, we minimize both our friction and our impact. At the same
time, we are able to use gravity effectively as a stable platform in
order to propel ourselves forward. With precise alignment in our
running form we learn to pinpoint gravity.

Alignment is equally valuable in responding to the condition of
suffering in our daily lives. We cannot avoid suffering any more
that we can avoid fear, impermanence, or gravity. If we choose resignation, we disempower ourselves as victims and forfeit the opportunity to challenge our spiritual fitness. If we choose to fight and
resist suffering, this only serves to strengthen it.

The Gravity of Suffering

So, how do we *align* with suffering? Let's look a little more at our
quest for gravitational alignment for some guidance. We begin to
align with *gravity* by first developing a high degree of sensitivity
and awareness to the pull of gravity and to its source at the center
of our Earth. Similarly, we begin to align with our *suffering* by
developing a high degree of sensitivity and awareness to all levels
of our suffering and to the nature and source of that suffering.

We explored the very simple tai chi wave walk as a practice of
gravitational sensitivity and as a way of strengthening our con-

templative steadfastness. Through this practice, we develop a keen and very accurate inner listening—even though we are in motion. This is after all the essence of zendurance—*moving* meditation.

Balance and Alignment

The ability to remain steadfast in our calm, still, silent, open, and empty space of deep inner listening and contemplation while we are engaged in activity gives us an accurate and precise sense of balance and alignment. In the spiritual fitness of our daily lives, we can strengthen the ability to remain steadfast with each experience by embracing and accepting the three conditions of human existence. The sense of balance that *this* requires is *more* than just a physical agility and alignment with gravity.

What is this sense of balance that enables us to align with the suffering of our daily lives—that enables us to minimize the friction of our suffering? Can we find a stable platform in our suffering—as we do with gravity—that will enable us to move forward through it? Our first notion is to identify that sense of balance as being our emotional and mental composure. Along with our physical sense of balance—which includes our physical health—this overall composure gives us a sense of *grounding*, of stability. Yet we know that the conditions of impermanence and selflessness will sometimes pull our sense of grounding and composure right out from under us.

The Gravity of Love

The condition of suffering is essentially a *loss* of physical, mental, and/or emotional balance. Our challenge is to discover a source of alignment, a sense of balance that transcends our physical, mental, and emotional states. All that remains for us in this experience of groundlessness is the choice to remain steadfast in our Zen center. Out of our Zen center—the clear and open window to our soul—arises *loving-kindness*, in the form of maitri and compassion. Loving-kindness is the *only* sense of balance that remains with us in the face of suffering—whether it is our own suffering or the suffering of others. *Loving-kindness is literally our spiritual gravity. This is why gravity is seen as the physical manifestation of love.*

Aligning with the Source

We become graceful, efficient, and enduring runners by aligning with gravity. As we align with gravity, we align with its source—the center of our planet Earth. We learn to focus and to pinpoint the pull of gravity like a laser in our bodies. Similarly, we become graceful, enduring and endearing human beings by aligning with our loving-kindness. As we align with our loving-kindness, we also align with its *source*—the clear and open window to our soul. We begin to *pinpoint* the light of our loving-kindness like a laser through our Zen center.

Since our primary source of gravity appears to be the center of Earth, gravity can be regarded as Earth's influence on us—as the *will* of Earth. Similarly, the source of our loving kindness appears to be our soul—ultimately the collective center of *all* of our souls— our divine spirit nature. When we align with our loving-kindness— when we *articulate* our loving-kindness by focusing and pinpointing—we are aligning with the will of our souls and with divine will. Through this alignment with divine will, we experience the same rebound, the same stable platform for forward movement that we experience as we run in alignment with gravity. It is this alignment with our divine will, with our loving kindness, that transforms the condition of suffering into an opportunity for spiritual fitness and intelligence.

Running has long been recognized as a form of spiritual practice. Alignment running is a profoundly powerful activity. We are transforming impact into rebound—suffering into triumph. With clear intention and a sacred approach, we can apply the spiritual intelligence and fitness of alignment running to our alignment with loving-kindness. This is the art of transforming our suffering into triumph. This is the divine will of our souls.

FINAL MILES: SUMMARY

Our initial response to the three conditions of human existence is to avoid them in every way possible. This is a very natural and healthy response—after all, no one *wants* to suffer. Yet we have to ask ourselves as athletes: If this is so, why do we choose to endure the *final miles* of a long race? These final miles can be a very intense and concentrated encounter with the three conditions of human existence—particularly suffering.

We make this choice because we know deep down that there is some profound value for us in the experience. We gain spiritual fitness throughout all our training and racing, but we are most challenged in those final miles. This is when we are really up close and personal with our suffering and pain, our fears and anxieties, our darkness and doubts.

During those final miles, we realize that our capacity to endure—through our *loving-kindness*—is much greater than the conditions of human existence. We experience true happiness, empowerment, and liberation when we *know* our fears rather than avoiding them. As ugly and intimidating as our impermanence, selflessness, and suffering may appear, the rewards for transforming them into opportunities for spiritual fitness and intelligence are immeasurable.

As we gracefully approach the finisher's chute, we feel the glow of our light and love. Although our race has been exhausting, we feel renewed and energized. This is the moment when we can see clearly that impermanence, selflessness, and suffering are the conditions that awaken and inspire our loving-kindness. This is certainly a cause for joy and celebration!

FINISH LINE

Finisher's Chute

We're entering the *finisher's chute* now! It's all *glory* from here on in! We sure have put a lot of blood, sweat, and tears into this race. With maitri and compassion, we have gracefully endured the suffering of those last painful miles. Our spiritual *fitness* has kept us steadfast in our resolve to stay centered and complete this race. With spiritual *intelligence*, we have responded creatively and brilliantly to our fears and anxieties, our pain and suffering, our doubts and darkness. After months of training—with a perfect blend of body, mind, heart and soul—we have dialed-in a brilliant performance here on race day.

Now it's time for bright lights, hugs and high-fives! We can feel the elation beginning to well up in our hearts. In all this glory, it feels so good to *humbly bow down* at the finish line and receive our finisher's medal. As it hangs over our heart, we can feel our pu'uwai resonating. We feel as though we are immersed in a sea of liquid love. Through this sea of love, we feel connected with everyone. We are all one race family.

Ah, the *glory* of finishing! I earnestly pray that each and every one of us may experience this glory and celebrate our spiritual fitness and intelligence at the finish line of many races together. And as we arrive at the finish line of our life race, may each of us bow down humbly to receive our finisher's medal and feel it resting over our hearts.

Finisher's Medal

On one side of this finisher's medal is birth and on the other side is death. Birth and death are just two sides of the same coin. And what about the coin—the medal itself? That's creativity—*divine* creativity.

Divine creativity wrote this book. Divine creativity is reading this book. Your unique way of perceiving, interpreting, implementing, and *playing* with *Zendurance* is a brilliant, divine, creative process. I am sincerely grateful to you for the sacred blend of creativity, brilliance, fitness, and intelligence that you contribute to our experience and our passion. Thank you.

ALOHA

Keep In Touch

As this book goes to press, I am constructing a website to provide information about the book and to establish a communications network for all of us. In the future, I would like to compile a sequel to *Zendurance* containing *your* personal accounts of experiences relevant to zendurance, spiritual fitness, and spiritual intelligence. This sequel will help clarify the principles and practices presented in this original text. I invite you to contribute to this project and to communicate. This network will help to strengthen our practice of zendurance and to foster our further development and growth. I don't promise to answer every correspondence that I receive, but I intend to read all of them. Please include your e-mail address to receive announcements of workshops and relevant activities and publications.

www.Zendurance.net

AWARDS CEREMONY

The first award goes to my spiritual partner of thirteen years—and that's just in this life—Maria de Fatima Cruz de Lacerda. Although our paths may diverge, our genuine love and empowering support for each other, as well as our ruthless commitment to the truth, will continue to unfold in a beautiful, graceful, and brilliant dance. *Zendurance* is a fruition of this inspiring dance we have shared. You are truly a remarkable spiritual master. Namaste Fatima. I love you.

And right here with Fatima is, of course, my mother, Katherine Reno Calvert. I look upon you sometimes as "Saint Kathi," but you are still my mom. Now in your seventies, your energy, focus, intensity and drive still amaze me. With absolute integrity and with an unyielding commitment to motherhood and service, you have brought so much guiding light to my path—ever since birth. That light continues to shine through my heart more brilliantly than the midday Kona sun! And to my stepfather Charles Calvert. I love you both.

Going back one more generation, I acknowledge my mother's mother, Katherine Reno, who just passed away at age ninety-eight. May we all live, grow, and age as gracefully as you. I am deeply grateful for all of the support you have given me throughout my life. Thank you for your empowering faith and for demonstrating so impeccably the function of a visionary. I love you.

I embrace my beloved siblings, Kevin, Regan, and Darcy. Throughout our childhood, we walked the path together hand-in-hand, graced with our mother's light. While our paths have branched out in unique and diverse directions, I still feel your comforting presence and love. I love you. And a special award to Darcy, her husband, Tom, and my niece, Ava, for giving me refuge in the final month of finishing this book.

I call to the Acknowledgment Stage: Erin—Fatima's daughter. You have always been an incredibly wise spiritual being—even at age seven, when I first met you. You never needed any parenting. (Whew!) You are more like an older sister than a stepdaughter. You demonstrate the true essence of *grace* and effortless power for me. Thanks for the divine wisdom you share and for the sublime and graceful way that you live and express that wisdom. I love you.

And rounding out the "Top Five," I welcome on stage the mighty Peaman and Mouse! (That's Sean "Peaman" Paggett and Linda

Jane "Mouse" Kelly.) You clearly demonstrate the true meaning of competition—a *celebration* of companionship. Far better than the hype and jive of Hawaii Ironman, our local-style Sunday morning Peaman Biathlon races are the purest and most playful expression of athletic Aloha ever! No sign-in, no entry fee and prizes for everyone! Peaman rules! To my beloved race family—the Peamana O'hana—I love you.

In the pro category, I want to honor Paula Newby-Fraser. From the first time we talked about *Zendurance*, your encouragement, exuberance and enthusiasm have provided me with the inspiration I needed to finish this book. This was especially true during the darkest times of doubt—when this whole vision looked like sheer lunacy to me. You are perhaps the greatest living example of Zendurance as a way of life. I appreciate not only your athletic mastery, but your humbleness and humility as well.

Now I bow down humbly. I get down on my knees, I press my forehead to the Earth and I kiss Pele. I kiss the Big Island of Hawaii and Mother Earth. I kiss all of the beloved ancestors. Thank you so very much for being my 'aina. And to all of the people of this powerful 'aina—aloha, I love you. Thank you so much for embracing me and including me in our family.

I sincerely thank Jim Medeiros, Wayne Leslie, Jack Kelly, Barbara DeFranco, Protect Keopuka O'hana, Keep Kealakekua Wild, Sierra Club Legal Defense, and all those who have worked so vigilantly and tirelessly to preserve the sacredness and the ecological health of our precious Kona 'aina. Thank you Hawaii Island Journal for providing the forum for our community voice.

Now let's hear it for Tanya Sunshine, Carole Jean "On-the-Scene," and the Intergalactic Irienational Fun Club. You are my guru-spiritual-teacher-masters of fun. Along with Wendy Marie, Gershon, Jeanie, Casey, Anata, Brian, and Barrie, I thank you all for derailing me into the vast fields and meadows of fun every time I was about to enter the tunnel vision of obsessive and myopic focus—training-writing-training-writing . . . After all, isn't that one of the responsibilities of family members—to enforce fun? Thanks for all your inane sanity. I love you all.

Thank you Bob and Cea Smith, my "big brother" and "big sister," for your encouragement, support, practical advice and abundant aloha. Aloha to the entire Filipino Clubhouse Road family. I love you all.

In the four-legged division, I want to honor Kahili and Kui—my "heart dogs" for more than nine years now. You witnessed the entire writing process, even if you both snoozed through most of it. Thank you especially for your companionship in the final snowy months of isolation in the woods that brought this vision to completion. The two of you were there at my feet, keeping them warm—and my heart warm, too! I love you girls!

I acknowledge Grant and Janet Miller, Oliver Kiel and the friendly, competent staff at HP Bikeworks in Kona. You have served and supported me with integrity and honesty.

I am grateful to Barb Kines for generously offering me the secluded writer's refuge during that cold winter retreat, in the woods of West Virginia, overlooking the Potomac River—frozen pipes and all.

I am also grateful to my longtime friend Barbara Ireland for proofreading the final manuscript. I always enjoy deleting superfluous and redundant material. Thank you for your encouragement and wisdom.

Thanks to Mark Allen, Dietrich Lawrence of Classic Physique, Craig Calfee of Calfee Bikes, Carla "Jamilla" Hannaford, Chris Erb, Cameron Widoff, Randy Cadell, Cowman, Tom and Gordana Leonard, Kawika Spaulding, Brian Clarke, and Fernando Olave—you have all been supportive and inspirational in this vision. Thanks also to Maryland Athletic Club for the use of your excellent facility.

Finally I present this special award of acknowledgment to *you*, my companion on this path of zendurance. Thank you again for the spiritual fitness, intelligence, and light you bring to our path of zendurance. All of us benefit from your presence. Together, we are never alone.

Loving Memory

This book is "live-icated" in loving memory to: my father, Alton Tony Smith, my grandparents, Russell Reno, Katherine Reno, Frank Smith, and Dede. And to Florence Griffith "Flo-Jo" Joyner, for showing me what God looks like when she is running with so much joy.

This book is also live-icated to Bob Marley, who demonstrated such remarkable spiritual fitness and intelligence. You are the true Iron-Lion-Zion-Man.

RECOVERY AND ADAPTATION

LOOKING BACK

Humble Introduction

It's been over ten months since I finished writing *Zendurance* and just weeks before the book goes to press. As the author of this book, I did not invent or discover Zendurance. The intelligent and conscious spirit of this sacred approach to endurance athletics—*and indeed to every moment of our lives*—is universal and eternal. My function here is simply to express some of the elements of this sacred universal approach in a language that is *tangible* for us as athletes—tangible enough to apply to our training and racing and, most importantly, to our daily lives.

Just One More Insight

If there is one more message I would like to include, one more insight I can share, it is this: I am in no way a master of any aspect of Zendurance. I am simply a student.

Diamonds . . .

Yes, I do experience brief glimpses of *satori*—that condition of perfect Zen centeredness in our calm, still, silent, open and empty space of deep inner listening and contemplation. Sometimes these moments of *satori* occur during endurance training or racing; more often now, they occur in the embracing presence of loved ones. During these moments of brilliant clarity, I seem to gradually and effortlessly glide through the five events of our Zen pentathlon. In these moments, every word of this book sparkles like a perfectly faceted diamond—in my every thought, word and action.

To Dust

As well, ten months ago when I finished writing Zendurance, I had lost almost all that was near and dear to me—my marriage to Fatima, our home including the farm I had nurtured for nine years and the enchanting house that Fatima had transformed into a sacred shrine, and my beloved Kona o'hana. I had lost my passion and enthusiasm for triathlon and my passion and love for life.

I went through a seven-month death process. During this period, I could feel my life energy slipping away. I was weak and frail physically, mentally and emotionally. I gave up cycling and running. My left shoulder, arm and hand became chronically numb, tingling all the time. I felt pain in the left side of my neck and occasionally I experienced total numbness of my lower jaw and the left side of my tongue. I am quite sure that a rigorous medical diagnosis would have identified some significant malady.

In the most acute moments of this experience, Zendurance was for me a total *failure*. I was incapable of any of the five steps of our Zen pentathlon and every word of Zendurance was invalid and worthless for me.

Like everything else in life, Zendurance can be a wonderful path to spiritual fitness or a distraction for *Edging God Out*—for our EGO. Sometimes we progress along our path of spiritual fitness gracefully and effortlessly. Sometimes we stumble and divert far off course. Among our gifts as explorers on this path of spiritual fitness, *grace* and *humility* stand out for me—enabling me to respond to the impermanence, selflessness and suffering of human existence with less resistance and resentment.

Heroism: Costly or Rewarding?

In stumbling and diverting off course, in slipping into ego, I have eagerly pursued my personal goals and agendas—athletic, artistic and otherwise. When this occurs, I become a prostitute to my achievements—all at the precious and dear expense of family and companionship. For this most painful experience, I apologize. I forgive myself to you and to all of our sacred o'hana.

I do thoroughly enjoy venturing deep into our *experiential wilderness* through endurance athletics, Tai-chi and other kinetic disciplines. The condition of isolation that I have chosen in doing so is sometimes soothing and exhilarating; however, at times it is terrifying and heartbreaking.

Being a successful triathlete is a worthless endeavor for me without HeartCore Zendurance—without integrity—and for that, I need you my sacred brothers and sisters. With grace and humility, I bow to *you* as my teacher. I honor our divine and sacred essence in you. Namaste.

Simple and Effortless

The spiritual fitness of our lives is not measured by our heroic achievements—physically, intellectually, financially, socially or otherwise. Spiritual fitness is simply and effortlessly manifest in our loving kindness towards ourselves and towards one another.

We exercise spiritual fitness through our genuine presence with one another—whether we are aerobically elite or plump and sedentary, whether we are intellectually brilliant or simple and naïve, whether we are financially savvy or subsist living hand-to-mouth.

As I pick up the pieces of my life and gradually begin to rebuild, I hold close to these realizations in my pu'uwai. I honor and appreciate the conditions of impermanence, selflessness and suffering as three valuable instruments for guidance along the path of spiritual fitness, rather than as obstacles to my personal success.

Above all, I love and honor the sacred and divine essence in each of us. What else is there?

LOOKING FORWARD

Sub Two-Hour Marathon

In November of 1998, on the eve of the New York Marathon, Sri Chinmoy spoke to many of his students who had come to participate in the epic event. He spoke on one of his favorite topics: running a sub two-hour marathon. He is certain it can be done on sixty miles of training per week, if a specific state of awareness and consciousness can be attained. Through our zendurance vocabulary, we can interpret this state of consciousness as a certain level of *spiritual fitness.*

To summarize briefly his requirements to attain this state of awareness that will break the two-hour barrier include these four elements: gratitude, peace of mind, purity of the vital (heart), and discipline of body.

Gratitude

With reverent and sincere gratitude, we honor the divine and sacred opportunity for spiritual fitness inherent in each experience and each moment of our lives. *"Gratitude is a miracle- action in us. This miracle-action strengthens our physical body, purifies our vital energy, widens our mental vision and intensifies our psychic delight."* Specifically, Chinmoy says that during our training sessions we must offer gratitude to *Mother Earth*—not just to our physical planet, but to our deeper Spirit, which has both male and female aspects. We offer gratitude to our *feminine* aspect, that brings forth and nurtures our existence.

Peace of Mind

We can interpret "peace of mind" as our capacity for contemplation—detaching from our ego-identification with our thoughts. We experience peace of mind when we abide in the Zen center of our energetic intelligence triangle. *"No price is too great to pay for inner peace. Peace is harmonious control of life. It is vibrant with life-energy."* "Harmonious control" is synonymous with our notion of effortless power. Harmonious control and effortless power arise from a calm and serene mind through the process of contemplation—our first event in the Zen pentathlon. *"The greatest misfortune that can come to a human being is to lose his inner peace. No outer force can rob him of it. It is his own thoughts, his actions that rob him of it."*

Purity of Heart

Chinmoy describes *"purity of the vital"* as *"the feeling of a living shrine in the inmost resources of your heart."* Purified vital energy is the true source of enthusiasm and eagerness in all of our endeavors. Through our pure hearts, we connect with and circulate our infinite sacred and divine essence. With this heart-connection, *anything is possible.*

Discipline of Body

The discipline we bring to our physical bodies is more than just fulfilling the mileage requirements and performance quotas of an endurance training program. It also includes the commitment to infuse our physical consciousness with our divine and sacred essence. In this physical discipline of integrating our peace of mind and purity of heart on a cellular level, our bodies become our living shrines, our *cellular conduits to God.*

Gratitude, peace of mind, purity of heart and discipline of body.

Sacred Language

Mana'o, pu'uwai and *na'au* come from the sacred Hawaiian language. We are consciously using these words to honor our minds, hearts and bodies as the three intelligent aspects of our divine and sacred essence. For us, *mana'o* expresses peace and serenity of mind, *pu'uwai* expresses purity of heart and intention, and *na'au* expresses the embodiment and activation of our tangible sacred intelligence.

The New Paradigm—Here It Comes!

In this new millennium, we are experiencing a deep and profound transformation—both as a global culture of human beings and as a collective *planetary intelligence* that extends beyond our human-scale experience. For some of us in our day-to-day experiences, this transformation is still quite subtle, even latent. For others, it is a clear vision that guides and instructs our every thought, word and activity. As athletes, we have the opportunity to deliberately support and participate in this new paradigm through a zendurance approach to our training and racing *and* in our daily lives.

Racing the New Paradigm

As this new paradigm begins to manifest through our global culture and our planetary intelligence, I am seeing a shift in our attitude towards competition—a shift towards the *empowerment* of companionship. (As individuals, this shift seems to occur naturally if we age gracefully and continue to race.) In this new paradigm, we are beginning to recognize and honor the more *sacred* qualities of athletic performance—those qualities that arise through gratitude, peace of mind and purity of heart, as well as our physical training and discipline.

As this new paradigm gains precedence over the old one, we will focus more on embracing and developing both the science and art of genuine effortless power. Through this enlightened approach, our athletic performances will appear as nothing less than *miraculous*. We will witness the sub two-hour marathon *not* as a result of scientific physical advances in technology—such as better equipment, improved conventional training techniques, or advancements in nutrition or performance enhancing substances. We will *celebrate* the sub two-hour marathon as a brilliant expression of our divine and sacred essence—our light and love.

Endurance athletics is a powerful and glorious arena for expressing our light and love, our faith and trust, our grace and balance, our harmony and integrity, our loving kindness and tenderness, our forgiveness and mercy, our patience and tolerance, our compassion and maitri, our health and vitality, our humbleness and humility, our flexibility and adaptability, our brilliance and clarity, intelligence and wisdom, creativity and playfulness, and our happiness and *joy*!

In our athletic competitions, we may always recognize and reward the fastest, the longest and the most enduring—but as this new paradigm gains critical mass, we are also developing and promoting criteria to recognize, reward and celebrate our divine and sacred essence beyond speed and endurance. Someday, the top award for a competition may go to the athlete who expresses most clearly our grace and integrity.

Soon, our athletic performances will defy the laws of science as we currently experience them. Runners will once again defy the law of gravity—just as the lungompa runners of Tibet did not so very long ago. We will understand clearly how the integrity of our daily lives not only enhances and improves athletic performance, but how it *sustains* our athletic performance as we age. Youth *is* a gift of nature. Age however, is a work of art—the sacred art of spiritual fitness.

Gratitude

I am sincerely grateful to you for your participation in this new paradigm, for your unique expression and embodiment of our divine and sacred essence, and for your commitment to spiritual fitness.

Namaste. Aloha.

READING RESOURCES

After the Ecstasy, the Laundry; Jack Kornfield.

Becoming an Ironman; Kara Douglass Thom; Breakaway Books; Halcottsville, NY; ISBN: 1-891369-24-5.

Bone Games, Extreme Sports, Shamanism, Zen, and the Search for Transcendence; Robert Schultheis; Breakaway Books; Halcottsville, NY; ISBN: 1-55821-506-9.

Cheng Hsin: The Principles of Effortless Power; Peter Ralston; North Atlantic Books; Berkeley, CA; ISBN: 1-55643-302-6.

In Fitness and in Health; Philip Maffetone; contact MAF Bionutritionals: (877) 264-2200.

Journey of the Heart; Jonathan Wellwood.

Ka Hana Pono; Connie Rios; www.KaHanaPono.Tripod.com

Magic and Mystery in Tibet; Alexandra David-Neel; Dover Publications, NY; ISBN: 0-486-22682-4.

New Pocket Hawaiian Dictionary; Mary Kawena Pukui, Samuel H. Elbert; University of Hawaii Press; Honolulu, HI; ISBN: 08248-1392-8.

Pure Pilates; Michael King; Mitchell Beazley Publisher; London; ISBN: 1-84000-266-2.

The Heart's Code: Tapping the Wisdom and Power of Our Heart Energy; Paul Pearsall; Broadway; ISBN: 0-7679-0095-2.

Seeking the Heart of Wisdom; Joseph Goldstein, Jack Kornfield; Shambala; Boston, MA; ISBN: 0-87773-327-9.

The Places That Scare You: A Guide to Fearlessness in Difficult Times; Pema Chodron; Shambala; Boston, MA; ISBN: 1-57062-409-7.

The Power of Now; Eckhart Tolle; New World Library; Novato, CA; ISBN: 1-57731-152-3.

The Seat of the Soul; Gary Zukav; Simon & Schuster; New York, NY; ISBN: 0-671-69507-X.

The Seven Spiritual Laws of Success; Deepak Chopra; Amber Allen Publishing; San Rafael, CA; ISBN: 1-878424-11-4.

The Triathlete's Training Bible; Joe Friel; Velopress; Boulder, CO; ISBN: 1-884737-48-X.

Shane Eversfield has pursued the path of mindful excellence through movement for over 30 years. His experience began with a B.A. in Modern Dance, serving as a principal dancer for two college resident companies (mid-1970s to late 1980s). He began practicing T'ai Chi in 1977, and regards this practice as the best investment of his life. It continues to inform and orient his pursuit of excellence as an endurance athlete. Inspired by his 13 years of living in Kona, he has trained and raced as a triathlete for over 12 years, including 2 Hawaii Ironman finishes and one Ultraman Hawaii finish.

In 2007, at age 50, he enjoyed a 4-month "Zen Rampage": Lake Placid Ironman (19th in age group), USMS 2-Mile Swim National Championship (5th in age group), 24 Hours of Triathlon (completing 8 miles swim, 141 miles bike, 42 miles run for 1st in age group), Virginia Double Iron (4.2M swim, 224M bike, 52.4M run), JFK 50-Mile Run and (7 days later) NCR Trail Marathon (3:36:18, missing Boston qualification by 19 seconds). "There is nothing super-human about this. It just requires graceful and efficient technique. That is the practice of zendurance. Many athletes have far exceeded this accomplishment." Continuing the pursuit of athletic excellence in 2008, he placed 8th in his age group at the ITU Long Course Triathlon World Championship and was recognized as a USAT All American.

Shane is a passionate educator within the multisport world, fueled by his love of camaraderie. He has published over 25 articles in triathlete magazines and is currently a contributing editor for Hammer Nutrition Endurance Magazine. Currently, he serves as a Master Coach for Total Immersion Swim, and travels extensively as a TI Workshop Leader and Coach, with his cherished companion, Betsy Laughlin. He is also a Serotta Advanced Bike Fit Specialist, received a USAT Level I Coach Certification in 2004, and periodically teaches T'ai Chi, Zendurance Cycling, and functional core strength for athletes. As of this printing, he is preparing to publish a "vook" (e-book with embedded video) on triathlon cycling technique, and a DVD "T'ai Chi for Endurance Athletes". Both will be marketed through Total Immersion. Contact Shane at ironzen@hotmail.com. Many of his writings are archived at www.zendurance.net.

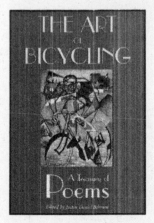

OTHER BOOKS OF INTEREST FROM **BREAKAWAY**

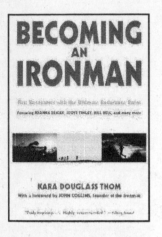

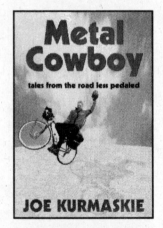

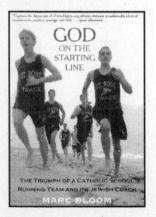

AVAILABLE IN BOOKSTORES EVERYWHERE
www.breakawaybooks.com   (800) 548-4348